Understanding Derrida

Understanding Derrida

Edited by

JACK REYNOLDS AND JONATHAN ROFFE

continuum
NEW YORK • LONDON

CONTINUUM

The Tower Building, 11 York Road, London SE1 7NX

15 East 26th Street, New York, NY 10010

First published 2004

British Library Cataloguing-in-Publication Data

A catalogue record for this book is available from the British Library.

ISBN 0 8264 7315 6 (HB)
    0 8264 7316 4 (PB)

Typeset by Aarontype Limited, Easton, Bristol

Printed and bound by The Cromwell Press, Trowbridge, Wiltshire

Contents

Contributors

David Allison is a professor of philosophy at Stonybrook, State University of New York, USA. As well as writing and editing several books on Nietzsche, he has translated and written the introduction for Derrida's important early work on Husserl: *Speech and Phenomena*.

Robert Bernasconi is a professor of philosophy at the University of Memphis, USA. He co-edited *Derrida and Différance* and has published many articles on Derrida's relationship with Heidegger and Hegel, as well as his book *Heidegger in Question*. He has also recently edited *The Cambridge Companion to Lévinas* with Simon Critchley.

Claire Colebrook is a senior lecturer in English literature at the University of Edinburgh, Scotland. She has published many articles on Derrida and Deleuze, as well as several books including *Ethics and Representation: From Kant to Poststructuralism*, *Irony in the Work of Philosophy*, and *Understanding Deleuze*.

Simon Critchley is a professor of philosophy at the University of Essex, England, and has recently taken up an appointment at the New School for Social Research. He has published widely on Derrida and written several important books including *The Ethics of Deconstruction: Derrida and Lévinas,* and *Ethics, Politics and Subjectivity*.

Simon Glendinning is a senior lecturer in philosophy at the University of Reading, England. He has edited a collection of essays on Derrida entitled *Arguing with Derrida*, written many articles on the philosophy of language, and authored *On Being with Others: Heidegger-Derrida-Wittgenstein*.

Kevin Hart is a professor of philosophy at the University of Notre Dame, USA. He has published numerous articles and books on Derrida, including *Trespass of the Sign: Deconstruction, Theology, Philosophy*. He has an ongoing interest in religion and poetry.

Fiona Jenkins is a lecturer in philosophy at the Australian National University. She completed her Ph.D. on Nietzsche at Oxford, and has a forthcoming monograph entitled *Gestures beyond Dialogue: Interruptions in the Politics of Speech*. She also has interests in practical philosophy, including philosophical counselling.

Christopher Norris is Professor of Philosophy at the University of Cardiff, Wales. He is the author of multiple books on Derrida, including *Derrida*, and *Deconstruction*, and has had an enduring influence upon the reception of deconstruction in the English-speaking world.

Paul Patton is Professor of Philosophy at the University of New South Wales, Australia. He is co-editor of *Between Deleuze and Derrida*, author of the influential *Deleuze and the Political*, and has edited a book of interviews with Derrida entitled *Deconstruction Engaged: The Sydney Seminars*. He has an ongoing interest in politics and issues pertaining to indigenous rights.

David Rathbone is a lecturer in philosophy at the University of Melbourne, Australia, has an M.A. from the New School for Social Research and an M.Sc. from the University of Melbourne. His research interests concern the history of idealism.

Jack Reynolds is a lecturer in philosophy at the University of Tasmania, Australia. He is the co-editor of this book, the continental area editor of the *Internet Encyclopedia of Philosophy*, and has published widely on Derrida. He has recently published a monograph entitled *Merleau-Ponty and Derrida: Intertwining Embodiment and Alterity* (Ohio University Press).

David Roden is a lecturer in philosophy at the Open University, England. He is the editor of a four-volume collection entitled *Jacques Derrida* (with Chris Norris) that offers a comprehensive survey of the secondary literature on Derrida, and he has published other articles on Derrida and film.

Jonathan Roffe is the co-editor of this book, and is the Convenor of the Melbourne School of Continental Philosophy. He is a contributor to the forthcoming *Deleuze Dictionary*, and has just completed a postgraduate thesis on Deleuze's ontology and subjectivity at the University of Melbourne, Australia.

Matthew Sharpe has been a lecturer in philosophy at the University of Auckland, New Zealand, and is currently lecturing at the University of Melbourne. He has published a number of important articles on Freud, Lacan and Žižek, and has a forthcoming monograph entitled *Slavoj Žižek: A Little Piece of the Real*.

Julian Wolfreys is a professor of English at the University of Florida, USA. He has edited a collection of essays on Derrida entitled *The Derrida Reader: Writing Performances*, authored *Deconstruction: Derrida*, and has written many other books on nineteenth- and twentieth-century British literary theory and cultural studies.

Acknowledgements

On an institutional level, thanks are due both to the University of Tasmania and the University of Melbourne for providing material support. At the former, Jack's colleagues Kim Atkins, James Chase, Robyn Ferrell and Jeff Malpas have helped facilitate this book by ensuring a supportive work environment. Above all else, thanks are due to each of the contributors, for without their involvement this book would not have been possible. This also applies to several people more aptly characterized as 'behind the scenes'. In particular, Sean Ryan, Ashley Woodward, Esther Anatolitis, Jo Shiells, Marion Tapper, Noha Khalaf, Rosemary Robbins, David Bartlett, as well as Jack's 'deconstruction and phenomenology' students, have all offered comments on the concept of the book, as well as the specific manuscripts, which have led to its improvement. We must also acknowledge Jackie Jones and Edinburgh University Press for allowing us to reprint extracts from Simon Critchley's *The Ethics of Deconstruction*. Finally, at Continuum, Tristan Palmer was very helpful during the formative stages of the book, and Hywel Evans saw us through to production

Abbreviations of texts by Derrida

Publication details can be found at the end of the book.

Acts of Literature (AL) 1992
Acts of Religion (AR) 2001
Adieu to Emmanuel Lévinas (AEL) 1997 (French 1997)
'On a Newly Arisen Apocalyptic Tone in Philosophy' (AT) 1993
Archive Fever (AF) 1995 (French 1995)
Arguing with Derrida (AD) 2001
'At This Very Moment in This Work Here I Am' (ATM) 1991 (French 1980)
'Circonfession' (C) 1993 (French 1991)
'Deconstruction in America' (DA) 1985
Demeure: Fiction and Testimony (DFT) 2002 (French 1998)
Dissemination (D) 1981 (French 1972)
The Ear of the Other: Otobiography, Transference, Translation (EO) 1986 (French 1982)
Edmund Husserl's Origin of Geometry: An Introduction (EHOG) 1978 (French 1962)
The Gift of Death (GD) 1995 (French 1992)
Given Time 1: Counterfeit Money (GT) 1993 (French 1991)
Glas (G) 1986 (French 1974)
'How to Avoid Speaking: Denials' (HAS) 1989 (French 1987)
Limited Inc. (LI, with Afterword) 1988
'Living On: Border Lines' (LOB) 1979 (French 1977)
Margins of Philosophy (MP) 1982 (French 1972)
Mémoires: For Paul de Man (MPM) 1986 (French 1988)
Memoirs of the Blind: The Self-Portrait and Other Ruins (MB) 1993 (French 1990)
Monolingualism of the Other, or the Prosthesis of Origin (MO) 1998 (French 1996)
Negotiations: Interventions and Interviews, 1971–2001 (N) 2002
Of Grammatology (OG) 1974 (French 1967)
Of Hospitality (OH) 2000 (French 1997)
Of Spirit: Heidegger and the Question (OS) 1989 (French 1987)
On Cosmopolitanism and Forgiveness (OCF) 2001

The Other Heading: Reflections on Today's Europe (OHE) 1992 (French 1990)
Points... Interviews 1974–1994 (P) 1995 (French 1992)
Politics of Friendship (PF) 1997 (French 1995)
Positions (POS) 1981 (French 1972)
The Post Card: From Socrates to Freud and Beyond (PC) 1987 (French 1980)
'Psyche: Inventions of the Other' (PIO) 1989 (French 1987)
Resistances to Psychoanalysis (RP) 1998 (French 1996)
Right of Inspection (RI) 1998 (French 1985)
Signéponge/Signsponge (S) 1984
The Secret Art of Antonin Artaud (SAA) 1998 (French 1986)
Specters of Marx (SM) 1994 (French 1993)
Speech and Phenomena (SP) 1973 (French 1967)
Spurs: Nietzsche's Styles/Eperons: Les styles de Nietzsche (SNS) 1979 (French 1978)
A Taste for the Secret (TS) 2001
The Truth in Painting (TP) 1987 (French 1978)
'The Villanova Roundtable: A Conversation with Jacques Derrida' (VR) 1997
'What is a Relevant Translation?' (WRT) 2001
Without Alibi (WA) 2002
Writing and Difference (WD) 1978 (French 1967)
The Work of Mourning (WM) 2001

Note that some of the book summaries at the end of each chapter have been written by the editors rather than by the authors of the respective chapters. Where this is the case, an asterisk has been placed after the title of the book.

CHAPTER I

An Invitation to Philosophy

Jack Reynolds and Jonathan Roffe

Academic status based on what seems to us to be little more than semi-intelligible attacks upon the values of reason, truth, and scholarship is not, we submit, sufficient grounds for the awarding of an honorary degree in a distinguished university. (P, 420–1)

Derrida is not now, nor has he ever been, a philosopher in any recognizable sense of the word, nor even a trafficker in significant ideas; he is rather a intellectual con artist, a polysyllabic grifter who has duped roughly half the humanities professors in the United States into believing that postmodernism has an underlying theoretical rationale. History will remember Derrida, and it surely will, not for what he himself has said but for what his revered status says about us. (Barry Smith, 30 January 2003, review of *Derrida: The Movie*, archived at http://listserv.liv.ac.uk/archives/philos-l.html)

Derridean deconstruction will have been the greatest ethico-political warning of our time. (Cixous, 1994).

The above statements were made and signed by leading academics and philosophers throughout the world. Even if you are coming to the work of Derrida for the first time, the excessiveness embodied in these quotations is obvious. Why does the work of this Algerian-born philosopher induce such diametrically opposed views? To what kind of excesses is his work prey? Why do some see him as a latter day Socrates, and some as a veritable hemlock to thought? What is it, from the point of view of some Anglo-American analytic philosophers, that predisposes French writers to 'semi-intelligibility' and a 'lack of Anglo-Saxon rigor'?

This book does not attempt to answer any of these questions, or at least not in a direct way. Rather, it submits them all to a prior imperative: do not judge until you have read. Indeed, if there is one theme in Derrida's work that perennially returns, it is this imperative.

Derrida's work has been criticized for its refusal to propound an obvious thesis, or formulaic response, to many of the most enduring philosophical questions – the relationship of language to the world, the degree to which metaphysical presuppositions condition our ways of thinking, and also ethico-political issues pertaining to the possibility (and the impossibility) of responsibility, democracy, hospitality, immigration, and so forth. This is not because there is a conceptual black hole in Derrida's work that means that such issues are ignored. On the contrary, his work not only negotiates with all of these issues but it also problematizes them and resists simplification wherever possible. This means that he is a thinker who should be read in his own words. The task of reading Derrida should not be replaced by introductory texts that say 'deconstruction says this', or 'deconstruction prohibits that'. Of course, this kind of supplementary text will always be possible, and perhaps even necessary, but one problem with focusing upon such texts is that it lends itself to reductive accounts of deconstruction like some of those cited at the beginning of this introduction. When Derrida's own work is ignored, an unsympathetic caricature of it is certainly much easier to establish.

Now there can be no doubt that this present volume also attempts to provide *some* kind of schematic outline for understanding deconstruction. Where this text differs from other introductory volumes is in its ongoing insistence on returning to Derrida's own writings. This is evident in the styles of the various essays contained in this volume and also in the annotated guide to further reading that accompanies each chapter. For example, at the end of the chapter on translation, many of the texts in which Derrida addresses the issue of translation are summarized so that the interested reader can pursue this single line of thought throughout Derrida's entire work. This book hence aims, above all, to facilitate access to Derrida's books *themselves*, and we think this is a means to a more detailed, exhaustive and correct interpretation of this important philosopher.

Our intent is not purely the negative one of trying to allow Derrida's own texts to speak for themselves against the caricatures of his work that abound. Rather, this book primarily addresses itself towards the many people who have an interest in what Derrida has said, having encountered some fragment or other of his work, or who have been puzzled by the prominence of his ideas without being familiar with them.

For those readers in this category, one obvious problem with attempting to read and understand Derrida's work more deeply is that he is amazingly prolific. He has written over 60 books that have been translated into English, not including the numerous as yet untranslated texts, and individual essays, that he has published. How can one negotiate this vast body of literature? Which texts of Derrida's are the important ones in trying to get an understanding of deconstruction? Anyone who has approached Derrida's books has had to deal with this problem.

Many philosophers will quickly respond that Derrida's early work remains pivotal – *Of Grammatology, Speech and Phenomena, Writing and Difference*, and 'Signature Event Context' – but this cannot be rigorously justified. As Derrida himself says, 'it is impossible to justify a point of departure absolutely' (OG 158, cf. MP 6–7). Which texts are deemed important will depend upon the particular interests that the reader brings to bear upon Derrida's texts, and Derrida's texts vary widely in the content with which they are concerned, if not in their strategic 'methodology'. While Derrida dislikes the concept of methodology because it assumes a stable distance between the observer and the observed, the frequently used term 'deconstruction' sums up his project. Deconstruction is *not* a simple rejection or negation of certain ideas in philosophy. Rather, as an initial definition and pointer, the strategy of deconstruction involves first the *reversal*, and then the *disruption* of traditional philosophical oppositions (LI 21). This double reading seeks the destabilization of philosophical positions and hierarchies in the hope of creating a new perspective.

Rather than trying to cover all of Derrida's work together, this book approaches his philosophy from a number of different perspectives, allowing the reader to find an entry point suited to their own interests.

A quick glance at the contents page of this volume will provide an outline of what this book offers by way of entry points. It introduces twelve main themes from Derrida's work: language, metaphysics, the subject, politics, ethics, the decision, translation, religion, psychoanalysis, literature, art, and Derrida's encounters with other philosophers who have been pivotal to his thought.

Each of these chapters deals thematically either with parts of Derrida's philosophy, or with the whole of it with an eye to one of his key concerns. David Roden's chapter on the subject is an example of the former: while subjectivity is not Derrida's perennial concern, he does deal with it quite substantially in a number of places. The chapter on ethics is an example of the latter: any careful reading of Derrida's work will discover various insistences that his work revolves around a certain, very specific, understanding of ethics, and this is the case even in very early books like *Of Grammatology* – this book was published in French in 1967, a watershed year for Derrida that also included the publication of *Speech and Phenomena* and *Writing and Difference*. There is also a third category of essays, which are the five 'encounters' that conclude this book. Each of these briefly discusses one of Derrida's key engagements with other important philosophers who have shaped his work in an important and enduring way: Hegel, Nietzsche, Husserl, Heidegger, and Lévinas.

Many of the academics included here have been at the forefront of Derrida scholarship in English-speaking academic life since his work began to be translated in 1973. They have consistently shown themselves both careful readers and clear expositors of this sometimes serpentine, always rich and elusive, body of work.

Their contributions here are significant and lucid, and their desire to participate in this project has also reinforced the value of, and need for, such a book.

In addition to these short introductory articles, there are two other important features to this book. As mentioned earlier, the first is the inclusion at the end of each chapter of select bibliographies that list, and briefly summarise, some of the relevant texts in Derrida's *oeuvre* that deal with the theme in question. These will help the interested reader to know where to begin further reading, given their own thematic interests. Secondly, there is a thorough bibliography to Derrida's work in English at the end of the text. All of his main works are included, and all of the key collections of interviews, along with individual texts that we judged to be significant. The bibliographical details cited in *Understanding Derrida* all refer to the year of Derrida's various books and essays being translated into English, and not to the original year of French publication. As a rough guide, after publication in French, Derrida's early works took seven or eight years before being translated into English. These days it is more commonly a year or two and translation is sometimes even contemporaneous.

There is a sense in which these two aspects form the real heart of this book, which is intended, in the final analysis, to be something like a 'users guide' to Derrida in English. There is no claim here that the essays included in this book provide a complete and total summary of Derrida's work; above all, as we have suggested, there is no way to replace actually reading his work. This book is meant to point out some of the larger paths that traverse, when considered together, a significant portion of Derrida's many interests. We trust that these essays are a helpful resource in navigating the difficult but rewarding territory of Derridean deconstruction. Finally, and perhaps most importantly, we also hope that this book has been able to further extend the invitation that Derrida himself offers in his work: an invitation to philosophy.

CHAPTER 2

Language

Simon Glendinning

SITUATING THE LINGUISTIC TURN

It is a commonplace today to suppose that the characteristic feature of Anglo-American philosophy in the twentieth century was that it made a decisive 'linguistic turn'. This meant that philosophical problems, especially problems in philosophy of mind and epistemology (the branch of philosophy concerned with knowledge), came to be regarded as fundamentally problems *about* language, or at least problems whose solution was fundamentally *dependent upon* a correct analysis of language. While Anglo-American philosophy was, in this way, developing as a 'language-analytic movement', those pursuing the various forms of phenomenology that dominated philosophy in continental Europe seemed determined, as the British moral philosopher R. M. Hare put it, to 'carry on in their old ways as if nothing had happened'. With the appearance of structuralism and then Derrida's studies of the structure of signs in the late 1960s, the situation on the continent appeared to be changing. There too, it seemed, language was starting to take centre-stage as the most fundamental object of philosophical investigation. So today, in the English-speaking world, Derrida's writings are frequently regarded as a particularly radical version of the general 'linguistic turn' in contemporary philosophy.

There are, without doubt, good grounds for this placement. Derrida explicitly and notoriously claims that 'there is nothing outside the text' (OG 158). Indeed, Derrida goes so far as to say that the 'person writing' and everything that is normally treated as 'the real life of these existences "of flesh and bone"' is not something 'beyond or behind' what we usually like to believe we can unproblematically circumscribe as 'so-and-so's text' (OG 159; cf. LI 148). On the contrary, he insists that this 'real life' is itself something 'inscribed in a determined textual system' (OG 160; cf. LI 136; POS 59–60).

So it seems that for Derrida everything is just language. In fact, however, what he is arguing for is quite different. To understand him properly, and to understand his relation to the linguistic turn, we need to make a careful distinction between language and text. That is, to understand a formulation like 'there is nothing out-side the text' we have first to acknowledge that the notion of 'the text' at work here does not relate to *a system of language* but, in a sense of 'writing' that I will explore and clarify in this chapter, to *a structure of writing*. For Derrida, language is made possible by, and must ultimately be understood in terms of, structures of writing (in his new sense) (OG 7).

With this affirmation it can be seen that Derrida's thought, far from being part of a distinctively linguistic turn in philosophy, is actually working already beyond it. Indeed as is emphasized at the opening of *Of Grammatology*, Derrida does not regard the current turn to language as a methodological must for a rigorous philosophy but as a kind of historical necessity within the metaphysical epoch that we still inhabit:

> However the topic is considered, the *problem of language* has never been simply one problem among others. But never as much as at present has it invaded, as such, the global horizon of the most diverse researches and the most heteroge-neous discourses . . . This inflation of the sign 'language' is the inflation of the sign itself . . . Yet, by one of its aspects or shadows, it is itself still a sign: this crisis is also a symptom. It indicates, as if in spite of itself, that a historico-meta-physical epoch must finally determine as language the totality of its problematic horizon. It must do so . . . because . . . language itself is menaced in its very life . . . when it ceases to be self-assured, contained, and guaranteed by the infinite signified which seemed to exceed it.
>
> By a slow movement whose necessity is hardly perceptible, everything that for at least some twenty centuries tended toward and finally succeeded in being gathered under the name of language is beginning to let itself be transferred to, or at least summarized under the name of writing (OG 6).

This vast historical sweep establishes an orientation to language from which Derrida has never wavered. The linguistic turn is regarded not as a fertile philoso-phical advance but as itself a symptom or sign. Language has come to the centre of every philosophical problematic because everything that seemed solidly to render its status as essentially *un*problematic, everything that had assured us that it *is* what we thought it *should* be, namely the system of signification of an order of pure intel-ligibility (classical 'meaning'), an order traditionally grasped in terms of the divine word or *logos*, has begun to melt into air.

While one might want to invoke the idea that 'God is dead' to interpret Derri-da's claims here, I would put things the other way around. That is, I recommend reading what Derrida has to say about the history of (or as) writing, and his pre-sentation of our present time as witnessing 'the end of the book', as a new and powerful way of giving content to that rather heady slogan. Of course, the possi-bility of making sense of such a massive motif through the seemingly unremarkable and insignificant topic of writing can seem extraordinary. But for Derrida there are systematic links between, on the one hand, the conception of the sign through which, still today, we generally obtain our understanding of writing and, on the other hand, the metaphysics of Christian creationism in its appropriation of classical Greek conceptual resources.

Central to this linkage is the construal of linguistic signs as the unity of a (worldly) sensible signifier and an (ideal) intelligible signified. While this signified need not everywhere be related to the divine *logos* of a creator God, as the 'pure face of intelligibility' it is still immediately caught up with the idea of the *logos* in general, the idea of an order of pure intelligibility. And this idea simply cannot be 'innocently separated' from its 'metaphysical-theological roots' in the thought of the divine *logos*, which, it is written, was 'in the beginning': ultimately inseparable therefore from the idea of the 'word or face' of God (OG 13). According to Derrida, then, 'the sign and divinity have the same place and time of birth. The age of the sign is essentially theological' (OG 14). And, in such an age, 'writing', the very image of the worldly or sensible signifier essentially exterior to the *logos* as pure intelligibility, can only find itself debased. What Derrida aims to show is that there never was nor could there be such an order of pure intelligibility, no *logos* or meaning that would be an ideal presence, a pre-existing and occult (that is, *hidden*) spiritual realm beyond what is denounced as (worldly) writing.

This is not to say that Derrida regards himself as in a position simply to *reject* the classical notions of the sign and language. Indeed, he accepts that any breakthrough that would hope genuinely to '*criticize* metaphysics radically' (OG 19) must (can only) make (inventive) use of the resources of the metaphysical heritage we actually inhabit. For Derrida, the fundamental lever of his criticism of metaphysics is the re-evaluation of that hitherto hardly philosophically central or unavoidable concept of writing. In what follows I will outline and explore what I take to be his central argument in this area: the argument from iterability.

GENERALIZED WRITING

I want to begin with a passage in which Derrida makes a cursory connection between writing and something he calls iterability:

> In order for my 'written communication' to retain its function as writing, i.e., its readability, it must remain readable despite the absolute disappearance of any receiver, determined in general. My communication must be repeatable – iterable – in the absolute absence of the receiver or of any empirically determinable collectivity of receivers. Such iterability – (*iter*, meaning 'again', probably comes from *itara*, 'other' in Sanskrit, and everything that follows can be read as the

working out of *the logic that ties repetition to alterity*) structures the mark of writing itself, no matter what particular type of writing is involved. (LI 7, emphasis mine)

Derrida represents his project here as developing an account of the conditions of possibility of writing in terms of something that he wants to call its 'iterability'. As the reference to the (etymological) connection to concepts of otherness aims to make vivid, this account of the kind of repetition that is a presupposition of the functioning of writing will not assume that what is in question must be pure and simple, a 'repetition of the same' identity. 'Working out the logic that ties repetition to alterity' will thus be an attempt reflectively to affirm a notion of the identity and unity of a written mark (an identity and unity that would belong to each and every specific instance of it) that is freed from the deeply tempting 'logocentric' idea of an (ideal) intelligible signified, an indefinitely repeatable 'meaning'.

But let me straight away highlight, noting what looks like a kind of immediate reflexivity of this point, that Derrida already wants to make room for a certain diversity within the field of writing here. 'Writing', he says, 'no matter what type'. Still, as we read this we have as yet no reason to doubt that we remain in a fairly familiar and well delineated, well circumscribed field – a field within the field of linguistic signs. There are, of course, all kinds of linguistic signs, we will agree. And within that there is a species (yes, OK, perhaps a fairly diverse species), that of writing. Now, such assured certainty regarding the place and limits of writing is not a theoretical mistake that Derrida is intending to remove. Responding with certainty here is little more than an attempt reflectively to endorse one's prereflective familiarity with the use of the word 'writing'. And Derrida is not interested in criticizing a particular usage of words as if it were defective or mistaken. What he is profoundly interested in, however, is the system or scheme of interpretation that we tend to develop when, in our epoch, we try to articulate this usage as picking out 'a species of sign'.

Now, according to Derrida, when it comes to giving a reflective articulation of the difference of 'writing', what we everywhere see is an appeal to the concept of absence. There is, we want to say, an 'absence that seems to intervene in a specific manner in the functioning of writing' (LI 8). Far from wishing to deny the rights of this appeal Derrida will expose in it an astonishing power of generalizability to all 'species of sign' of whatever type. This generalization does not leave the logic that has hitherto dominated our reflective understanding of writing intact: it will no longer be possible to regard writing (in the usual sense) as a secondary 'fallen' signifier. Indeed, we will no longer be compelled to regard what we call 'linguistic signs' in general, whether spoken or written, as sensible signifiers that represent ideal thought contents or 'meanings'. On the contrary, we are likely to see a profound point to affirming that anything that accompanied writing (anything that would seem to give these dead marks 'life') would just be more writing.

What, then, is the absence that is supposed to be so specific to writing? Derrida invokes a tradition of interpretation on this subject for which he claims an astonishing ubiquity – 'not a single counterexample can be found in the entire history of philosophy' (LI 8). According to this traditional interpretation, writing is conceived as a technique or technical instrument for communicating an ideal meaning-content over a far greater distance than is possible by speaking. Specifically, it makes it possible to communicate these contents 'to persons who are *absent*' (LI 4). As Derrida notes, the concept of absence in play here is really a 'concept of absence as the modification of presence' (LI 6). That is, on the traditional interpretation, writing emerges as a technical device when the desire or need arises to extend the field of communication to addressees who are present but who are 'outside of the entire field of vision and beyond earshot' (OG 281). It is with his interrogation of this concept of absence as the modification of presence that Derrida's analysis challenges the traditional interpretation of writing.

WRITING AND ABSENCE

On the interpretation that seems to belong to philosophy, the absence that characterizes the use of writing relates to the (current) non-presence 'here' of the addressee. The addressee is, from the point of view of the sender of a letter, for example, a distant presence. So the notion of absence in this analysis is really a modified form of presence. In his reading of this analysis, Derrida considers whether in fact and in principle the absence in question here 'must be capable of being carried to a certain absoluteness' if writing is to be possible (LI 7). In short, Derrida's question is whether the absence of the addressee that is supposed to specify writing should be characterized in terms not of communication to those who are currently, *in fact*, absent from me (distantly present), but, rather, in terms of the structural *possibility* of the addressee's radical or absolute absence; for example, the non-presence which is brought about by his or her death.

If we consider again the passage in which Derrida first employs the concept of iterability we can see that his response to this question is affirmative: writing, Derrida insists, 'must remain readable despite the *absolute disappearance* of any receiver, determined in general'. The claim is that the readability of the written mark is possible on *this* occasion only if *another* repetition is always possible, up to and including, a repetition in the absolute absence of the 'living presence' of an empirically determinable addressee. It must be capable of doing without their presence, of functioning without them.

I write a letter and address it with a proper name. To do this is to write to an empirically determinable receiver or addressee. Of course, it is always possible that before receiving my written message this addressee will die. Does this prevent my writing from being read? Of course not. However, Derrida does not want the obviousness of this point to be taken to reflect a common-sense supplement to the traditional interpretation of writing. On the contrary, with the re-evaluation of the relationship of writing to absence Derrida wants radically to transform the conceptual economy in this area, as I will explain.

Note first of all that the traditional interpretation of writing does not mention the absence of the producer of the written mark who sends it away to be read elsewhere. It is clear, however, that parallel considerations must hold here too:

> To write is to produce a mark ... which my future disappearance will not in principle, hinder in its functioning ... For a writing to be a writing it must continue to 'act' and to be readable even when what is called the author of the writing no longer answers for what he has written ... The situation of the writer is, concerning the written text, basically the same as that of the reader. (LI 8)

Derrida is not concerned here with death or writing (in its usual sense) as an empirical eventuality. Rather his concern is with the logical and not merely the physical conditions of possibility for a written text to remain readable when the absence of the sender or the addressee is no longer a mode of presence but a radical or absolute absence. And his claim is that the possibility of it functioning again beyond (or in the absence of) the context of its production, or its empirically determined destination, is part of what it is to be a written mark: to be what it is all writing must be capable of functioning beyond the death of any empirically determinable user in general. We can thus propose the following 'law' of writing: a mark that is not structurally readable — iterable — beyond the death of the empirically determinable producer and receiver could not be writing.

The general claim then is that the *possibility* of 'functioning in the absence of' implied by the classical conception of writing must be capable of being brought to an absolute limit if writing is to constitute itself as such. Any particular event of writing or reading, if it is to take place as such, presumes as its condition of possibility the possibility of an iteration in the radical absence of this one. Hence, for any actual language user, the functioning of his or her current use necessarily presumes the possibility of the absolute absence of his or her current presence, as well as the absence of any specific receiver. Again, the written mark must be able to function in the absence of any user's current presence. An event in which this possibility of absence is excluded is, in fact and in principle, not an event of writing.

THE LOGICAL SPACE OF WRITING

According to Derrida's argument, these two possible absences — the absence of the sender and the absence of the receiver — 'construct the possibility of the message itself' (LI 50). That is, and *pace* the traditional interpretation, it is not the relative 'permanence' of the writing message that makes iterations possible in the absence of the sender or receiver; rather the written mark is precisely made to make up for, or supplement, these *possible absences*.

It is with this conclusion that the idea of a strategic generalization of the term 'writing' becomes forceful. According to Derrida's argument the absence that characterizes writing is not a function of the fact of physical persistence but of logically necessary preconditions of its status *as* readable writing. It is true that these preconditions are most perspicuous in the case of writing, but what if these possibilities of absence can be acknowledged to be part of the structure of *every* event of 'communication' no matter of what kind, whatever the 'species'?

The idea here is that a 'singular event' could be a case of 'communication' (could be, say, 'an event of speech') only on condition of a necessary or structural relation to an iteration that is *another such* 'singular event' that is *not present* at the time of its production or reception, another such event which is not what it *is* except in its relation to *another such* event, and so on (see the section on Husserl in Chapter 13). The claim here is not that there must have been a certain multiplicity of iterations for a sign to be, or to be recognizable as a sign. Rather, it is that the iterability of a sign is not just a supplementary benefit for something that could conceivably occur just once: usability on more than one occasion is not an added bonus but an internal feature of every event that is recognizable as being 'a use of signs'. This is what Derrida is insisting upon when he states that the 'unity of the signifying form' that is 'required to permit its recognition . . . only constitutes itself by virtue of its iterability' (LI 10). The point is that an instance of language use that could not function again in the absence of the current context (and anything simply present within it 'inner' or 'outer') could not *be* a 'piece of writing' – *no matter of what kind*.

'Writing' (in Derrida's fresh 'no matter of what kind' sense) is, therefore, structurally, *for every possible user in general* (LI 8). That is to say, the logical space of 'writing' is 'immediately *not* private' (AD 106). In every case, an event of writing detaches itself from its 'author'. *What* I *do* now must, in its iterability, be able to detach itself from what *I* do *now* for it to function and to be what it is 'here and now': it is, from the start, essentially 'beyond my absolute re-appropriation' (AD 106). Hence there can be, Derrida notes, no system of signs that cannot in principle be used by another (LI 8). Even in the case of a language only spoken by one person, the possibility of repeating the marks that is entailed by such behaviour (if it is such behaviour) makes it in principle iterable for another in the radical absence of the first.

On this account the factual emergence of what we usually call writing, the eventual emergence of a relatively permanent mark that can do without the current presence of a determinable sender or recipient, is possible because, in principle, the possibility of this absence is part of the logical structure of any sign, linguistic or not, human or not; it is part of the conditions of possibility of any means of communication in general. Language, Derrida urges, is not just a 'sort of writing', nor even simply 'a species of writing' but, ultimately, 'is a possibility founded on the general possibility of writing' (OG 52).

That this structure of iterability is most evident in writing provides a *raison d'être* for its generalization, ensuring thereby an effective intervention into the fabric of the system of interpretation that has hitherto dominated the subject. As we have seen, a fundamental motif of that system is that it relegates writing to a position of debased secondariness: the graphic representation of the phonetic representation of an (ideal) meaning-content. If, however, anything that could function as 'a means of communication' presupposes writing (in Derrida's new sense) as its condition of possibility, then the traditional conception of linguistic signs in terms of signifiers of a realm of pure signified intelligibility must give way to an understanding of iterable marks (of diverse kinds) functioning within a general text (a structure of writing) that that does not depend for its significance on something outside it.

MAJOR TEXTS ON LANGUAGE

Speech and Phenomena (SP) 1973
In this text Derrida critically examines the conception of language that is presupposed by Husserl in his *Logical Investigations*. The argument is marked by its analytic rigour and textual detail. It also contains an early version of the argument from iterability. Related material: *Introduction to Edmund Husserl's Origin of Geometry* (EHOG) 1978; the section on Husserl in Chapter 13.

Of Grammatology (OG) 1974
In this text Derrida launches his new approach to and understanding of the structure of writing. The book has two major parts. In the first, Derrida outlines his new account of writing and situates it in relation to classical metaphysics and modern structuralist linguistics. In the second, this theoretical conception is brought to bear on an interpretation of the anthropological writings of Lévi-Strauss and Rousseau. Related material: *Positions* (P) 1981.

Margins of Philosophy (including '*Différance*', 'White Mythology' and 'Signature Event Context') (MP) 1982
This book comprises a number of essays bearing directly on issues about language. The essay '*Différance*' introduces the now famous orally imperceptible neologism for describing the structure of ('spatial') differences and ('temporal') deferrals that are constitutive for all linguistic signs. Developing the critique of structuralist linguistics elaborated in *Of Grammatology*, Derrida adds to the structuralist doctrine of identity through 'synchronic' differentiation, a supplementary principle of

'diachronic' differentiation. The connection of this account to the argument from iterability is brought out in *Limited Inc* (LI 53). White Mythology investigates the philosophical presuppositions incorporated within the distinction between literal and metaphorical language. Signature Event Context is the source for the most explicit and most accessible presentation of the argument from iterability. It also contains a reading of J. L. Austin's theory of performative utterances that forms the background of the exchanges with John Searle.

Limited Inc. (including 'Signature Event Context', 'Limited Inc abc . . .' and 'After-word: Towards an Ethics of Discussion') (LI) 1998
This text brings together in a single volume the essays centrally involved in the exchange with Searle. Searle tends to think that Derrida is simply 'confronting' Austin's ideas, but a more careful examination reveals that Derrida is both impressed by and attracted to Austin's work on the performative dimension of language, as well as critical of some his procedures. Related material: *Arguing with Derrida* (AD) 2001.

CHAPTER 3

Metaphysics

Christopher Norris

INTRODUCTION

Derrida has always been clear about one thing: that 'metaphysics' is not just a specialized branch of philosophical enquiry having to do with certain issues – among them issues concerning the ultimate nature of mind and reality – which transcend any knowledge attainable through the natural, social, or human sciences. No doubt this is one well-established usage of the term whose currency goes back to the ancient Greeks and that has figured centrally in philosophical debates down to the present. Still there is a wider, more inclusive sense whereby every aspect of everyday human thought, language, knowledge and experience involves a 'metaphysical' aspect, that is to say, a range of beliefs or presuppositions that enable us to make sense of the world and our various dealings with it. It is this dimension that Derrida refers to when, in an early interview, he remarks that '[t]here is *not* a transgression, if one understands by that a pure and simple landing into a beyond of metaphysics' (POS 12). The context here is that of a question concerning the relationship between Derrida's deconstructive project and Martin Heidegger's famous attempt to think through and beyond the heritage of Western (post-Hellenic) concepts and categories. For Heidegger, it is chiefly a matter of recovering that authentic, primordial experience of truth that had once been glimpsed in certain fragments of the Pre-Socratics but thereafter obscured by those various 'metaphysical' accretions – from Plato and Aristotle to Descartes, Kant, and Husserl – that replaced it with other, more technically refined but existentially impoverished conceptions.

There is no room here for a complete account of Derrida's complex, ambivalent, and constantly evolving dialogue with Heidegger over the past four decades (see the section on Heidegger in Chapter 13). Suffice to say that, on the one hand, Derrida is far from rejecting Heidegger's claim that philosophy has long been embroiled in problems of its own 'metaphysical' engendering and needs guiding back to those contexts of everyday, situated 'being-in-the-world' that provide its authentic subject-matter and vocation. On the other hand, Derrida doubts whether this can be achieved through a thinking that purports to break so decisively with all those inherited 'metaphysical' concepts that Heidegger summons to account. For it is Derrida's point that such concepts are inextricably bound up with all of our knowledge and experience, to the extent that any deconstructive questioning of them will have to take a more oblique, qualified, and highly circumspect form. Thus 'even in aggressions or transgressions, we are consorting with a code to which metaphysics is tied irreducibly, such that every transgressive gesture re-encloses us – precisely by giving us a hold on the closure of metaphysics – within this closure' (POS 12). That is to say, we shall err if we equate 'metaphysics' with a certain kind of chronic delusion to which philosophy is especially prone, the delusion that results (as Wittgenstein put it) from allowing language to 'go on holi-day' and that thereby creates all manner of hyper-induced puzzles and perplexities. Hence the argument of commentators such as Richard Rorty that deconstruction is best viewed as a range of therapeutic strategies for talking us down from the giddy heights of metaphysical abstraction to a sensible acceptance that truth is just what-ever is 'good in the way of belief'. However this reading has to steer a tactful path around everything that is most distinctive about Derrida's work. That is to say, it ignores Derrida's insistence that the deconstruction of metaphysics must go by way of a close engagement with Western metaphysical thought, which questions received concepts and categories meticulously rather than simply rejecting them *tout court*.

There are two main points that need making if we are to grasp these issues. One is the extent to which our everyday beliefs, practices, language-games, cultural 'forms of life', and so forth, are themselves bound up with all manner of deep-laid metaphysical presuppositions (POS 18–19). The other is Derrida's claim that we *can and must* examine those presuppositions from a standpoint that neither pla-cidly accepts them, nor purports to escape from all such metaphysical beliefs. This applies especially to his ethico-political thought, starting out with the early essay, 'Violence and Metaphysics', where he offers a detailed deconstruction of the ethics of radical 'alterity', or respect for the absolute otherness of the Other, propounded by Emmanuel Lévinas (WD 126; see the section on Lévinas in Chapter 13). This discussion is continued in more recent texts such as 'Force of Law' (AR) and *Spectres of Marx*, where Derrida engages issues of legal, moral, and political justice (see Chapter 4 of this volume). These writings are themselves 'metaphysical' – inescapably so – to the extent that they involve a sustained meditation on issues that inherently transcend the realm of physical experience or sensory acquaintance. What chiefly characterizes Derrida's philosophical approach is its willingness to raise such speculative issues while maintaining a vigilant critical awareness of their tendency to slip into other, more doctrinaire forms of metaphysical thought.

DECONSTRUCTING METAPHYSICS

Let me therefore resume by clearing away some of the misconceptions that surround Derrida's (supposed) 'attack' on metaphysics, or – more accurately stated – his deconstruction of the various forms that metaphysical thinking has taken in the history of Western philosophy from Plato to the present. If 'metaphysics' has lately acquired a bad name among thinkers in both the mainstream-analytic and the broadly continental traditions, then this has to do with a tendentious, misconceived, or polemical usage of the term. Here I shall take 'metaphysics' – conventionally enough – to denote that particular branch of philosophy that raises certain distinctive issues concerning the *conditions of possibility* for thought, knowledge, and experience in general. That is to say, metaphysics has always involved some version of the claim (most explicitly advanced by Kant) to deduce those conditions from a rigorous enquiry into the *a priori* structures and modalities of human understanding. No doubt it is the case that Derrida has come up with some complicating arguments which may be seen to challenge received ideas of what counts as an instance of *a priori* truth, or a form of transcendental deduction from first principles that would serve to secure or to validate any such claim. Nevertheless his thinking belongs very much to that same tradition of enquiry, whatever the problems that come to light when he examines the various forms it has taken down through the history of Western post-Hellenic thought.

Still, there is a version of Derrida put around, for the most part, by literary and cultural theorists that assigns an exclusively pejorative sense to the term 'metaphysics'. Thus it needs saying straight off that when Derrida alludes to the 'metaphysics of presence' (see the sections on Heidegger and Husserl in Chapter 13) or to various 'metaphysical' traits and motifs in thinkers such as Plato, Aristotle, Rousseau, Kant, Husserl, Heidegger, Freud, Saussure, and Lévi-Strauss, he is *not* referring to the kind of aberration that might have been avoided had they only exercised a greater degree of critical acumen. On the contrary: he often goes out of his way to insist (1) that there simply is no thinking 'outside' or 'beyond' the remit of metaphysics, and (2) that moreover these thinkers are exemplary in so far as their texts strikingly exhibit the kinds of logical complexity that result from the inextricable co-presence of metaphysical (or 'logocentric') and deconstructive elements. Indeed, as we have seen, the ambivalence of Derrida's commentaries on Heidegger has much to do with the latter's occasional claims to have 'overcome' the heritage of Western post-Hellenic metaphysical thought along with all its hitherto dominant structures of logic and representation. For Derrida, the critique of metaphysics cannot be carried on except by means of those various metaphysical concepts and categories that belong to the very history of thought which deconstruction both 'inhabits' – necessarily so – and sets out to challenge at just those points where its presuppositions come most visibly under strain (OG 24; MPM 72–9).

As Derrida has noted, arguments regarding the 'end of metaphysics' are often simultaneously couched in terms of the 'end of philosophy' (AT 3–37). Kant was the first to announce an end to those varieties of speculative ('metaphysical') thought that purported to derive substantive truths about the world from an exercise of pure reason that transcended the furthest bounds of human knowledge and experience. Such ideas no doubt had a proper place in our thinking about matters of a moral, political, or religious import that by very definition exceeded the limits of our cognitive dealing with the world, matters having to do with freedom, autonomy, social justice, the existence of God, or the immortality of the soul. However they could only produce all kinds of metaphysical bewilderment – and also give rise to epistemological scepticism – if allowed to encroach upon the cognitive domain whose first rule was that sensuous (phenomenal) intuitions must always be 'brought under' adequate concepts. So it was that, in Kant's well-known dictum, 'concepts without intuitions are empty' while 'intuitions without concepts are blind' (*Critique of Pure Reason*). This was despite the fact – as he ruefully conceded – that thinking exhibited a constant tendency to overstep these cognitive limits, like the dove that imagines that by soaring to a height beyond the earth's atmosphere it will at last break free of the friction and resistance that have hitherto impeded its flight.

As mentioned, Heidegger also laid claim to have thought his way through and beyond the entire 'metaphysical' epoch whose closure was marked by his own project of fundamental ontology. That epoch started out with Plato (more specifically: with the turn toward a realm of transcendent 'forms' or 'ideas'), continued with Aristotle's definition of truth as correspondence, and thereafter took in every major episode in the Western philosophical tradition, from Descartes, via Kant, to Hegel, Nietzsche, and Husserl. One prominent feature of Derrida's commentaries on Heidegger, both early and late, is his claim that the project of fundamental ontology gives voice to a craving for origins, or for the pure, unmediated 'presence' of Being and truth, which itself belongs squarely to that same metaphysical tradition that Heidegger claims to have 'overcome'. Thus, when Derrida questions Heidegger's strong-revisionist reading of Nietzsche as the 'last metaphysician', he does so from a deconstructive standpoint that affirms the radicality of Nietzsche's texts – in particular, their sheerly irreducible play of multiple, heterogeneous styles or idioms – as against Heidegger's 'hermeneutic' drive to reduce and contain their disruptive energies (OG 19; see also the section on Nietzsche in Chapter 13).

Derrida's reservations in this regard are also made plain when he remarks on Heidegger's failure to achieve anything like so radical a break with the subject-centred discourse – or humanist 'metaphysics of presence' – that he (Heidegger) claims to have shaken to its very conceptual foundations. Derrida notes how each occurrence of the term *Dasein* ('being-there', deployed by Heidegger as a means of avoiding such unwanted metaphysical commitments) is really just a stand-in for that range of other terms or personal pronouns – 'man', 'human being', 'the subject', 'I', 'we', and so forth, – whose substitution would scarcely affect the sense of any given passage (M 127, 133–4). In comments like these, it *appears* that Derrida is out to subvert every last vestige of the 'metaphysics of presence', because deconstruction seeks nothing more than to reveal the various blind spots or aporias engendered by a logocentric discourse that has always (from Plato down) equated truth with the authentic 'voice' of inward, self-present consciousness. Such is indeed one major part of the Derridean project, broached at the outset in his early texts on Husserl and continued through the readings of Rousseau, Saussure and Lévi-Strauss that constitute *Of Grammatology*. However it will soon become clear that Derrida is not merely purporting to go one better and assert the credentials of deconstruction as a yet more radical thinking-through of those issues that Heidegger raises.

METAPHYSICAL OPPOSITIONS AND LIMITED INC.

We can best take some further bearings here from Derrida's encounters (in his essays 'Signature Event Context' and *Limited Inc.*) with the speech-act theorists J. L. Austin and John Searle (LI). These have to do with various kinds of performative or speech-act commitment, such as promises, treaties, contractual obligations, marriage vows, declarations of trust, and so forth. Austin sets up a hierarchy and a 'natural' order of subordination between serious and non-serious, normal and deviant, or proper and improper uses of language that Derrida regards as symptomatic of all metaphysical thinking (LI 13–19). What emerges through his reading of Austin is the impossibility of fixing conditions for what shall count as a 'genuine' or, to use Austin's term, a 'felicitous' speech-act as opposed to other – non-genuine or merely 'parasitical' – samples of the kind that carry no such commissive or obligatory force. Among these latter would be promises spoken in jest, by actors on the stage, by characters in a novel, or indeed by speech-act theorists (like Austin) who deploy them as handy instances by which to make a point about language in its performative aspect. Such utterances are in some way 'peculiarly void or hollow' because they lack the animating force of self-present speaker's intent, as do promises made with a purpose to deceive or with 'mental reservations' of various sorts. Yet in many cases – as Derrida notes – these sincerity conditions simply do not apply, in so far as what counts as a 'genuine' (legally or contractually binding) speech-act is the right form of words uttered on a given occasion under some appropriate set of circumstances. Thus it would not invalidate a marriage ceremony if the minister were to say 'I declare you man and wife' and then, shortly afterwards, 'sorry, I was joking', or 'no, I didn't mean it', or 'that was just a practice-run' (LI 17). But if the appeal to speaker's intention does not get us very far in distinguishing 'felicitous' from 'infelicitous' speech-acts then neither does Austin's alternative proposal, that it is a question of the right form of words uttered in the right sort of context. For this ignores the point that speech-acts acquire their conventional force only in virtue of what Derrida calls their 'iterable' character (see Chapter 2), or their capacity – to function to carry that force – across a vast and theoretically limitless range of varying contexts.

Thus the very language of Austinian theory is such as to imply that performatives (including 'felicitous' samples of the kind) are *performed* according to some pre-existent script, or that speech-acts are likewise *acted* in a sense of that word with certain distinctly theatrical connotations. This is *not* to claim – as some have supposed – that Derrida is perversely out to 'deconstruct' the very notion of good-faith performative utterance, or to flatly deny that we can ever say what we mean or mean what we say. Rather, it is his way of drawing attention to the impossibility of classifying speech-acts according to well-defined sincerity conditions or straightforward contextual criteria. 'If things were that simple', as Derrida put it in one of his responses to Searle, then 'word would have gotten around' (LI 119). What clearly will not work, when it comes to defining those conditions, is a direct appeal to thoughts or meanings 'in the mind' of some utterer placed in just the right context – and with just the right authority – to issue this or that performative. Derrida insists that we must question such communal norms (OH 9–11) even while acknowledging the necessary role they play in our everyday linguistic and practical dealings. In short, it is the difference between a philosophic outlook which, in Wittgenstein's words, 'leaves everything as it is' (*Philosophical Investigations*) and an outlook that reserves the right to reflect critically on those taken-for granted or 'common-sense' verities which define what conventionally counts as a sample of good-faith utterance. For if there is always the chance that speech-acts will 'misfire' – fail to function in the usual, communally sanctioned way – then this necessary possibility must be accounted for by any adequate speech-act theory and not, as theorists like Searle would have it, brusquely set aside for the purposes of 'serious' philosophic debate (LI 39–45, 88–96). For Derrida, this is to fall into a kind of naïve or unwitting metaphysics as one term of the opposition is unjustifiably accorded a value of 'self-evident', 'natural' priority at the expense of the other which is thereby treated as marginal or accidental (MP 195; POS 41).

DIFFÉRANCE

Thus 'iterability' is another name for that element of *différance* that Derrida finds to be all-pervasive in the texts of Western philosophy (POS 39–44). *Différance* cannot be exhaustively defined in any satisfactory manner, both because Derrida employs it in several different contexts and senses, and because it problematizes the very act of definition. Among other things, it is an attempt to conjoin the two main traits that

Derrida associates with writing – those of *differing* and *deferring*. On the one hand, writing is split (differed) by the absence that makes it necessary, one example of which is the fact that we write something down because we may soon forget it, or to communicate to someone who is not there. Writing also involves deferral because the meaning of a text is never punctually present, never perfectly captured by the author's intention to convey some particular idea, experience, memory, semantic nuance, or whatever. That meaning is endlessly deferred, subject to the chances and vicissitudes of the text's unpredictable reception-history. *Différance* conjoins these two aspects – differing and deferral – in a term that itself plays upon the distinction between the spoken and the written. After all, what differentiates *différance* and *difference* (in the French language) is itself an inaudible, hence strictly graphic, trait, and their existence in written form is therefore prerequisite in order for any such distinction to be drawn. Writing is hence a structurally necessary 'condition of possibility' for language, and not just a derivative, accidental, or 'supplementary' addition to speech, as linguists like Saussure have held (OG 27–44).

Derrida finds *différance* everywhere at work in the texts of Western philosophy even, or especially, where they strive to keep it bay. It is what emerges in his deconstructive readings of Plato, Rousseau, Husserl, Saussure, Lévi-Strauss and others as a counter-logic that upsets or subverts the manifest (intentional) sense of their discourse, and which hence gives rise to moments of *aporia*, that is to say, problematic moments in a text that undermine its apparent coherence or stability and result in an impasse that cannot be decided simply through further textual analysis (see Chapter 6 in this volume). At these moments, certain classical binary distinctions (such as those between nature/culture, speech/writing, presence/absence, origin/supplement, and so forth) are subject to a kind of dislocating wrench that inverts or unsettles their usual, metaphysically sanctioned order of priority. That is, deconstruction takes aim at that deep-laid 'metaphysics of presence' that has governed the discourse of occidental thought from its ancient-Greek origins to its manifestation in the texts of philosophers like Husserl and Austin, linguists like Saussure, or anthropologists such as Lévi-Strauss. To this extent, Derrida may plausibly be thought of as an *anti*-metaphysician, one who (along with Wittgenstein and Heidegger) seeks to loosen the grip of certain misconceptions about language, truth, and reality that have so far held philosophers captive. However this fails to acknowledge the fact that he has continued to engage critically with the texts of that same 'logocentric' tradition and has done so, indeed, with a maximal regard for the coexistence within them of metaphysical motifs and complicating details of the kind briefly summarized above. For it is just Derrida's reiterated point that anyone who thinks to 'turn the page' on philosophy by adopting a radically different approach and without the most attentive working-through of the texts of that tradition from Plato to Husserl is sure to fall back into some form of naïve or pre-critical thinking.

HUSSERL AND GEOMETRY

Thus Derrida's typical strategy is to show not only how those texts run up against certain constitutive aporias in their own undertaking, but also that these are *strictly unavoidable* for any rigorously argued project of philosophical critique. To take a further example from the work of Husserl, such an aporia is that which results from an attempt to vindicate the 'absolute ideal objectivity' of certain *a priori* truths (like those of logic or mathematics) while also providing an adequate account of how such truths were progressively discovered or arrived at through a process of thought with clearly marked stages of historical development. On the one hand they can only be conceived (in realist terms) as pre-existing and hence as potentially transcending any state of knowledge at this or that point in the history of thought up to now. That is to say, such truths are 'recognition-transcendent' in so far as our statements might always be objectively true (or false) quite apart from the scope and limits of our knowledge concerning them. Such is the realist argument according to which any truth-apt statement in mathematics, logic, or the physical sciences has its truth-conditions – fixed irrespective of whether or not we are able to confirm it – by the way things stand (objectively so) with regard to their particular subject-domain. Yet those disciplines also manifest a sequence of changes, advances, or progressive refinements of knowledge which cannot be explained except on the premise that any truths concerning them are subject to a process of historical ('genetic') development, such as that which led from Aristotelian to modern (post-Fregean) logic, or from Euclidean to non-Euclidean geometry, or from Ptolemaic to Copernican astronomy. So if thinking is compelled to posit the existence of objective truths it is also compelled to confront the necessity that these took rise within a certain tradition of thought whose progress was marked by various stages of discovery, whether with regard to the abstract (*a priori*) realms of mathematics and logic or as concerns our knowledge of the physical world. In order to gain a knowledge of them we must somehow be enabled to grasp – or 'reactivate' – the thought process through which they first occurred, such as the kinds of primordial intuition that have characterized the progress of geometrical enquiry from Euclid down. Hence the problematic relation between 'structure' and 'genesis' that Derrida finds most strikingly revealed in Husserl's essay *The Origin of Geometry* and in his other writings on philosophy of logic and mathematics (see the section on Husserl in Chapter 13 of this volume). Indeed it is one that cannot but arise with any project that strives to comprehend both the character of 'absolute ideal objectivity' possessed by certain axioms or grounding principles in the formal sciences and the fact of their having been brought to light through successive (historically situated) acts of discovery.

Moreover, as Derrida notes, it is the condition of possibility for progress in these disciplines – and likewise for our knowledge of previous such episodes, right back to Euclid or the 'original geometer' – that primordial intuitions be somehow conserved, transmitted, or recorded in a form (that of writing) whereby they become part of a continuing and developing history of thought. From a 'metaphysical' standpoint, in one sense of the term, that condition should be treated as merely an accidental feature, a contingent fact about the limits of oral tradition, or the need for writing as a kind of prosthetic device, a 'supplementary' adjunct to those truths vouchsafed through the geometer's otherwise wholly autonomous and self-sufficient powers of intuitive-conceptual grasp. Yet this is to impose another of those value-laden (hierarchical) binary distinctions since 'structure' is then regarded as intrinsically more fundamental than, and indeed ideally separable from, any consideration of 'genesis'. However in Husserl's case – as in Derrida's readings of Plato, Rousseau, Saussure, Lévi-Strauss, and others – it is the 'supplement' of writing – the possibility of graphic inscription – which turns out in fact to be no such thing but rather to constitute the enabling condition for all thought and knowledge.

Thus it is precisely the 'iterable' character of signs – their capacity somehow to function and communicate across and despite vast differences of cultural-historical context – that explains both the possibility of science (in so far as it aims toward a realm of objective truths) and the existence of a history wherein we can recognize the various stages of scientific progress to date. A conflict develops between, on the one hand, Husserl's appeal to an order of *a priori* intuitions or truths self-evident to reason and, on the other, his appeal to a certain historical tradition of thought wherein those truths have successively emerged and of which we could acquire no knowledge were it not for the existence (or the standing possibility) of writing as their means of transmission. Thus, for Derrida, it is writing, not speech, that best exemplifies this feature of iterability, despite Husserl's strenuous efforts to maintain the opposite thesis (SP; see also the section on Husserl in Chapter 13 of this volume). It is this power of writing to signify despite its detachment from the original context of utterance – or without the appeal to some animating force of self-present speaker's intent – which ensures the possibility of communication not only through written signs but also through spoken language in so far as the latter likewise depends upon various conventional structures of signification. Thus Derrida's point with regard to the constitutive tensions or aporias in Husserl's philosophy of language carries over into his treatment of themes in Husserl's philosophy of logic, mathematics, and the formal sciences.

Approaching these issues via his intensive early reading of Husserl, Derrida makes due allowance *both* for those 'absolute ideal objectivities' which are taken to transcend any merely 'genetic' or developmental account, *and* for the fact of their having been arrived at through successive (historically specific) stages of thought. This is characteristic of deconstruction which tends to adopt a 'both-and' approach to such issues, rather than the exclusive binary logic of an 'either-or' which attempts to enforce a choice between one or the other response. At the same time, Derrida is at pains to insist that this stage can be arrived at only after – and in consequence of – the most rigorous process of textual analysis according to the norms of a classical (two-valued) logic of truth and falsehood. It involves him in a form of transcendental, or quasi-transcendental, reasoning that respects those norms right up until the point when analysis reveals the conditions of *im*possibility for resolving, in this case, the issue between structure and genesis (WD 154–68). This is the most distinctive aspect of his work on philosophy of language and logic, and one that clearly raises metaphysical issues of the greatest importance. Indeed, I would venture to suggest that if analytic philosophers could be persuaded to engage closely with Derrida's texts then they might gain a deeper, more adequate grasp of those problems that have often re-surfaced in the wake of old-style logical empiricism with its hard-line veto on 'metaphysical' talk of whatever kind.

However, if this is the case, then his disciples (or some of them) are wide of the mark when they seek to enlist Derrida on the side of a 'post-philosophical' culture that would have no time for those endless (since plainly unresolvable) disputes. Metaphysical issues have a way of returning to haunt those who declare them off-bounds for all legitimate philosophic purposes. Derrida's approach to these issues in his writings on Plato, Kant, Husserl, Austin and others is one that involves nothing like any wholesale (for example, Rortian) version of the present-day 'linguistic turn'. Indeed, as he is often at pains to insist, it is only on a grossly inadequate (not to say wilfully distorted) reading of his work that deconstruction can be taken to deny or reject the existence of a language-independent reality or of truth-values that in principle transcend its various modes of linguistic or discursive representation (see Chapter 2). No doubt there are passages that, taken out of context, might seem to commit him to some such 'strong' anti-realist position but this idea rests on a highly selective (not to say partial and distorting) account of his work. Derrida emphatically rejects any notion that philosophy could somehow escape or surpass the discourse of 'Western metaphysics' without thereby giving up its primary vocation. For it is here – on the essentially contested ground of metaphysical concepts and categories – that deconstruction has staked its most distinctive claims with respect to the 'unthought axiomatics' of Western philosophical tradition.

MAJOR TEXTS ON METAPHYSICS

Speech and Phenomena (SP) 1973
The best known product of Derrida's intensive early researches into various aspects of Husserlian phenomenology. Includes the classic essay *Différance*, where he teases out the movement of differing-deferral that exerts a constant disruptive effect on Husserl's attempts to isolate a moment of authentic, self-present meaning in spoken

language and likewise to locate a punctual 'now' in the past-to-future flux of internal time-consciousness.

Of Grammatology (OG) 1974

Derrida's most extensive and closely argued engagement with various texts by Rousseau, Saussure and Lévi-Strauss which he takes to typify the Western tradition of thought. Develops his thesis concerning the ubiquitous 'logic of supplementarity' as it works to unsettle their preconceptions with regard to the 'natural' order of priority between nature and culture, male and female, speech and writing, and so forth. Fairly tough going in places but probably the best place to start for readers wishing to familiarize themselves with the intricacies of Derrida's deconstructive thought.

Writing and Difference (WD) 1978

Contains some of Derrida's most important early essays, including texts on Husserl, Lévinas, Foucault, and Lévi-Strauss. Of particular interest for its tracing of the various tensions, aporias, or conceptual fault-lines that Derrida finds in the two great projects of thought that most influenced his own work at that time – Husserlian phenomenology and the structuralist movement descending from Saussure.

Dissemination (D) 1981

This includes 'Plato's Pharmacy', an essay that reads Plato's dialogue the *Phaedrus* as focused on the issue about speech and writing, or the (assumed) superiority of self-present spoken language over the mere simulacra of written signs. In this and other chapters – devoted to a range of philosophical and literary texts – Derrida broaches a deconstruction of the deep-laid Platonist 'metaphysics of presence' that has hitherto structured predominant conceptions of philosophic truth and method. Still he is insistent that one cannot 'turn the page' on those conceptions without the most rigorous (philosophical) thinking-through of their conceptual problems and dilemmas.

Margins of Philosophy (MP) 1982

Essays on a wide range of themes including the relationship between concept and metaphor in philosophical discourse ('White Mythology') and the aporias resulting from various attempts – chiefly those of Aristotle, Hegel, and Heidegger – to conceptualize temporal experience from a standpoint dominated by the Western logocentric metaphysics of presence (for example *Ousia* and *Gramme*). It also contains The 'Ends of Man', an early piece where Derrida complicates various then-fashionable 'post-metaphysical' (or 'post-humanist') modes of thought, among them those of Heideggerian depth-ontology, Sartrean existentialism, and Althusserian Marxism. The 'Supplement of Copula' is another essay that turns certain preconceptions about Derrida very firmly on their head, in this case the idea that he is some kind of far-out 'textualist' thinker who treats all philosophical concepts and categories as products of this or that language, discourse, or conceptual scheme.

Spectres of Marx (SM) 1994

A brilliantly inventive intertextual meditation on various works of Marx (including the *Communist Manifesto* with its famous opening sentence: 'A spectre is haunting Europe') alongside Shakespeare's *Hamlet* and other ghostly intimations. Marx and his opponents (past and present) have this much in common: that they seek to exorcise the 'spectre' of a justice yet-to-come by invoking the evidence of how things stand – or will surely turn out – at some given (present or future) stage of economic or socio-political development. This can also be seen as a continuation – albeit in more expressly political and ethical terms – of Derrida's earlier project: his deconstructive critique of the 'metaphysics of presence'.

CHAPTER 4

Politics

Paul Patton

For a long time Derrida did not write about political issues or political concepts. Throughout the highly politicized years of French intellectual life before and after 1968 he remained apart from the debates over Marxism that dominated philosophical thought about politics in France, resisting questions about the relationship between his work and the materialist dialectic and theory of history (POS 60–7). Although he taught alongside Althusser at the École Normale Supérieure throughout much of this period and was familiar with the issues and with many of the central figures, he declined to comment on the efforts to redefine Marx's philosophy and theory of history. His silence was in part due to his philosophical reservations about the terms in which these debates were conducted. His awareness of the relationship between these debates and ongoing efforts to reform the French Communist Party, and reluctance to appear critical of those efforts, provided an additional reason for refraining from raising the kinds of deconstructive question about Marx and Marxism that he willingly pursued in relation to other philosophers during this period (N 158–63).

Since 1980, by contrast, Derrida has written about a variety of explicitly political themes and taken public positions on many political issues of the day. He has written about justice, responsibility, Europe and the ideals of the Enlightenment; about hospitality, forgiveness, friendship, democracy, equality and a range of other concepts implicated in modern social and political thought. He has spoken out in defence of imprisoned intellectuals and writers in many parts of the world, campaigned against apartheid and taken increasingly forceful positions on political issues such as the treatment of illegal immigrants, the politics of reconciliation, the death penalty and rogue states (N). In 1993, in the aftermath of the collapse of Eastern European socialism and in the face of the widespread belief in the death of Marxism as a political force, he published an essay on Marx's ambivalent relationship to the theme of spectrality, which haunts his writing, in which he aligned deconstruction with a radicalization of the spirit of Marxism (SM 92). In full awareness of the chequered history that Marxism has inspired, and conscious of the contradiction at the heart of the injunction to remain faithful to the heritage of a revolutionary tradition, *Specters of Marx* promotes the idea of a new 'international' in support of international peace between just and democratic states. In 2003, he published a wide-ranging interview, 'Autoimmunity: Real and Symbolic Suicides', on the nature and consequences of international terrorism in which he discusses the conditions of major global events such as September 11 and speculates on the future of state sovereignty (cf. WA 207) in an increasingly cosmopolitan world order (cf. OCF). In this context, he outlines an overtly political conception of the present task of philosophy, namely to analyse and draw 'the practical and effective consequences of the relationship between our philosophical heritage and the structures of the still dominant juridico-political system that is so clearly undergoing mutation' (Autoimmunity, 2003, 106).

Clearly, Derrida has become less inhibited than he was about addressing political issues. Does this imply a change in his political orientation over the years? There is little evidence to suggest that it does. He has never sought to conceal his allegiance to both the political left and the emancipatory and democratic ideals of the Enlightenment. Contrary to the suggestion that he is an anti-Enlightenment thinker, Derrida affirms his belief in progress: 'I am for the Enlightenment, I'm for progress, I'm a "progressist"' (Affirmative Deconstruction, 2001, 100). However, while he affirms the possibility of progress in human affairs, 'progress' here must be understood in a formal and negative sense, in the manner of Foucault's characterization of the ethos of Enlightenment as the commitment to identifying and supporting those dimensions of the present in which it is possible to move beyond 'the contemporary limits of the necessary' (Foucault, 1997, 313). Thus, whereas *Specters of Marx* endorses a 'radical and interminable' critique of the present, this is a non-teleological critique carried out in the name of 'an experience open to the absolute future of what is coming, that is to say, a necessarily indeterminate, abstract, desert-like experience that is is confided, exposed, given up to its waiting for the other and the event' (SM 90).

Does the overtly political character of much of Derrida's writing since 1990 accompany a change in his philosophy? Again, there is little evidence that it does. Derrida always endorsed the view, widely accepted in France during the 1960s and 1970s, that philosophy is itself a form of political activity. Deconstruction, he insisted, 'is not *neutral*. It *intervenes*' (POS 93). In *Positions*, he summarizes the strategy of deconstructive intervention against hierarchical oppositions such as presence versus absence, literal versus metaphorical meaning, or speech versus writing: first, an overturning that establishes that the term supposed to be secondary is already implied in the primary term. For example, the presence of an abstract entity such as a word or a law also implies its non-presence or absence. Similarly, speech is already a form of writing to the extent that it is an articulated series of marks supposed to express pre-formed meanings or mental contents (see Chapter 2). In its second phase, deconstruction creates a new 'concept', one 'that can no longer be, and never could be, included in the previous regime' (POS 42). For example, the concept of writing-in-general, which refers to any kind of instituted mark or trace, '*simultaneously* provokes the overturning of the speech – writing hierarchy, and the entire system attached to it, *and* releases the dissonance of a writing within speech, thereby disorganising the entire inherited order and invading the entire field' (POS 42). This new 'concept' of writing-in-general is not a concept in the sense of designating a determinate set of properties but rather a name for an open-ended series of related characteristics or themes. It embodies and expresses the refusal of limits, determinate forms, or ultimate vocabularies, which characterizes the conceptual politics of deconstruction.

Derrida's early work showed how the logic of essence and identity that governed traditional philosophical approaches to language and meaning failed to account for their conditions of possibility and suggested that these conditions were more adequately expressed by the deconstructive 'quasi concepts' of writing or citationality. In common with other French poststructuralist philosophers of this period, he sought to intervene on the side of openness against closure, difference against identity, perpetual movement against stasis. Deconstruction intervened in particular philosophical contexts by exposing the limits of all attempts to provide secure metaphysical foundations, grounds or final vocabularies. It sought to open up the possibility of transformation, reinterpretation, or movement, within established structures of thought and action. To the extent that political life is also played out within and against certain institutional structures, it could also be considered subject to the general conditions of such institutionality. The permanent possibility of citation or iteration is also a possibility of transformation. Nevertheless, in the absence of explicit connections between the conceptual politics of deconstruction and recognizably political issues or concepts, critics argued that it was a form of nihilist obscurantism, or irrationalism, which stood for nothing and provided no grounds for political action. Alternatively, they argued that its emphasis on *différance* and the undecidability of its a-conceptual figures such as the pharmakon, supplement, mark, or trace, lead to indecision, to a refusal to take sides and therefore to a political relativism. Either way, the deconstructive refusal of closure or foundations was considered to involve a primarily negative critical stance.

Whatever the basis in Derrida's early writings for criticisms of this kind, from at least the early 1980s he begins to present deconstruction in a more positive light. Whenever the question of the purpose or the politics of deconstruction is raised, he points to the undesirability of having a 'good conscience' about established ways of acting and thinking and the desirability of questioning and challenging what is currently accepted as self-evident in our ways of thinking and acting. In response to criticisms of deconstruction as an 'inherently conservative' activity, he argues that deconstruction is not anything 'inherently'. Indeed the logic of essence, of the proper and of the 'inherent' as opposed to the extrinsic 'is precisely what all deconstruction has from the start called into question' (LI 141). In response to the charge that deconstruction stands for nothing, he argues that what it stands for is what it does, namely to destabilize existing grounds for political thought and action. These grounds are also limits that must be overcome if anything new is to appear, so it follows that deconstruction is also a revolutionary gesture. In 'Force of Law' (AR), he appeals to the idea of 'a deconstruction that would like, in order to be consistent with itself, not to remain enclosed in purely speculative, theoretical, academic discourses but rather . . . to aspire to something more conse-quential, to *change* things and to intervene in an efficient and responsible, though always, of course, very mediated way' (AR 236).

DECONSTRUCTION AND INVENTION

In 'Psyche: Invention of the Other', first presented as a series of lectures in 1984, Derrida announces that 'deconstruction is inventive or it is nothing at all' (AL 337). He immediately adds that, in *order* for this to be true, deconstruction must call into question the traditional concept and status of invention. Traditionally, 'invention' refers to the coming of something new, something that is therefore other to what has gone before and that 'at the moment when it comes about' conforms to no pre-existing status or rule (AL 338). At the same time, to the extent that an invention is able to be received into some pre-existing practice or institution, it must be legit-imized by rules and procedures that are compatible with those already in existence. In this manner, an invention that is recognizable and receivable as such will always have been possible in accordance with the rules and procedures of a given prac-tice or institution. Understood in this manner, an invention would not break with current institutions, laws or procedures. It does no more than make explicit that which was already possible within 'the economy of the same' (AL 341). It fol-lows that invention 'would be in conformity with its concept . . . only insofar as, paradoxically, invention invents nothing, when in invention the other does not come' (AL 341).

But would an invention that did not break with existing institutional procedures really be an invention? Would not an invention that really did invent something new require the advent of something truly 'other'? Would it not require the com-ing about of something that did not fall within the existing space of the possible and that was therefore, strictly speaking, impossible? It is in this sense that decon-struction is inventive. It serves a political function to the extent that it assists in opening up the present in order to 'let the other come'. This deconstructive 'inven-tion', Derrida argues, 'can consist only in opening, unclosing, destabilizing fore-clusionary structures so as to allow for the passage towards the other' (AL 341).

Derrida argues in 'Psyche' that, in so far as it involves the coming about of something other in this more radical sense, 'the interest of deconstruction . . . is a certain
experience of the impossible' (AL 328).

   In subsequent writings, this apparently paradoxical formula provides a provocative way of describing the political ambition of deconstruction. For example,
'Force of Law' contrasts the law, which is subject to historical conditions and is
therefore open to modification or change, with justice, which is that in the name
of which the law is modified and which therefore remains essentially undeconstructible. Justice is manifest both in particular applications of the law, and in particular
improvements or modifications of the law, but, Derrida argues, neither of these
implies an experience of justice as such. Justice as such is an impossible object of
experience and, in so far as deconstruction is concerned with justice, it is concerned
with the experience of the impossible (AR 243). The French *experience* can mean
'experiment' as well as 'experience', so the interest of deconstruction involves
more just than the phenomenological experience of pushing against the limits of
what is currently possible: it also involves the attempt to bring about that which is
truly other. Derrida points out that any decision and therefore any responsible
action necessarily involves an aporetic or contradictory experience of this kind.
On the one hand, if it is to be properly a decision and not simply a mechanical
procedure, it must involve more than simply acting in accordance with a given
rule. On the other hand, a decision must have some relation to a rule and not be
simply capricious or unmotivated. In this sense, any decision must pass through
this experience of the impossible, an 'undecidable' oscillation between different
and conflicting requirements (LI 116; see also Chapter 6 in this volume).

APORETIC ANALYSIS AND THE 'BEYOND'

The distinction between two kinds of invention in Psyche exemplifies one of two
principal strategies or styles of deconstructive analysis prevalent in Derrida's later
writings. This is the aporetic analysis of concepts practised in a series of discussions
of the gift, justice, responsible decision, democracy, the cosmopolitan right of hospitality and a number of other concepts. In each case, he offers a redescription of
an existing concept, which invents or reinvents the distinction between a contingent or conditioned form of the concept and an absolute or unconditioned form.
For example, in *On Cosmopolitanism and Forgiveness*, Derrida points out that the
Christian or Abrahamic tradition from which our use of the term 'forgiveness'
derives is torn between a concept of pure, unconditional forgiveness and a concept
of forgiveness that is possible only upon certain conditions, such as the repentance
of the perpetrator. Strictly speaking, it is only the existence of the unforgivable that
gives force, or meaning, to the idea of forgiveness: 'Must one not maintain that an

act of forgiveness worthy of its name, if ever there is such a thing, must forgive the unforgivable and without condition?' (OCF 39). If one forgave only that which is forgivable, then the concept of forgiveness would lose its force, just as the concept of a gift would lose its force if it meant that one gave only that which one was able to give, or the concept of justice would lose its force if it were reduced to the idea of procedural justice in accordance with law.

Derrida points out that we could never 'in the ordinary sense of the words', practise a politics or law of forgiveness in this unconditional sense. Forgiveness proper remains heterogeneous to the order of political or juridical thought, as this operates in particular historical circumstances where forgiveness or reconciliation is required, but this unconditional form of the concept is necessary in order to inflect politics or bring about change. In the case of justice, 'deconstruction takes place in the interval that separates the undeconstructibility of justice from the deconstructibility of *droit*' (authority, legitimacy and so on) (AR 242). In the case of forgiveness, 'it is between these two poles, *irreconcilable but indissociable*, that decisions and responsibilities are to be taken' (OCF 45). The fact that the two heterogeneous poles of the concept are irreducible to, but indissociable from, one another guarantees that the question remains open of the conditions under which justice or forgiveness can occur. Just as it is by appealing to justice that the law can be modified or improved, so it is by reference to the paradoxical idea of the unforgivable that we can 'orient' an evolution of the law or 'inspire' new forms of responsibility (OCF 53).

In *Of Hospitality*, Derrida identifies a parallel antinomic structure within the law or the concept of hospitality. On the one hand, hospitality as it is practised in particular contexts is always conditional: it is always offered to certain determinate others, endowed with a particular social status and subject to certain reciprocal duties in relation to the rights of the host, who must remain in control to be the host at all. On the other hand, the conditional practice of hospitality derives its force and its meaning from a concept of absolute or unconditional hospitality that would welcome the other in the absence of any conditions and without any restrictions with regard to behaviour while in the domain of the host:

> . . . absolute hospitality requires that I open up my home and that I give not only to the foreigner (provided with a family name, with the social status of being a foreigner, etc.), but to the absolute, unknown, anonymous other, and that I *give place* to them, that I let them come, that I let them arrive, and take place in the place I offer them, without asking of them either reciprocity (entering into a pact) or even their names. The law of absolute hospitality commands a break with hospitality by right, with law or justice as rights. (OH 25)

Like unconditional forgiveness, absolute hospitality remains heterogeneous and irreducible to ordinary, conditional hospitality and, as in the case of unconditional forgiveness, the idea of unconditional hospitality underpins the possibility of improvement or progress in the existing conditional forms of welcome extended to foreigners:

> It is a question of knowing how to transform and improve the law, and of knowing if this improvement is possible within an historical space which takes place *between* the Law of an unconditional hospitality, offered *a priori* to every other, to all newcomers, *whoever they may be*, and *the* conditional laws of a right to hospitality, without which *The* unconditional law of hospitality would be in danger of remaining a pious and irresponsible desire, without form and without potency, and of even being perverted at any moment. (OCF 22–3)

The point of this distinction between the heterogeneous orders of the conditional and unconditional is to remind us that we are not completely defined by the existing practices that determine our political being: 'Must we not accept that, in heart or in reason, above all when it is a question of forgiveness, something arrives which exceeds all institution, all power, all juridico-political authority?' (OCF 54). It is this 'something beyond' that inspires the possibility of change in each determinate context. Through the recurrent analysis of this distinction in relation to concepts such as invention, justice, forgiveness, hospitality, friendship and democracy, deconstruction invents a series of descriptions of this impossible 'beyond': invention of the absolutely other; pure or unconditional forgiveness, hospitality; justice, equality and democracy to come.

The Other Heading undertakes this kind of deconstructive analysis with regard to the idea of European cultural identity and its leading ideals. Derrida argues in favour of a traditional idea of Europe as the source and leading purveyor of Enlightenment ideals, but also in favour of the necessity to go beyond that idea in the name of an idea of another Europe, less Eurocentric and more open to its other than it has been in the past: 'it is necessary to make ourselves the guardians of an idea of Europe, of a difference of Europe, *but* of a Europe that consists precisely in not closing itself off in its own identity and in advancing itself in an exemplary way toward what it is not, toward the other heading or the heading of the other' (OHE 29). Above all, he draws attention to the contradictory double injunction at the heart of the project of defending European ideals. Responsibility to and for the ideals that make up European identity calls both for remaining faithful to Europe's heritage but also opening it up 'onto that which is not, never was and never will be Europe' (OHE 77). The same duty enjoins us to respond to equally divided and contradictory ideals of hospitality, and to assume the 'uniquely European heritage of an idea of democracy, while also recognizing that this idea, like that of international law, is never simply given, that its status is not even that of a regulative idea in the Kantian sense, but rather something that remains to be thought and to come …' (OHE 78).

THE GENEALOGY OF CONCEPTS AND THE 'TO COME'

The second style or strategy of affirmative deconstruction employs a genealogical approach to the history of particular concepts. The discussion of invention in *Psyche* included a discussion of the ways in which this concept has been recognized in legal, literary, intellectual and technological domains. Similarly, the discussion of law and justice in 'Force of Law' called for an historical genealogy of different concepts of law, right and justice, and of the manner in which these are bound up with responsibility and the network of concepts related to this, such as property, intentionality, will, freedom, conscience, and consciousness (AR 247–8). In *Politics of Friendship*, the history of philosophical discussions of friendship provides a pathway into the history of democracy. Philosophers since Plato have defined democracy in terms of friendship. Aristotle in particular defined the *polis* as the work of friendship. Politics, like friendship, is a matter of living together with others, in the aim of achieving a 'good life' (PF 199). Derrida situates his interest in friendship within the context of an attempt to deconstruct the 'given concept of democracy' in order to open up the possibility of a different way of understanding democracy (N 178). His approach is genealogical in that it examines how the idea of democracy arose in the West, in what terms it has been thought, and in relation to what other concepts or philosophemes it has been defined. However, it also follows the analysis of aporia outlined above in relation to forgiveness and hospitality: the idea of democracy encompasses irreconcilable obligations to the singularity of each individual member of the *demos*, and to the universality of the law before which all citizens are equal (PF 22).

The political problem around which this book is constructed is reflected in the fact that philosophers have defined friendship and along with it concepts such as equality and democracy in familial, patriarchal and fraternal terms. From an historical point of view friendship, like democracy, has been an affair among men. Derrida's deconstructive genealogy asks:

> is it possible to think and to implement democracy, that which would keep the old name 'democracy', while uprooting from it all those figures of friendship (philosophical and religious) which prescribe fraternity: the family and the androcentric ethnic group? Is it possible, in assuming a certain faithful memory of democratic reason and reason *tout court* – I would even say the Enlightenment of a certain *Aufklärung* (thus leaving open the abyss which is again opening today under these words) – not to found, where it is no longer a matter of *founding*, but to open out to the future, or rather to the 'to come', of a certain democracy? (PF 306)

It is this orientation towards an impossible future, or towards the other, encapsulated in the phrase 'to come', which underwrites the affirmative politics of deconstruction. By this phrase Derrida means the future understood not as a possible future present but rather as something that can only ever remain in the future because of its aporetic character. This is an absolute or structural future, a messianism without a messiah (see Chapter 7), but it is also the condition of possibility of change in the present. Even though this absolute future will never be actualized in any present, it remains capable of acting in or upon the present. It is precisely because justice always remains 'to come' that 'justice, insofar as it is not only a juridical or political concept, opens up for *l'avenir* the transformation, the recasting or refounding of law and politics' (AR 256). This impossible future has the structure of a promise in that, like a promise, it is a means by which an imagined future can intervene in or act upon the present. Just as a promise in relation to some future state of affairs has consequences for one's actions in the present, so the appeal to justice or to a democracy to come will have consequences in the present. It is this structure of action in the present in the light of an impossible future that Derrida calls the 'to come' and which he distinguishes from the possible future that only reproduces or continues the present. This other future remains to be determined, determinable yet perpetually open. It is a 'to come' understood as 'the space opened in order for there to be an event, the to-come, so that the coming be that of the other' (N 182).

MAJOR TEXTS ON POLITICS

'Afterword: towards an ethics of discussion', (LI 111–54) 1988 *

This extremely important text by Derrida, in the context of his 'debate' with Searle, answers a number of familiar criticisms of his work (that he advocates the free play of meaning, that deconstruction is politically conservative) by clarifying: (1) the socio-political nature of his concepts of text and context; (2) the importance of philosophical rigour, traditionally understood; and (3) the importance of supporting certain socio-political contexts in order for this rigour, not to mention relevant and efficacious political intervention to exist (even if, finally, there must be a supplement to any such context for true political or ethical decisions to be possible).

The Other Heading (OHE) 1992 *

Contains two discussions of the future and political life of Europe, and in particular the way that the figure of democracy has been used and abused – and the ways in which democracy still is and must be the guiding concept for any rethinking of Europe, and of Western political life in general.

Specters of Marx (SM) 1994 *

Derrida argues that the spectre of Marxism is, and should, continue to haunt liberal capitalism. Divested of its teleology (for example, the talk of definitive epochs in history and the exaggerated reliance on the motif of class struggle), Marxism should inspire resistance to capitalism, as well as state sovereignties, by helping to create/perpetuate what Derrida calls a spirit of 'new Internationalism'.

Of Hospitality (OH) 2000 *

This book contains reflections on the aporia that afflicts the notion of hospitality – that it inevitably involves a certain violence, in that hosts, with all of the property rights implicated in the notion of hosting, must keep the hosted under control and must place certain conditions on the behaviour of their guests – otherwise it could not be said that they are hosting at all.

On Cosmopolitanism and Forgiveness (OCF) 2001 *

Derrida expands on the above aporia, via a more explicit consideration of the plight of refugees, and he considers a related aporia, or paradox, that is at work in the concept of forgiveness.

'Force of Law' (AR 230–98) 2002 *

In this illuminative essay, Derrida emphasizes that every deconstruction is undertaken in the name of something that is undeconstructible – for example, justice, openness to difference, the wholly other, the marginalized, the 'to come', or the future. These are all roughly synonymous, and Derrida argues that justice (as opposed to the law) is always 'to come', deferred, and can never finally arrive. Instead, justice is the radical future that haunts the time of the present, or the law of the same, and is 'impossible' in an important sense. You cannot claim that this or that particular social organization is just, as justice is not a present thing. It is an openness towards difference (the future) that is always both betrothed to the law, while simultaneously interrupting the calculations of the law.

Negotiations (N) (including 'Politics and Friendship' and 'Ethics and Politics Today') 2002 *

In Politics and Friendship, an interview with Michael Sprinker, Derrida explains his apparent ethico-political reticence when he was first appointed to the École Normale. To outwardly reject his Marxist/Althusserian counterparts would have risked his position being co-opted by a conservative politics that he has always disavowed. In 'Ethics and Politics Today', Derrida represents ethics as the non-negotiable and politics as the art of negotiation. He suggests that what is required in the many issues confronting us today (including terrorism), is a means of negotiating the non-negotiable and, by implication, a breaching of any arbitrary divide between politics and ethics.

CHAPTER 5

Ethics

Jonathan Roffe

DECONSTRUCTION AS ETHICS

The most frequent criticism of Derrida's philosophy, alongside the claim that it forms a 'modern' or 'postmodern' linguistic scepticism (MO 4), is that it offers no serious basis for any kind of ethical or moral claim – or, even more strongly, that it attempts to destroy any kind of ethical thinking at all, in favour of a form of relativism or moral nihilism. This is despite numerous claims from Derrida himself along the lines of the following: 'from the point of view of semantics, but also of ethics and politics, "deconstruction" should never lead either to relativism or to any sort of indeterminism' (LI 148). I hope to show in what follows that Derrida's texts have been, since the very beginning, *overtly concerned with topics we normally consider to be moral or ethical, fundamentally oriented in an ethical way*, and *increasingly centred on ethical themes*. The first of these three claims is obvious to anyone who spends even the smallest amount of time examining Derrida's work, and it is the task of this chapter to demonstrate the latter two.

In one of his very first texts, *Of Grammatology*, published in French in 1967, we find the following claim:

> The general structure of the unmotivated trace connects within the same possibility, and they cannot be separated except by abstraction, the structure of the relationship with the other, the movement in temporalisation, and language as writing. (OG 47)

Without going into detail concerning the nature of this 'unmotivated trace', it is enough to note, at this early stage, the intertwining of ethics with two other themes that will preoccupy Derrida from this point on: the concept of generalized writing (see Chapter 1); and a reconsideration of temporality that is undertaken, for example, in 'Ousia and Gramme' (MP 29–67), as well as *Given Time* and *Spectres of Marx*. This citation indicates something further, however: it is not just any understanding of ethics that is involved here, irreducibly tangled up with the rest of Derrida's philosophical concerns. He is concerned with *the relation with the other*. What exactly does this mean?

To take one of the other examples he mentions, that of writing, as something of an introductory guide, Derrida has been concerned to show that language use, in order to be anything like language, to communicate anything at all, relies upon the ability of any given 'statement' (a word, a sentence, a book or even a whole language) to mean something *other* than what it means in any particular context: this is Derrida's concept of general writing. In other words, alterity, otherness, is at the heart of language. More than this, and here is where Derrida's idea of context becomes so important (cf. LI 136), each such 'statement' is indebted to others in order to *work*: no particular language use makes any sense without a whole range of other language uses to which it refers and which make it coherent and 'meaningful'.

As the above citation indicates, the same structure holds for ethics as the relation to the other. Derrida's general claim is going to be that the self is nothing without an other, or others, to which it has a fundamental and fundamentally constituting relationship. It is this central kernel of the ethical that Derrida develops in many ways throughout his work, and which will be investigated here.

Obviously there have been many different ways of engaging with moral or ethical questions throughout the history of philosophy (utilitarianism, Kant's categorical imperative, the Platonic meditation on the good life, and so forth). However disparate these various schemes are, we can extract from them all a common thread, which would be the perennial attempt to *generalize* a rule-for-all, or set of rules, that all activities would fall under. Indeed, this is the activity of philosophy itself, according to Derrida, which consists in the attempt to attain universality.

Now, not only does Derrida frequently turn a deconstructive glance the way of some of these traditions directly (such as Kant in AR 40–101, OCF 20–3, 135–88), he more importantly begins by putting in question this generality *itself*, which is inherent in theories *of* ethics, philosophical understandings *of* the ethical. Derrida suspects that it is here, in the attempt to universalize that characterizes the very first step in any philosophical ethics or morality, that we destroy the key characteristic of ethics, and become unethical and violent towards ethics itself. Derrida suggests that 'When ethics is not . . . dissociated from metaphysics . . . when law, the power of resolution, and the relationship to the other are once more part of the *archia*, they lose their ethical specificity' (WD 81). In other words, he argues that the generalizing nature of philosophy – that is, metaphysics – is itself a threat to ethics. The moment that we make a general claim, we lose the very thing we wished to preserve. More precisely, what is excluded or reduced is the otherness of the other, the singular strangeness or non-identity with the self (whether it be my own self, a nation-state, a racial group, and so forth) that ethics is most concerned to preserve and nurture.

Furthermore, given this point, Derrida's ethical orientation can be extended to deal with not only those texts that deal with obvious ethical themes, like friendship (PF, N 147–98), 'illegal' immigration (N 133–44) or ethnocentrism (OG 123), but also to those that concern themselves with understanding the way that philosophy in general excludes problem cases, such as 'parasitic' language use (LI), marginal phenomena (MP), supplements (OG), singularity (GD, DFT), creation (AL), chance (MC), and many other problems that the history of philosophy has put to one side in its hunger for truth, unity and meaning. In other words, Derrida's philosophical interests *as a whole* are avowedly ethical. This way of considering ethics and the relation between philosophy and ethical thinking is not specific to Derrida alone – it is derived centrally from another philosopher whose importance for his work cannot be exaggerated, Emmanuel Lévinas.

DERRIDA'S DEBT TO LÉVINAS

Derrida's relationship to the philosophy of Lévinas is complex and ambiguous, and is dealt with in greater depth in the section on Lévinas in Chapter 13. For the purpose of this discussion, three complementary arguments, which Derrida endorses up to a point, need to be raised: Lévinas' understanding of the history of Western philosophy since Parmenides, his understanding of ethics in relation to this tradition, and the alternative view that he proposes (which we have seen briefly above).

For Lévinas, the cornerstone of philosophy in the West since the Greeks has been an identity that grounds thinking by excluding everything that can be brought under the heading of *alterity*. The whole history of metaphysics (to use a Heideggerian/Derridian term), in its search for foundations, certainty, presence-to-self, unity, and so forth, has proceeded by subsuming alterity, except for the briefest glimpses here and there (Lévinas gives the examples of Plato's Good beyond Being in the *Republic*, and Descartes' conception of infinity). Lévinas' preferred term for this millennia-long skewing of thought is ontology – philosophy concerning the nature of being. Of course Heidegger, who characterized his thought at various times as fundamental ontology, is the main contemporary philosopher towards whom Lévinas directs himself at here, but the whole history of thought insofar as it insists on the primacy of being (the concern of ontology) over and above the concern with alterity, what is otherwise than being, is being accused of a fundamental mistake.

This is clearly a total failure in terms of Lévinas' conception of the ethical as the relation to the other, since it operates by at once excluding alterity, and in turn bringing about a reign of identity and similarity, which perpetuates this exclusionary violence at the heart of Western thought. The philosophy of Lévinas is an attempt to release ethics from this burden – or, better yet, ethics is the name that

Lévinas gives to the relation to the Other that does not totalize, or render similar, that Other. Now, given what has just been said about Western philosophy, Lévinas' understanding of ethics puts him in the position of denouncing enormous amounts of this history of thought, this long error of reducing otherness to similarity that he calls the 'imperialism of the same'. The fundamental problem with the history of philosophy is not that it has casually decided to exclude otherness, a choice that Lévinas is now retrospectively criticizing; rather, the failure to glimpse the radical otherness that structures our existence is precisely co-extensive with the success of theoretical knowledge in general. In other words, philosophy exists only insofar as alterity is marginalized.

In contrast to this monolithic picture, the work of Lévinas offers (in very broad terms) two themes that attempt to bring alterity back to the heart of philosophical thought. The first is signalled in the following citation from Lévinas found in Derrida's text on his work 'Violence and Metaphysics': 'It is . . . toward a pluralism which does not fuse into unity that we wish to make our way; and, if it can be dared, to break with Parmenides' (WD 89). This Lévinasian pluralism needs to be further qualified, however, for it is not merely a non-hierarchical community or neutral plurality of equal citizens that is being indicated here, but a radical incommensurability between the other who exists before the self, and a self that is broken open, demanded of, or called to by the other, before it can hole itself up in the ivory tower of self-sufficiency, self-consciousness and mastery.

Reversing the traditional hierarchies of being over alterity, ontology over ethics, Lévinas' thought insists that before there is any identity of any kind, there is an other who calls me forth, who constitutes me as that being who is responsible for the other. Ethics, far from being concerned with rights or equality, has as its key terms hostage, infinite debt and respect. This forms the basis of Lévinas' general theoretical position, *ethics as first philosophy*, displacing the focus on identity, reason, being, and so forth.

The second of these two themes is to be drawn from Lévinas' *Otherwise than Being or Beyond Essence*: the distinction between the *saying* and the *said*. The *said* is a term that describes the monolithic movement of sameness that discursive knowledge in philosophy, and language more generally, are predicated upon. The kernel of the said would be the verb 'to be [*être*]', a word, incidentally, that Lévinas does not use at all, in any of its forms, in the whole of *Otherwise than Being*. In other words, 'Isness', selfness or 'ipseity' is the index of ontology. The *saying*, on the other hand, is the moment of irreducible alterity, the event of meaning that sameness, ontology or philosophical discourse cannot produce but only cloak or subjugate. Every said must have a saying that makes it possible, just as every self is brought forth by the singularity of the other that calls it (see the section on Lévinas in Chapter 13).

DERRIDA BEYOND LÉVINAS

I said earlier that Derrida endorses up to a point these three Lévinasian claims about the history of philosophy and ethics. We will deal with each in turn.

Firstly, Derrida agrees with Lévinas that Western philosophy is predicated on a fundamental necessary exclusion of alterity in order to create order, truth, subjectivity, and all of those deep philosophical values. In fact, as we have seen already, it is fair to claim that all of Derrida's philosophy can be subsumed under this heading. To take the example of writing again, a large amount of Derrida's early work revolves explicitly around showing how this 'parasitic' entity writing is excluded from speech, that form of language that manifests the self-presence of truth to itself, and to the speaker, who is self-present in the act of speaking (see Chapter 2 and the section on Husserl in Chapter 13). The fact that the many texts where Derrida addresses precisely this concern about the relation between speech and writing *in terms of* a concern for alterity is a good indication of the depth at which his work is concerned with ethical themes. On this point, he and Lévinas are in agreement.

Secondly, Derrida takes on board the Lévinasian point about the nature of the ethical, as we have already seen. For both philosophers, an ethical relation is based on avoiding all forms of totalization, and responding to the call of the other without thereby reducing that otherness to sameness. At this point, however, Derrida makes a decisive shift away from Lévinas. On the latter's account, the relationship between the self and the other is structured absolutely hierarchically: the other transcends the self, precedes and makes the self possible. For Derrida, this hierarchy itself, just like the traditional self-other dyad, must be undone: there is no fundamental, transcendent asymmetry between self and other in either direction, but a radical and universal disequilibrium, where all sameness is dissolved into a web of otherness. If we recall Rimbaud's famous line, 'I is an other [*Je est un autre*]', we will get the sense of Derrida's point here. Consequently, the failure of ethical relations can occur not just in the direction diagnosed by Lévinas; just as much as the other can be appropriated by the self (LOB 102), the self (as 'an other') can be appropriated, for example, by an imperial other, as Derrida shows in his discussion of colonialism in *Monolingualism of the Other* (MO 69–70).

Consider the following difficult but important passage from Derrida's paper, 'Force and Signification':

> The same is nothing, is not (it)self before taking the risk of losing (itself). For the fraternal other is not first in the peace of what is called intersubjectivity, but in the work and the peril of interrogation; the other is not certain within the peace of the response in which two affirmations espouse each other, but is called up in the night by the excavating work of interrogation. (WD 29–30)

Among other things, this passage indicates Derrida's basic contention about the mutual interrelation of self and other. Derrida's starting point here is the same as that of Lévinas: a rejection of 'intersubjectivity', the kind of ethics-as-equality at work in most moral philosophy from Kant to utilitarianism. As we have seen, however, Lévinas goes on to add that the other precedes the self and makes it possible, retaining a kind of primordial purity. For Derrida, this is precisely what is not the case: there is no priority or purity of the other that does not immediately implicate the unity of the self (WD 126); as he frequently notes, one of the fundamental tasks of deconstruction is to put in question any such purity (LI 130). In contrast, self and other emerge together through what Derrida here calls 'the work and peril of inter-rogation' – an unsure, difficult and risky process.

Thirdly, in concert with the above, Derrida agrees that the activity of philoso-phy as a unified discourse about the truth, reality, and so forth, the *said*, constitutes itself only by excluding the moment of alterity, the *saying*. Indeed, the 'margins of philosophy' are the places Derrida looks to find a glimmer of this saying at work in the canonical tradition: strange words, concepts that fit uncomfortably in concep-tual schema, disavowed commitments, and slips of the pen, are the bread and butter of much of Derrida's close readings. However, a complication again becomes necessary in turn concerning the radicality and purity of this distinction in Lévinas. In line with the complexification he offers concerning the mutual implication of self and other, Derrida's thought continually insists that the pure alterity of the saying is ensnared in an economy of the said from which it cannot be disentangled: Derrida expresses this thought, among other things, in his infamous claim that 'There is nothing outside of the text [*Il n'y a pas de hors-texte*]' (OG 158). For Derrida, there are indeed moments of alterity at work, sayings, but they are *always* mutually com-plicit with the instances of the said that express them.

THE NATURE OF THE ETHICAL HORIZON
IN DERRIDA'S THOUGHT

Given the discussion so far, we can conclude something further about ethics in Derrida's sense: if there is always a mutual implication of self and other, a perennial and perilous interrogation, then the possibility of either purely ethical behaviour (total openness to the other) and a complete violent exclusion of the other (total appropriation of alterity) does not exist. This in turn allows us to discern what we might call two ethical horizons in Derrida's work, which can be found throughout.

The word 'horizon' here is doubly important. On the one hand, a horizon is that towards which we move but will never reach (there is, as we have just seen, no absolutely ethical stance or act, but only an ethical horizon); on the other, a horizon is a structure that we can describe, using a concept centrally derived from Immanuel

Kant and that Derrida frequently engages with, as *transcendental*, that is, a condition for the possibility of something. Just as the visible horizon makes it possible for us to experience things in terms of distance, the ethical horizon in Derrida's work is the condition of possibility for any ethical act. The radical otherness of the other, despite the fact that we can never attain it as a state, makes possible any *attempt*.

These two horizons are outlined in a response Derrida gave to an interviewer on the topic of narcissism:

> Narcissism! There is not narcissism and non-narcissism; there are narcissisms that are more or less comprehensive, generous, open, extended. What is called non-narcissism is in general but the economy of a much more welcoming, hospitable narcissism, one that is much more open to the experience of the other as other. I believe that without a movement of narcissistic reappropriation, the relation to the other would be absolutely destroyed, it would be destroyed in advance. The relation to the other – even if it remains asymmetrical, open, without possible reappropriation – must trace a movement of reappropriation in the image of oneself for love to be possible, for example. (P 199)

This passage condenses a number of important themes to be found in Derrida's treatment of ethics. First of all, the two horizons mentioned before are here evident: a horizon of hospitality, and a horizon of appropriation, where the first involves a movement towards openness to the other, and the second an appropriation or dissolution of the otherness of the other. Secondly, it indicates again Derrida's departure from Lévinas in a slightly different fashion from the above, by insisting on the irreducible need for an element of self-preservation if there is to be any relation, ethical or otherwise. Thirdly, in line with this point, the two concomitant forms of ethical disaster are also indicated. The movement towards hospitality would be 'absolutely destroyed' if I were to be radically self-less; there would be no relation whatsoever in this case. On the other hand, according to the earlier points, the move away from hospitality towards a narcissistically self-centred theory and practice destroys by degrees the ethical relation.

The same point is registered by Derrida with regard to the aporia of hospitality. I can invite the other in, host them within my home, be generous with what I have, only insofar as it is *my* home, and they are *my* possessions (OH 135). Similarly, a country can only allow in refugees on the condition that it does not allow in *everyone*, since this would mean the dissolution of the country in question, its sociocultural and political borders (OCF 39; OH 151–5).

The further consequence of this particular lack of absolutes is manifested in Derrida's growing concern with the nature of *deciding*. If there is no pure abstract law to guide ethical conduct, as Plato, Kant, and many others have claimed in one way or another, then making an ethical decision involves a moment of radical undecidability, a leap of faith (GD; see also Chapter 6 of this volume).

Why is this the case? As Lévinas and Derrida both demonstrate, the relation to the other cannot go by way of generality, but must respect the singularity, strangeness and non-totalizable nature of the other. Thus any ethical decision must involve in the final instance the abandonment of general rules and the affirmation of the singularity of the other about, or according to, which one is making a decision. Whenever we 'decide' according to a set of general rules about an ethical issue, according to Derrida, we neither really decide (we only follow a rule), nor do we act ethically, because we subsume the otherness of the other under a general category. Here, the overturning of the general ethical ideal (following a just rule of whatever form) takes its most bold form: following the law, whatever law, is *unethical*, at least insofar as the singular otherness of the other does not have the final say. As Derrida puts it in a pithy phrase: 'There is no moral or political responsibility without this trial and this passage by way of the undecideable' (LI 116).

CONCLUSION

Let us touch again on the three claims opening this chapter: 1. that Derrida's work is concerned with traditionally delineated ethical questions; 2. that it is fundamentally oriented in an ethical direction, and; 3. that Derrida's work has increasingly turned toward meditations on ethical themes.

The first and third of these claims are on the surface of Derrida's texts, for anyone who cares to read them. *Of Grammatology*, for example, takes as one of its explicit aims a critique of ethnocentrism in the human sciences. And the last 20 years of Derrida's work is saturated with reflections on profound ethical themes, like death (MDM, GD, AEL, WM, *Aporias*), hospitality (OH, AR 356–420), and the plight of refugees (OCF 3–23).

In the end, however, what makes Derrida's work a work of ethics is less these surface features, but this second point: the profound undercurrent or orientation that is the most fundamental level of his thought. In summary, taking and modifying the Lévinasian theme of the relation to the other, Derrida tries to pursue the eradication of alterity throughout the history of philosophy in all of its multifarious manifestations. The relation to the other, that is, concerns the other person, but also the other meanings of a text, the other ways of seeing things, other races, other genders, another time (such as the future, the messianic), other languages, other traditions, and so forth. If we claim, then, that deconstruction is ethics, it is because of its constant commitment to all of these others. Derrida's work, considered in this way, has, since the very earliest texts, been travelling down the side-streets of Western thought, well off the monotonous motorway (MO 72, P 295), drawn on by the ethical demand to open itself up to the other, to all the others.

FURTHER READING ON ETHICS

Violence and Metaphysics (WD 79–153) 1978
At This Very Moment in This Work Here I Am (ATM) 1991
Adieu to Emmanuel Lévinas (AEL) 1999
These three texts form the main body of Derrida's engagement with Lévinas. Violence and Metaphysics is the primary text here, difficult yet rich and rewarding. It deals with Lévinas' relation to the philosophical tradition (particularly Husserl and Heidegger), and also to the issue raised in the section on Derrida beyond Lévinas above, concerning the purity of the other. At This Very Moment responds to the fundamental motive behind Lévinas' thought, that of giving to the other, and problematizes this position, *vis à vis* language and sexual difference. *Adieu* is the text of two addresses given by Derrida after Lévinas' death, and touches on themes of hospitality, religion and, of course, the *adieu*.

The Gift of Death (GD) 1995
In this book, which is discussed at length in the next chapter, Derrida argues that responsibility is always precarious, and there is a sense in which living by a rule, or ethical code, is irresponsible to the demands of a singular other (such as a loved one, or God), but he also suggests that a pure affirmation of singularity is itself irresponsible. We must negotiate the tension between generality and singularity.

'Ethics and Politics Today' (N 295–314) 2002
This recent little text is an excellent introduction to Derrida's concern to understand what makes ethical decisions *ethical*, and of the relation to ethics and politics. The question of terrorism is also raised in the conversation recorded at the end of this piece.

CHAPTER 6

Decision

Jack Reynolds

UNDECIDABILITY

Before attempting to understand Derrida's account of the decision, it is necessary to examine an associated notion that has pervaded much of his work — undecidability. An undecidable is one of Derrida's most important attempts to trouble dualisms, or, more accurately, to reveal how they are always already troubled. An undecidable, and there are many of them in deconstruction (for example, the ghost, *pharmakon*, hymen, and so forth), is something that cannot conform to either polarity of a dichotomy (such as present/absent, cure/poison, and inside/outside in the above examples). For example, the figure of a ghost seems to be neither present nor absent, or alternatively, it is both present and absent at the same time (SM). This may seem to be a banal philosophical point, but Derrida consistently shows that this kind of undecidability actually reveals a very important aspect of the various texts that he is examining. This kind of equivocation breaks open the meaning that an author seeks to impose upon their work and exposes it to alternative understandings that undermine the explicit authorial intention. For example, in his essay 'Plato's Pharmacy' (D 63–171), Derrida shows that the undecidable status of the term *pharmakon* in Plato's work (it means both cure and poison) actually undermines Plato's own attempts to distinguish between serious philosophy and mere sophistry (for the Greeks, sophistry is basically a rhetorical use of argumentation for fun, or for profit, that is not grounded in any search for the 'truth').

Derrida contends that in all texts there are inevitably points of undecidability that betray any stable meaning that an author might seek to impose upon his or her text. The process of writing always reveals that which has been suppressed, covers over that which has been disclosed, and breaches the very oppositions that are thought to sustain it. This is why Derrida's work is so textually based and it is also why his key terms are always changing, because depending upon who or what he is seeking to deconstruct, that point of undecidability will always be located in a different place.

The logic of the supplement, which is such an important aspect of Derrida's famous early book *Of Grammatology*, also has an undecidability attached to the notion. A supplement is something that, allegedly secondarily, comes to serve as an aid to something 'original' or 'natural'. For example, we might supplement our main income by doing some other paid work, after hours. Now Derrida's main purpose in discussing the supplement is to problematize any suggestion that the supplement is, in fact, secondary (and this is a complicated argument that I cannot address here). For my purposes, however, it is important to recognize that there is a constitutive undecidability involved in the notion of the supplement. In order to understand this, it is helpful to consider two more examples of the supplement: masturbation, as Derrida suggests in relation to Rousseau (OG 153), and the use of birth control precautions. What is notable about both of these examples is an ambiguity that ensures that what is supplementary can always be interpreted in *two ways* (there are two determinate possibilities involved in an undecidable – a double-bind – and this is why undecidability is not the same thing as indeterminacy). For example, our society's use of birth-control precautions might be interpreted as suggesting that our natural way is lacking and that the contraceptive pill, or condom, hence replaces a fault in nature. On the other hand, it might also be argued that such precautions merely add on to, and enrich our natural way. It is always undecidable whether the supplement adds itself and 'is a plenitude enriching another plenitude, the fullest measure of presence', or whether 'the supplement supplements … adds only to replace … represents and makes an image … its place is assigned in the structure by the mark of an emptiness' (OG 144). Ultimately, Derrida suggests that the supplement is both of these things, accretion and substitution (OG 200). The supplement resists the binary logic of presence/absence, as well as any other either/or designations. Its status cannot be decided according to these metaphysical ways of thinking, and it is this component of his earlier work (the difficulty of actually deciding) that Derrida returns to in detail in many of his more recent texts.

DECISION

Much of Derrida's recent work is united by his analysis of a related kind of undecidability that is involved in the concept of the decision itself. In this respect, Derrida regularly suggests that a decision cannot be wise. Posed even more provocatively, he argues that the instant of the decision must actually be mad (AR 255; GD 65; OCF). Drawing on the work of Kierkegaard, Derrida tells us that a decision requires an undecidable leap beyond all prior preparations for that decision (GD 77). According to him, this applies to all decisions and not just those regarding the conversion to religious faith that preoccupies Kierkegaard. To pose the problem in inverse fashion, it might be suggested that for Derrida, all decisions are a faith and a tenuous faith at that, because were faith and the decision not tenuous they would cease to be a faith or a decision at all (GD 80). This description of the decision as a moment of madness that must move beyond rationality and calculative reasoning may seem paradoxical, but it might nevertheless be agreed that a decision requires a 'leap of faith' beyond the sum total of the facts. Many of us are undoubtedly stifled by the difficulty of decision-making, and this psychological fact aids and, for his detractors, also abets Derrida's discussion of the decision as it appears in texts like *The Gift of Death*, *Negotiations*, 'Force of Law', *Demeure: Fiction and Testimony*, *Adieu to Emmanuel Lévinas*, and *Politics of Friendship*.

In *Adieu to Emmanuel Lévinas*, Derrida argues that a decision must always come back to the other, even if it is the other 'inside' the subject, and he disputes that an initiative that remained purely and simply 'mine' would still be a decision (AEL 23–4). A theory of the subject is incapable of accounting for the slightest decision (PF 68–9), because, as he rhetorically asks, 'would we not be justified in seeing here the unfolding of an egological immanence, the autonomic and automatic deployment of predicates or possibilities proper to a subject, without the tearing rupture that should occur in every decision we call free?' (AEL 24). In other words, if a decision is envisaged as simply following from certain character attributes, then it would not genuinely be a decision. Derrida is hence insisting upon the necessity of a leap beyond calculative reasoning, and beyond the resources of some self-contained subject reflecting upon the matter at hand. A decision is never simply about weighing up pros and cons, and figuring a problem out like a mathematical equation. We may ask ourselves questions like, 'should I leave my partner?' or 'should I use my knight or my bishop for this particular chess move?' We may even work out that it is definitely in our best interests to leave our current lover, or to use the knight in order to best facilitate a checkmate. However, the decision itself does not automatically follow from this. It still needs to be taken, and that requires a leap beyond any prior preparations for that decision. What Derrida is insisting on, is that for a decision to genuinely be a decision, it must invoke that which is outside of the subject's control, and it must hence be partially 'mad'.

If a decision is an example of a concept that is impossible within its own internal logic and yet nevertheless necessary, then not only is our reticence to decide rendered philosophically cogent, but it is perhaps even privileged. Indeed, Derrida's work has been described as a 'philosophy of hesitation', and his most famous neologism, *différance*, explicitly emphasizes deferring, with all of the procrastination that this term implies. Moreover, in his early essay Violence and Metaphysics, Derrida also suggests that a successful deconstructive reading is conditional upon the suspension of choice: on hesitating between the ethical opening and the metaphysical totality (WD 84). Even though Derrida has suggested that he is reluctant to use the term 'ethics' because of logocentric associations, one is led to conclude that 'ethical' behaviour (for want of a better word) is a product of deferring, and of being forever open to possibilities rather than taking a definitive position.

ABRAHAM AND ISAAC

The problem of the decision is perhaps most dramatically illustrated in *The Gift of Death*. In this text, Derrida seems to support the sacrificing of a certain notion of ethics and universality for a conception of radical singularity similar to that evinced by the sacrifice that Abraham decides to make of his son Isaac, according to both the Judaic and Christian religions alike (GD 71). At the very least, Derrida makes clear that the paradox of responsible behaviour means that there is always a question of being responsible before a singular other (such as a loved one, or God), and this necessarily exists in tension with our responsibility towards others generally and to what we share with them. When he is asked to sacrifice his only son upon Mt Moriah, Abraham confronts this problem: on one level, he has communal responsibilities; on another level, he has a very singular responsibility before God. While many of us may have reservations about the particularities of Abraham's decision, Derrida insists that this type of aporia, or tension, is too often ignored by the 'knights of responsibility' who presume that accountability and responsibility in all aspects of life is quite easily established (GD 85). These are the same people who insist that concrete ethical guidelines should be provided by any philosopher worth his or her 'salt' (GD 67) and who ignore the difficulties involved in a notion like responsibility, which demands something importantly different from merely behaving dutifully (GD 63).

Derrida's exploration of Abraham's strange responsibility before the demands of God, which consists in *deciding* to sacrifice Isaac (God intervenes and Abraham does not have to go through with his decision), but also in betraying the ethical order through his silence about this act (GD 57–60), is designed to problematize any ethical concern that exclusively locates responsibility in the realm of generality. This more common notion of responsibility, which insists that one should behave according to a general principle that is capable of being rationally justified in the public realm (GD 60), will always run up against the demands of a singular other (for example a singular person whom we love such as a member of our family, or God). These two aspects of responsibility are incommensurable (GD 61, 66) and any decision must hence always involve an undecidable leap that can never be reduced to any kind of rational calculation

Derrida will not say whether Abraham's willingness to murder is an act of faith, or simply an unforgivable transgression. He suggests that, 'Abraham is at the same time, the most moral and the most immoral, the most responsible and the most irresponsible' (GD 72). This equivocation is a defining trait of deconstruction, but it is clear that Derrida thinks that there is something about Abraham's decision that we must all face in our own decisions. Ethics, with its dependence upon generality, must be continually sacrificed as an inevitable aspect of the human condition and its aporetic demand to decide (GD 70). As Derrida points out, in writing about one particular cause rather than another, in pursuing one profession over another, in spending time with one's family rather than at work, one inevitably ignores the 'other others' (GD 69), and this is the general state of affairs in which we live. He argues that: 'I cannot respond to the call, the request, the obligation, or even the love of another, without sacrificing the other other, the other others' (GD 68). For Derrida, it seems that the Buddhist desire to have attachment to nobody and equal compassion for everybody is an unattainable ideal. He does, in fact, suggest that a universal community that excludes no one is a contradiction in terms. According to him, this is because:

> I am responsible to anyone (that is to say, to any other) only by failing in my responsibility to all the others, to the ethical or political generality. And I can never justify this sacrifice; I must always hold my peace about it . . . What binds me to this one or that one, remains finally unjustifiable. (GD 70)

Derrida hence implies that responsibility to any particular individual is only possible by being irresponsible to the 'other others', that is, to the other people and possibilities that haunt any and every existence. To represent Derrida's position more precisely, true responsibility consists in oscillating between the demands of that which is wholly other (in Abraham's case, God, but also any particular other) and the more general demands of a community. Responsibility is enduring this trial of the undecidable decision, where attending to the call of a particular other will inevitably demand an estrangement from the 'other others' and their communal needs. Whatever decision one may take, according to Derrida, it can never be wholly justified (GD 70) and one can also never finally know whether that decision was the right one (N 232).

CONCLUSION

Of course, Derrida's emphasis upon the undecidability inherent in all decision-making does not want to convey inactivity or a quietism of despair, and he has insisted that the madness of the decision also demands urgency and precipitation (AR 255–8). While the decision is in some sense 'impossible', as it must involve a mad leap beyond any rational calculations, Derrida also asserts that it is equally impossible to simply remain within an undecidable (DFT 16). This means that Derrida is *not* denying the imperative to make decisions. Rather, he suggests that the experience of the 'trial of undecidability' (LI 210) is necessary for any determinate ethico-political decisions, and it also structures those decisions. Moreover, what is involved in enduring this trial of undecidability would seem to be a relatively anguished state of being. In an interview with Richard Beardsworth, Derrida characterizes the problem of undecidability as follows:

> However careful one is in the theoretical preparation of a decision, the instant of the decision, if there is to be a decision, must be heterogeneous to the accumulation of knowledge. Otherwise, there is no responsibility. In this sense not only must the person taking the decision not know everything ... the decision, if there is to be one, must advance towards a future which is not known, which cannot be anticipated. (N 231)

This suggestion that the decision cannot anticipate the future is undoubtedly somewhat counter-intuitive, but Derrida's rejection of anticipation is not only a rejection of the traditional idea of deciding on the basis of weighing-up and internally representing certain options. By suggesting that anticipation is not possible, he means to make the more general point that no matter how we may anticipate, any decision must always rupture those anticipatory frameworks. A decision must be fundamentally different from any prior preparations for it. As Derrida suggests in *Politics of Friendship*, the decision must 'surprise the very subjectivity of the subject' (PF 68), and it is in making this leap away from calculative reasoning that Derrida argues that responsibility consists (PF 69).

MAJOR TEXTS ON THE DECISION

Writing and Difference (including Violence and Metaphysics) (WD) 1978
As the title suggests, this essay describes the way in which metaphysical thinking is necessarily betrothed to a certain kind of violence in that it engenders hierarchies that exclude and marginalize the 'lesser' term of an opposition. Through a sustained discussion of Lévinas, Husserl and Heidegger, Derrida suggests that although one cannot ever simply escape metaphysics, a successful deconstructive treatment of a text, or an idea, must hesitate between metaphysics and that which is non-metaphysics. Deconstruction's own status *vis-à-vis* metaphysics is hence also importantly undecidable (see Chapter 3).

Dissemination (D) 1981
In his early work *Dissemination*, Derrida accords a lot of attention to the undecidable figures, such as the *pharmakon* and Mallarmé's hymen, that unravel the metaphysical logic of particular texts and that also resist the binary oppositions that have

dominated much of the tradition of Western philosophy (for example, presence/absence, inside/outside, speech/writing).

Limited Inc. (including 'Afterword: Towards an Ethics of Discussion') (LI) 1988
Following his interaction with John Searle in *Limited Inc.*, in the 'Afterword' to this text Derrida repeatedly insists that undecidability is not the same thing as indeterminacy. As Derrida suggests, 'there would be no indecision or double-bind were it not between *determined* (semantic, ethical, political) poles' (LI 148). Undecidability hence involves a 'determinate oscillation between possibilities', and this is a frequently ignored point.

Spectres of Marx (SM) 1994
Rather than Marxism being dead and buried, Derrida contends that a spectre of Marx continues to haunt and inform modern Western democracy. The logic of this 'hauntology', as Derrida puns, is undecidable. After all, the ghost of Marxism is neither present nor absent, or it is both present and absent. As mentioned above, this kind of undecidability troubles the dichotomies that pervade much of the Western philosophical tradition.

The Gift of Death (GD) 1995
This book examines two important but divergent accounts of responsibility. It begins with an analysis of Jan Patočka's politics, before considering the individualism, or 'radical singularity' of Kierkegaard's account of the decision. In this text, which revisits Abraham's decision to sacrifice his only son Isaac, Derrida addresses the concept of the decision at length and extends the logic that governs Kierkegaard's discussion of the religious 'leap of faith' to all decisions.

Politics of Friendship (PF) 1997
In this text, orientated around a consideration of the famous Aristotelean proclamation 'O my friends, there is no friend', Derrida examines two alternative conceptions of friendship: Montaigne's, in which the friend is a soulmate who is known and understood absolutely; and, alternatively, a conception of friendship in which the other is not known but always resists our understanding of them and hence surprises us. Considering various other theorists of friendship, including Aristotle, Kant, Schmitt, Blanchot and Nietzsche, Derrida examines the paradoxical sense in which a friend must also be an enemy. In relation to the decision, Derrida's engagement with Nietzsche in Chapter 3 also contains the provocative suggestion that the *'decision is unconscious* – insane as that may seem' (PF 59).

Adieu to Emmanuel Lévinas (AEL) 1999

Following Lévinas' death, Derrida traces the presence in Lévinas' work of themes like the *adieu*, and he also emphasizes the sense of *hospitality* towards the other person that pervades Lévinas' philosophy despite the enduring absence of this term from his work (see the section on Lévinas in Chapter 13). In this text, Derrida's discussion of the decision also takes on board the Lévinasian suggestion that we are originarily called by the other person, and even held hostage by the other, prior to any conception of subjectivity. In deciding, Derrida argues that we decide by and for the other: any genuine decision must invoke that which is outside of the subject's control. Related material: *Of Hospitality* (OH) 2001; 'Hostipitality' (AR 358–420) 2002.

On Cosmopolitanism and Forgiveness (OCF) 2001

In this accessible text, Derrida confronts a number of pressing ethical and political questions currently being debated, including refugees, immigration, asylum seekers, the political role of the writer, and the nature of national borders. Referring in a number of places to Immanuel Kant, he argues that the position of the refugee or asylum seeker is in some sense exemplary of social subjects in general, and not just a current issue. He confronts the issue of the decision through the theme of amnesty and reconciliation: the decision genuinely to forgive another person, or nation, must remain heterogenous to political and moral calculations, however necessary they may be. Derrida contends that this 'impossible' aspect of the decision is too often ignored in the current international discussions pertaining to colonialist reparations. Related material: colonialism – *Circonfessions* (1994); *Monolingualism of the Other* (1998). 'Forgiveness – As If It Were Possible' (N) 2002.

Force of Law (AR 232–98) 2002

In this collection of essays on the (im)possibility of justice, and particularly juridical justice, Derrida insists in 'Force of Law' that his emphasis upon undecidability is not a vacillation that neglects the necessary political task of deciding. Rather, he argues that undecidability structures any determinate decisions that we might make, and it also impels them with a sense of urgency.

Negotiations (including 'Nietzsche and the Machine') (N) 2002

In this interview with Richard Beardsworth, Derrida offers a particularly lucid overview of his understanding of the decision, emphasizing that no preparation for a decision, and no anticipatory structures, including our habitual comportment towards our environment, can assuage the moment of undecidability that is involved in all decisions. Other essays in *Negotiations* illustrate the importance of the experience of undecidability to any responsible political decision-making, but particularly in relation to questions concerning the death penalty, the human genome, and the problem of the *sans-papiers* (immigrants without passport papers).

CHAPTER 7

Religion

Kevin Hart

While Jacques Derrida's early writings displayed little obvious interest in religion, his work has become increasingly attentive to religious themes and concepts. This chapter will explain this development through an analysis of the main religious themes in Derrida's work in something like chronological order.

ONTO-THEOLOGY

In his early work, Derrida's primary critical object is what he calls the 'metaphysics of presence' (see Chapter 3 of this volume), which, as he points out, has structured Christianity in part although not in whole. The expression 'metaphysics of presence' is not to be found in the collected works of Martin Heidegger but the concept is. Heidegger argues that Western metaphysics is constituted in a highly determined way, and when naming that way he borrows a word from Immanuel Kant: 'onto-theology'. For Kant, onto-theology is a way of trying to apprehend God by way of being: as the *highest* being, the *original* being, and the *being* of all being. Kant argues that onto-theology is ultimately a failure: we can have no theoretical knowledge of God. Yet the deity can be known practically, he thinks. We can please God by adhering to the categorical imperative: 'Act only according to that maxim whereby you can at the same time will that it should become a universal law' (*Critique of Practical Reason*). That imperative falls squarely within the realm of reason, and everything else associated with religion – such as works of grace, miracles, mysteries, and means of grace – merely border upon religion considered within the limits of reason alone. I look over Heidegger's shoulder to Kant because some of his ideas will become important for the older Derrida. In particular, Derrida will contest the categorical imperative and reformulate the project of religion considered within the limits of reason alone.

For the early Derrida, though, it is Heidegger rather than Kant who is the principal philosopher to be reckoned with. Onto-theology, for Heidegger, is the consequence of an ambiguity in the very idea of metaphysics as conceived by Aristotle: the study of being as being. On the one hand, this formula denotes the study of being in general (*on he on*), and is therefore known as ontology. On the other hand, it indicates the study of the highest being (the *theion*), which is known as theology. Since the highest being accounts for being in general, and since we cannot know the highest being unless we account for the essence of being in general, Heidegger argued that metaphysics is constituted as 'onto-theology' (see the section on Heidegger in Chapter 13). The ambiguity in Aristotle's definition of 'metaphysics' is not merely an accident, Heidegger said: it has given rise to the history of metaphysics from Plato to Nietzsche. Onto-theology arises in Greek philosophy long before the advent of Christ and the development of Christian theology.

The metaphysics of presence has always been linked to one or more varieties of deconstruction, Derrida tells us. A movement of endless difference and deferral, *la différance*, inhabits and disturbs any claim to presence. This insight leads to two issues in his thought that concern Christian theology. The first is, as he points out in *Of Grammatology,* that Christianity becomes metaphysical when it bases itself on certain assumptions, for example the founding notions of Greek philosophy: *ousia* (substance), *nous* (reason), *logos* (thought/speech), *telos* (goal), and so on. Christianity has a complex history of appropriating Greek conceptuality; it begins in the New Testament, and is heavily marked in the writings of many Church Fathers and the medieval schoolmen. It should be noted that Judaism, with its profound commitment to commentary on the Torah, has been drawn far less into the history of metaphysics (WD 152–3). That said, one should not infer that Derrida is offering an oblique Jewish apologetics. Although he was born a Sephardic Jew, his intellectual culture has been European and Christian. In general, we might say that the position he develops allows for the possibility of a non-metaphysical theology (in his extended sense of 'metaphysical') in Christianity, although it is not something that he has explored in any detail.

Of course, there is no reason why a Jew who, as he says, can 'quite rightly pass for an atheist' (C 155) would be interested in contributing to Christian theology. Yet Derrida has reason to doubt that a non-metaphysical theology could be developed along the lines that have often been envisaged for it. His reservations come into focus when we consider the second consequence of his general position. If *la différance* is beyond being and unable to be captured by our concepts, it resembles the God of negative theology.

NEGATIVE THEOLOGY

In Christianity, a positive theology reveals the Father in the Son through the Spirit; it sanctions the deity to be spoken to and spoken of affirmatively. Negative theologies are intertwined with positive theologies: they reflect on how the predicates ascribed to God in positive theologies ('good', 'light', 'beauty', 'love', and so forth) cannot properly be ascribed to the deity. They ascend to God by way of denying the adequacy of speech. Because God transcends the world, God also transcends our language about the world; and if we are to ascend to the deity we can do so only by a negative way, by suspending, contesting or denying the predicates that are revealed in positive theologies. When talking of *la différance* Derrida often mimics the syntax of negative theologies ('neither this nor that'), but it does not follow from this practice that it is divine. God is transcendent, while *la différance* is quasi-transcendental: a condition of both possibility and impossibility (see Chapter 11). Besides, even the most negative of negative theologies, Derrida suspects, covertly construes God as full presence, and therefore gets entangled in the metaphysics of presence. Negative theology would therefore be an unlikely guide to a non-metaphysical theology.

Would we be correct then to claim that negative theology is simply another version of metaphysics? Yes and no. That there are moments of metaphysics in the *Divine Names* and *Mystical Theology* of the Pseudo-Dionysius, for instance, is not to be disputed. But that the Pseudo-Dionysius affirms a deity whose hyper-essentiality is a blazing moment of self-presence is not supported by his writings. The God evoked in the *Corpus Areopagiticum* is neither present nor absent, neither being nor non-being, neither one nor many, and is entirely free to determine itself. More generally, we should be sceptical about claims by some of Derrida's followers that Christianity belongs in a simple or straightforward way to the history of metaphysics. There have been movements of deconstruction at work in Christianity from its earliest times, and it might be argued that the very word 'deconstruction' has a partial heritage in Luther's word *destructio* in the *Heidelberg Disputation* (1518) which is formed as a response to Paul's words 'I will destroy the wisdom of the wise' (1 Corinthians 1:19), itself a quotation of Isaiah 29:14. Luther's criticisms of the Catholic 'theology of glory' influenced Heidegger when thinking about his word *Destruktion* ('destructure'), which, along with *Abbau* ('unbuild'), is one of the immediate forebears of the word 'deconstruction' (see the section on Heidegger in Chapter 13).

If Derrida has reservations about negative theology indicating a non-metaphysical theology, he is more sanguine about the chances of a deconstructive theology. The aim of such a movement would be 'to liberate theology from what has been grafted on to it, to free it from its metaphysico-philosophical super ego, so as to uncover an authenticity of the "gospel"' (DA 12). We are not to imagine deconstruction coming from an imagined outside to tamper with theology; rather, it would already be at work within theology, calling (as he says) 'Aristotelianism or Thomism' into question, criticizing 'a whole theological institution which supposedly has covered over, dissimulated an authentic Christian message'

(DA 12). Reading these words, we can see that a certain deconstruction is already theological, and that its theology arises out of the Reformation. Yet it is easy enough to see how a deconstructive theology of another stripe could call into question Protestant assumptions about a return to a pure origin and an unmediated relation with God. There is no *one* deconstruction, Derrida says; it might be added that there is no *one* deconstructive theology, either.

Derrida's engagement with negative theologies is mostly confined to the mid-1980s and early 1990s, although it must be said that Derrida never loses interest in the topic. One or more 'negative theologies' is always at issue when talking of *la différance*, and the scare quotes are never to be removed, for they remind us that *la différance* is unsayable because it is quasi-transcendental and not because it is transcendent in the religious sense of the word.

RELIGION WITHOUT RELIGION?

From the early 1990s, however, another emphasis can be detected in Derrida's interest in religion. Now it is not a matter of showing that deconstruction is not a disguised negative theology, or that negative theology relies on presence. Instead, it is a question of 'religion today', of how we are to rethink faith and the holy, evil and the messianic, prayer and sacrifice. Derrida's later thoughts on religion can be organized around his phrase 'religion without religion' (GD 49). Religion without religion? The phrasing recalls Augustine's when he evokes God as 'Measure without measure', 'Number without number' and 'Weight without weight' (*The Literal Meaning of Genesis*, I, 108). In all three instances, 'without' signals divine transcendence. Equally, the phrasing recalls the work of Maurice Blanchot, a French writer and literary critic that Derrida much admires, who frequently uses expressions like 'death without death', 'being *without* being' and 'relation without relation'. Blanchot has recourse to this syntax precisely in order to refuse the very transcendence that Augustine wishes to affirm. The relation without relation, for instance, is a way of being in the world other than that of dialectical transformation of the other person (Hegel) or immediate fusion with the Other (the mystics). Blanchot comes upon the idea when critically reflecting on Lévinas' *Totality and Infinity*. In this text, Lévinas rethinks ethics along the lines of an asymmetry between myself and the other person. There never has been a time when I have not been called to help another person, Lévinas says. The other calls to me as though from on high, and this asymmetric relation can never be reversed without erasing ethics. Wanting to leave God out of ethics, Blanchot argues that the 'relation without relation' is not asymmetric, in favour of the other person, but doubly dissymmetric: you remain other for me, and I remain other for you. We two are held together and apart by an infinite relation. Like Lévinas, Blanchot insists on the word 'infinite' because there can be no calculating of a final responsibility that I have for the other person, and that the other presumably has for me. Much as he admires Augustine, Derrida's phrasing – 'religion without religion' – falls into line with Blanchot.

The expression 'religion without religion' also comes up when Derrida notices that the Czech philosopher Jan Patočka's thought coheres, in various ways and to different extents, with that of several other philosophers he admires: Lévinas, Ricœur and Marion, Kant and Hegel, Kierkegaard and Heidegger. This powerful tradition, cued into a much longer sequence of western philosophy, proposes, he says, 'a nondogmatic doublet of dogma, a philosophical and metaphysical doublet, in any case a *thinking* that "repeats" the possibility of religion without religion' (GD 49). We can approach this claim by way of any of the philosophers Derrida names, and no two would take us to exactly the same place. Marion, a devout Catholic, will lead us where we can find phenomenological justification for the possibility of revelation, while Kant proposes to see if Christianity can be brought within the limits of bare reason.

REVELATION AND REVEALABILITY

For the sake of concision, let us again follow Heidegger whose distinction between *Offenbarung* and *Offenbarkeit*, revelation and revealability, is one that Derrida has adapted to his own ends (HAS 123–7). The Heidegger who does not accept the Christian revelation nonetheless keeps open the possibility of a new revelation of the divine, the traces of which will be registered by the poets. This hope in the spiritual receptiveness of poets is alien to Derrida, and yet the distinction is of use to him: it indicates an aporia that can be found in all periods but that has perhaps been especially significant since the Enlightenment. Revelation and revealability do not arrange themselves by way of a strict distinction, as Heidegger thought. Not at all: each answers to a general structure of iterability, a repetition that begins in and leads to difference and deferral (see Chapter 2 of this volume). Is it revelation or revealability that leads us to the transcendental ground of religion? In other words, does revelation make manifest the conditions of possibility for revelation after the fact? Or is it that the conditions comprising revealability must precede any revelation merely for us to know that it *is* a revelation? An aporia must be negotiated, Derrida tells us (VR 23–4); we must undergo the experience of being pulled in two directions without any possibility of those forces ever being resolved. Why not? Because they are incommensurable: revealability can be calculated but revelation cannot. Theologically, this negotiation would mean that we would think revelation and revealability together. It would have been fascinating to see how Derrida would have explored this new relation. His interest, however, has been in revealability more than in revelation because that enables one to talk of faith without dogma.

MESSIANISMS AND THE MESSIANIC

To put the problem in slightly different terms, Derrida is interested in a general structure of what he will come to term 'messianicity' (SM), without relying on a historical messianism – whether it be Christian, Jewish or Islamic – which proffers a Messiah of known characteristics who is expected to arrive at a particular time and place. Whereas the historical messianisms calculate the unknown and the future, the messianic refers to a structure of our existence that involves openness towards a future that can never be anticipated or circumscribed by the horizons of significance that we bring to bear upon it. While Derrida concedes the possibility that this general structure of messianicity cannot be detected without one or more historical messianisms (VR 23–4), his implication seems to be that the revealed messianisms, or religious orthodoxies, can be transformed into an archive that opens the future and keeps it open.

Consider Judaism as a case in point. Derrida is drawn to 'what constitutes Jewishness *beyond all Judaism*' (AF 74). Jewishness is interminable while Judaism is terminable. So runs Yerushalmi's distinction in *Freud's Moses* (1991), and Derrida finds it of considerable help when specifying messianicity. Yerushalmi maintains that Jewishness is an affirmation of a radical future, a hopeful waiting for what can come only from the future as such: justice. Only the Jew has this hope, Yerushalmi insists: it is an absolutely unique trait of being Jewish, one that survives the loss of belief in God and the rejection of the corporeal election of Israel. It is the absolute character of this trait that Derrida disputes. On his analysis, the singularity of 'being Jewish' is divided in advance, for there can be no unique mark without the possibility of its being repeated. Yerushalmi does not affirm revelation yet he does endorse without reservation the absolute uniqueness of being Jewish, and in considering his understanding of interminable Jewishness Derrida points to the priority of revealability: in this case, the possibility of a singular people.

Unlike Yerushalmi, Derrida argues for a messianicity that exceeds Jewishness as well as Judaism. At issue here is a claim that needs to be inspected: there is a faith that is prior to the determinate faiths of all positive religions. All human interaction presumes that a certain faith – let us call it 'credence' in order to distinguish it from all specific acts of faith – has been extended. In order for me to talk with you, I ask you to trust me to tell the truth. Even if I intend to lie to you, I promise you, through the very act of addressing you, that I will be truthful. What Derrida calls messianicity comes down to be a general structure of the promise – one that inhabits the speech of each and every person, regardless of whether he or she believes in a particular Messiah. It is this archi-promise, structurally informing all our talk, that opens the future, Derrida argues. The 'yes' of the archi-promise must be confirmed, however; it must always be followed by another 'yes' or the promise will remain empty. Openness towards the future is not an endless, passive waiting for justice to

come. Our responsibilities already press hard upon us (AR 255). Only in acting
now, in affirming the archi-promise with a 'yes', can we bring about justice. But
justice itself will never come. There will never be a time when freedom and justice
are embodied fully in a constitution or a society. When people speak in such terms,
freedom and justice have already congealed into law. In such a society there may be
a tomorrow and a next week and a next year, but there is no future. The future
consists of there being always more justice to come, not because we converge
only slowly upon utopia but because material circumstances are always changing.

Derrida greatly admires a passage in *The Writing of the Disaster* where Blanchot
tells the story of the Messiah, the most just of all the just, sitting among beggars and
lepers at the gates of Rome. 'When will you come?' he is asked by someone who
recognizes him. The question indicates that there is a disjunction between the Messiah's presence and his coming. Messianic time cannot be calculated in terms of a
past present, the present day, and a future present. No, it is the time when justice
occurs, a wholly other register of temporality. Justice does not happen, it occurs.
To grasp why this is so we must distinguish between law and justice. An act might
be passed in the Legislature and become law: on a particular day, over a given political space, new liberties or obligations are declared that concern you and me. The
law happens. No matter what the law says, however, I cannot set a bound on
my responsibility to you. Quite simply, I can have no *theoretical* knowledge of my
obligations. Contracts, programmes and rules, along with other judgments of a
theoretical kind, can point out the *sort* of responsibilities I might have, but the
extent of those responsibilities cannot be determined, and I cannot have foreknowl-
edge of situations to come that might call for further acts on my part. No matter
how much I work to help you – teaching you, caring for you, fighting for your
rights, and so on – I cannot say at a given time that I have behaved justly to you
(GD 70). Justice does not occur in any time that has or will be present to my consciousness (AR 255). It occurs, if it does, in the archi-promise that is prior to each
and every specific promise and in the radical future from which justice comes.

I said at the beginning that the early Derrida looked over Heidegger's shoulder
to Kant but that his relationship with Kant is worked out only when he is much
older. It was Kant's view that we can have no theoretical knowledge of God: none
of the traditional proofs for the existence of the deity work. Yet we can have practical knowledge of God. We can please God if we follow the categorical imperative.
This moral law is irreducibly Christian, Derrida argues; it is complicit with an evan-
gelization that seeks to exclude all religious differences. Now Derrida does not wish
to affirm anything that licenses cultural violence in the way that the moral law does.
However, in advocating a messianicity without messianism he is urging a general
structure that impinges on all people. Messianicity, he tells us, constitutes *'a univer-
salizable culture of singularities'* (AR 56). Unlike the Kantian categorical imperative,
messianicity can be universalized without bringing all people under the one law,

without erasing each person's singularity. Where Kant commends a programme in which it is possible to please God without relying on dogma, Derrida affirms that which exceeds all programmes and answers to the impossible. Kant proposes an experiment: to think religion *within* the limits of bare reason. Derrida attends to an experience: religion *at the* limits of reason alone, namely messianicity without messianism. The parallel is not exact, for Derrida says nothing about pleasing God.

As we have seen, Derrida is the first to point out that 'religion without religion' is not a new movement in philosophy. Doubtless one could go back past Kant to Averroës (Ibn Rushd) who maintained in the twelfth century that there is one truth that can be approached in various ways, including revealed theology and philosophy. That the teachings of the Qu'ran are true is not disputed, but their deep truth is to be found by the philosopher who extracts it from the shell of representation. Philosophy thus becomes the judge of theology. This juridical relationship is found everywhere one finds 'religion without religion', and nowhere more clearly than in Kant. Now Derrida wishes to revise Kant's *Religion within the Limits of Reason Alone*, and in particular wishes to preserve and extend the democratic impulse he discerns there. Religion is to be freed from the ecclesiastical hierarchy and grounded in the universal, namely the moral law. We pass from revealed faith to reflective faith, from theology to philosophy; and in doing so we keep fanaticism at bay. Leaping forward from the late eighteenth to the late twentieth century we find Derrida repeating the gesture. Messianicity without messianism passes from revealed faiths to reflective faith; and in doing so it removes us from contemporary fanaticisms and the growing danger of violence. In fact, Derrida goes further than Kant, past the opposition of dogmatic and reflective faith, and certainly past the polarity of revelation and revealability, towards faith as the quasi-transcendental condition of all meaningful existence.

Religion without religion would be a radical openness to the future, an endless calling for justice. It would figure faith as the credence we extend to the other person, and the holy as the singularity of the other person. This is indeed religion without *religion*, without priests and liturgies, without dogmas and superstitions. Notice, though, that it is not religion without *hierarchy*: philosophy remains the judge of theology. Far more seriously, it might also be argued that it is also a religion without *God*, that it merely reworks a classical ideal of virtue without religion. This is not quite fair. Derrida maintains that the other person is other in every way. If we agree with this anthropology, and figure the other person as addressing me from on high, then it is impossible to say whether my relations with him or her are ethical or religious (GD 84). Strictly speaking, I cannot tell if I talk with or pray to the other person.

This revision of religion is unlikely to satisfy any but the most liberal of believers. Religion without religion seeks to adjust positive religions to forestall fanaticism. As Derrida suggests, people will indeed kill for a messiah (PIO 60). They will not

die for messianicity, however, and while this has political import, it counts against
the success of 'religion without religion' as a phenomenology of religion. In the
light of this, it might be asked if one could develop messianicity *with* messianism.
One way of doing this would be to think revelation and revealability together, and
so take a path that Derrida indicated but did not follow himself.

MAJOR TEXTS ON RELIGION

'How to Avoid Speaking: Denials', *Derrida and Negative Theology* (HAS) 1992 *
Derrida addresses the relationship between deconstruction and negative theology at
length, paying particular attention to Meister Eckhart and Pseudo-Dionysius. While
Derrida denies any absolute proximity with them, he does, however, claim that he
does not trust any philosophy that is not 'contaminated by negative theology'.

The Gift of Death (GD) 1995 *
In this text, Derrida considers Kierkegaard's *Fear and Trembling*, as well as its famous
examination of Abraham's decision to sacrifice his son Isaac upon Mt Moriah. Kierkegaard attempts to keep the religious and the ethical apart, but Derrida suggests
that Kierkegaard's own work ultimately undermines any such distinction, and he
argues that this is also the case with Lévinas (GD 84).

'Faith and Knowledge: The Two Sources of 'Religion' at the Limits of Reason
Alone', *Acts of Religion* (AR) 2001
The problematic of religion without religion is raised and discussed in this text in
detail.

CHAPTER 8

Psychoanalysis

Matthew Sharpe

INTRODUCTION

In one way, it is strange that an essay on Derrida's relation to psychoanalysis should be included in this volume. Freud was, after all, no philosopher, and psychoanalysis, if it is anything, is never just a philosophy, even in its most philosophically sophisticated forms. However, in at least several other ways, it is absolutely in order that this collection should feature an engagement with psychoanalysis. For Derrida has always insisted that his work, and its importance, is characterized by a *complex* relationship with mainstream Western philosophy. His entire *œuvre* has been concerned to locate, and to have responded to, the Other or Others – for it is not clear, he says, that there could ever be 'one' Other – excluded by what he designates as canonical logocentric philosophy (see Chapter 5 of this volume). From the earliest essays, accordingly, Derrida's work is characterized by an ongoing, sometimes explicit, often only implicit or marginal, dialogue with psychoanalysis as a theoretical body situated at the margins of philosophy. 'Freud', alongside of 'Lévinas', and 'Nietzsche', is one of the proper names cited by Derrida in the programmatic piece '*Différance*' (MP 3–27) as having pointed the way towards his own notion of the 'trace'. At a crucial moment of this essay, Derrida describes Freud's thought as 'another diaphoristics, which in its entirety is both a theory of the figure (or of the trace) and an energetics' (MP 18).

From very early on, Derrida hence acknowledges a filial debt owed by deconstruction to psychoanalysis. Alongside Nietzsche, Heidegger, Saussure and Lévinas, the theory inaugurated by Freud stands as one of his primary (re)sources. Derrida is attracted to psychoanalysis 'putting into question the primacy of consciousness' (MP 18). He sees the founding Freudian postulation of an unconscious as of epochal importance. *Writing and Difference* talks of 'that moment of world history subsumed under the name "Freud"' (WD 228). In recent years, Derrida has hence even offered defences of psychoanalysis against those who would simply dismiss it. Talking of Lacan, Derrida for instance remarks in *Resistances*: 'nothing of that which managed to transform the space of thought in the last decades would have been possible without some coming to terms *with* Lacan, without the Lacanian provocation, however one receives it or discusses it' (RP 46).

In the background of Derrida's praise of psychoanalysis is his central understanding of the history of Western philosophy. Derrida has consistently maintained that this tradition is characterized by a set of founding commitments to the values of presence (over absence), speech (over writing), the same (over the other), identity (over difference), truth (over fiction and falsehood), life (over death), and the ideal (over the material). His further bold position is that all of these prioritizations originate in what he calls (borrowing from Kant) a 'transcendental illusion'. This is the illusion that an individual subject could fully control the meaning of everything they say, think, and do: an illusion promoted by the situation of an isolated and fully self-conscious subject 'hearing itself speaking' without any external interruption, or 'leakage' of the meaning. The importance of this *phonocentric* illusion (from *phone*/the voice: 'voice-centric'), according to Derrida, is proven by the fact that the philosophy of the modern age, 'from Descartes to Hegel', is that of 'presence as consciousness, self-presence conceived within the opposition of consciousness and unconsciousness' (WD 198).

Now it is precisely such an equation of meaning with consciousness, that Freud, no less than Derrida, was concerned to challenge. Mentally ill people are living proof, Freud argued, that individuals are not in full mastery of their own thoughts and behaviours. Neurotic symptoms and 'parapraxes' (slips of the tongue, or the pen) are moments in subjects' behaviours and speech that they cannot even consciously understand, let alone control. 'Symptoms are, therefore the unconscious is' is something like Freud's version of Descartes' *cogito*. In Derridean language, we could say that, for Freud, symptoms testify to *an irreducible surplus of meaning over conscious intentionality*. The desires to which these symptoms are tied must have been *repressed*, Freud argues. Moreover, far from being meaningless, symptoms are explicable as 'returns of the repressed' that can be interpreted as such.

Derrida's first extended essay on Freud, 'Freud and The Scene of Writing' (WD 196–231), thus opens with a reflection on the appearance of a resemblance between deconstruction and psychoanalysis:

These appearances: the analysis of a historical repression since Plato. This repression constitutes the origin of philosophy as *episteme*, and of truth as the unity of *logos* and *phone* . . . Repression, not forgetting; repression, not exclusion. An unsuccessful repression, on the way to historical dismantling . . . The *symptomatic* form of the return of the repressed: the metaphor of writing which haunts European discourse, and the systematic contradictions of the ontotheological exclusion of the trace. The repression of the writing as the repression of that which threatens presence and the mastering of absence . . . (WD 197)

At the close of this piece, moreover, Derrida suggests a series of research programmes in fields 'whose specificity . . . could be opened to a thought fecundated by psychoanalysis': a new psychopathology of everyday life; a more developed history of writing; a new literary criticism or theoretic of literature; and what Derrida calls a psychoanalytic graphology (WD 230–1).

In line with the way psychoanalysis understands filial relations, though, it needs to be stressed that Derrida's relationship with psychoanalysis is not a wholly simple one. In Freud and the Scene of Writing, Derrida qualifies the impression that might be created by the similarities between his deconstruction of logocentric philosophy and psychoanalysis. In his own words, Derrida evinces: 'a theoretical resistance to utilise Freudian concepts, except in quotation marks' (WD 196), and as he puts it, archly, later in the essay, 'we never dreamed of taking it [Freud's theory of dreams] seriously, outside of the question which disturbs and disorganises its literalness' (WD 229). Derrida talks of the 'neurological tales' of the early Freud, and the 'metapsychological fables' of Freud's work after the ground-breaking *Interpretation of Dreams* (WD 228). All of Freud's concepts, he argues:

> Without exception, belong to the history of metaphysics; that is, to the system of logocentric repression which was organised in order to exclude or to lower (to put outside or below) the body of the written trace as a didactic and technical metaphor, as servile matter or as excrement. (WD 197)

In short, Freud's work – and the work of psychoanalysis in general – is situated at the margins of philosophy, and this in the double sense of marginality that Derrida has made famous. On the one hand, it promises a way out and steps forward with regard to the age-old figures of thought which 'call for a deconstructive questioning (a questioning which is obviously by definition both philosophical and eccentric . . .)' (RP 54). On the other hand, psychoanalysis is inevitably 'guilty by association', as it were. For all the steps beyond metaphysics it initiates, it does not avoid contamination by, and subscription to, the system of logocentric valuations that it promises to destabilize.

In Derrida's texts on psychoanalysis, then, how does he proceed? For the purposes of this chapter, I want to suggest that there are two 'types' of Derridean engagement with psychoanalysis. These two 'types' can and often have interpenetrated in the same written text, although they will be separated out in what follows in this essay.

The first, to be pursued in the next section, is Derrida's more avowedly negative relation to psychoanalysis. In this respect, his concern is to show that psychoanalysis is not 'wholly Other' to logocentric philosophy, despite its attempted steps beyond it. It bears its stamp, Derrida argues, even (especially) in the work of Jacques Lacan, Derrida's contemporary, and the most philosophically sophisticated successor of Freud (PC). There are two central issues here that will be discussed in this essay: the first is the continuing attempts of psychoanalysis to wholly secure what Derrida calls its 'archive'; the second is the question of what Derrida calls a 'psychoanalysis of literature respectful of the *originality of the literary signifier*' (WD 230).

The second, more affirmative aspect of Derrida's engagement with psychoanalysis is borne out by following statement, again from Freud and the Scene of Writing:

> Our aim is limited: to locate in Freud's texts several points of reference, and to isolate, on the threshold of a systematic examination, those elements of psycho-analysis which can only uneasily be contained within logocentric closure, as this closure limits not only the history of philosophy but also the orientation of the 'human sciences'. (WD 199)

FREUD'S LEGACY: LITERATURE AND THE TRUTH

ARCHIVING: IN THE NAME OF THE FATHER

As I commented above, there are two recurrent concerns that Derrida's (broadly speaking) 'critical' deconstructions of psychoanalysis turn around. The first is the attempt of psychoanalysts, especially those after Freud, to secure what Derrida calls the psychoanalytic 'archive'. The central texts here are 'Freud's Legacy' in *The Post-card*, and *Archive Fever*. Derrida is referring primarily, of course, to the written documents wherein the history of psychoanalysis is publicly recorded. Psychoana-lysis has always aspired towards a scientific status. As such, its practitioners have always been keen to differentiate texts and notions that are 'proper' to it from 'deviations'. These must be excluded from the archive. Yet, unlike other sciences, the destiny of psychoanalysis has remained, Derrida stresses, irrevocably tied to the legacy of 'Freud': the man Sigmund Freud and his proper name (a name which has – of course – outlived its 'owner'). Lacan, as we shall comment later, presented his entire work as a 'return to the meaning of Freud' (*Ecrits*).

As we shall see in Part 2, however, Derrida is repeatedly concerned to show that what certain moments within psychoanalysis itself should have made clear is that the psychoanalytic archive (as with *any* body of writings) can always be contami-nated, or be put to (ab)uses beyond the imagination of the founder or his followers. Derrida's own texts on psychoanalysis, for example, are texts in which, as he says, he reads psychoanalysis 'as it pleases him' (RP 51). In both *The Postcard* and *Archive Fever*, also, he interweaves analysis of the canonical texts of Freud with citations from documents – Freud's letters, memoirs, and so forth – not usually included in the archive of psychoanalysis.

THE FATHER HAS NO CLOTHES

The second deconstructive concern that Derrida's writings on psychoanalysis circle around is the question of how psychoanalysis treats works of literature. In the opening section of Le Facteur de la Verité, he singles out Freud's reading of Hans Christian Andersen's famous fable of the emperor who has no clothes. Freud analyses the tale in the context of an attempt to explain the recurrent dream people have of being naked, wherein no one else but the dreamer notices. Freud thinks that Andersen's strange tale, in which no one but the emperor notices his nakedness, gives voice to the fantasy structuring these dreams, which hail from the period of our early infancy (the only time when we were widely seen naked by unconcerned adults).

Derrida's first objection to Freud's appropriation of Andersen's tale is that it reduces the tale to the mere purveyor (*facteur*) of a truth more directly stated in his own theoretical works. Psychoanalysis, as Derrida thus opens Le Facteur de la Verité by musing, tends to find itself, and confirmations of itself, in everything that it encounters.

However, Derrida makes the further claim that the very content of Andersen's tale calls into question Freud's way of interpreting it. Derrida's point concerns how both the garment and the nakedness it would conceal in the story are invisible. The emperor's nakedness, far from being a hidden truth to be uncovered, is always visible in the first place. Hence, drawing a parallel between the 'textile' of the emperor's gown, and the 'text' itself, Derrida points out that the idea that the text veils some hidden truth, like the hidden truth Freud reads into or behind Andersen's story, is made problematic. Rather than being the object of Freud's un-covering interpretation (which peels away the unnecessary contents of the tale), the tale, as it were, already comments on (or re-marks) its interpretation (see Chapter 9 of this volume).

FRAMING CONCERNS

Derrida finds the same questionable interpretive procedure that he contests in Freud – of extracting the supposed truth of the fictional tale from everything 'inessential' about it – even more strongly at play in Jacques Lacan's reading of Poe's famous story 'The Purloined Letter'. Lacan's reading appears to be an advance on the more standard psychoanalytic way of reading a literary text, but for Derrida the same problem repeats itself, in part because 'Lacan's refinement and competence, his philosophical originality, have no precedent in the tradition of psychoanalysis' (RP 47). The truth that Lacan seeks to extract from Poe's story is the truth of truth *per se*, which is a wholly more problematic and philosophical question.

Lacan sees 'The Purloined Letter' as turning around a peculiar repetition, in the Freudian sense of this word. What repeats is a three-way, or three-person ('triangular'), social situation. In the first key scene, the three actors are the Queen, the King, and a Minister. The Queen has just received a letter, whose content we never know, but which the Queen, for whatever reason, absolutely does not want to fall into the hands of the King. The King, the second person, is blind to the situation. The Minister (third person), however, is cunning enough to see clearly the disempowered position that the Queen is in, when she is interrupted reading the letter by the King. He calmly 'purloins', or steals the letter knowing that, although she can see him doing it, the nature of the letter will prevent her from intervening. His possession of the letter, he also knows, will mean that the Queen is under his control. The Queen hence calls in the Prefect of Police, without notifying the King, in order to relocate the letter.

The second key situation ensues at the Minister's chambers. According to Lacan, the three parties in this situation (the Minister, the Prefect of Police, and 'our' hero Dupin) are in social positions that precisely replicate those of the first situation. First, we have the holder of the letter. In the first scene, it was the Queen, in the second, it is the Minister. The second position is that of the blind authority. In the first scene it was the King, this time it is the police, who cannot find the letter. The third player in the second scene, which replicates that of the Minister in the first scene, is the detective Dupin. He sees what the Police do not. This is that the letter, far from being hidden, is placed openly atop the Minister's fireplace. Just as the Minister had in the Queen's chambers, he accordingly purloins the letter, and replaces it with one of his own.

According to Lacan, this repetition reveals the nature of the Freudian repetition compulsion as such. This compulsion or 'drive' hails from the subjection of human individuals to the 'agency of the signifier'. Humans may imagine themselves to be the autonomous authors of their behaviours, Lacan says, yet their meaning is determined by how we are situated socially, in relation to other people. The 'signifier' in question in the story is the purloined letter. Its 'agency' or power, Lacan observes, is like that of a repressed desire in the unconscious. Whoever possesses the letter is immediately disempowered *simply by virtue of the social ramifications of having it*. It possesses its possessor, and what repeats when humans repeat, Lacan argues, is their subjective position *vis-à-vis* the prohibited letter(s) of the unconscious. The truth of the unconscious is that 'the letter always arrives at its destination' (*Ecrits*).

So Lacan thinks that by extracting or purloining the truth of Poe's fiction of the purloined letter, he too can return the letter 'Freud' to its proper destination, and restore the psychoanalytic archive against Freud's unfaithful followers. Yet, Derrida argues, Lacan can only perform this purloining activity at the cost of a number of telling omissions.

The most significant of these is that, in order to extract the supposed truth of 'The Purloined Letter', Lacan omits to consider the *fourth* person involved in the two scenes, who is none other than the narrator, Dupin's side kick. Now this narrator is not Poe, Derrida notes, and Poe is writing a fiction (PC). Moreover, because the story is told in the past tense, the narrator is already doubled into a narrator-narrating and a narrator-narrated. Is it then legitimate to omit considering the narrator at all, so as to treat the story as merely a 'purveyor [*facteur*]' of truth, as Lacan does? In fact, in 'Le Facteur de la Verité', Derrida makes a claim about 'The Purloined Letter' parallel to that of 'The Emperor's New Clothes'. Derrida argues that Poe's story, wherein the 'hidden' purloined letter is overlooked precisely because it is so evident above the fireplace, itself pre-empts and disempowers Lacan's attempt to peer behind the surface of the literary written text to disclose the story's supposed truth.

CONTENT: POSTAL PROBLEMS AND LACAN WITH THE PHILOSOPHERS

Derrida's concerns about Lacan's interpretive procedure in his framing Seminar on the Purloined Letter are also informed by a series of more lasting philosophical points. Derrida reflects that at the same moment as the method of deconstruction called 'one to think the philosophical from a place that could not longer be simply philosophical or non-philosophical', it was also 'possible to witness a theoretical binding of the Lacanian discourse that made the most strenuous, and powerfully spectacular, use of all of the motifs that were in my view deconstructible, undergoing deconstruction' (RP 54).

In 'For the Love of Lacan' (RP), Derrida lists eight points of difference from Lacan, from which I will take only two that lie at the heart of what Derrida calls the 'chiasmus' of his encounter with Lacan:

● *On 'the' letter.* Lacan talks of 'the' letter in the unconscious, and in Poe's story. He argues that the agency of the letter that he refers to – the letter to the Queen – will not be effected should the physical letter be cut up or divided, because its 'agency' depends only on what people (will) think about its relation to the King's Law. Derrida, by contrast, contends that – Lacan's protestations notwithstanding – this idea is an indefensible and 'idealist'. It is not just that a letter, when it is on a piece of paper, can be crumpled, cut up, broken into little pieces so that its written letters, for example, can be cut and pasted onto other pieces of paper in totally different contexts. This obvious empirical fact, for Derrida, points towards what he calls, in 'Signature Event Context' the *iterability* of the signifier (LI 7). This is the idea that one necessary condition for the possibility that a letter or signifier can 'make sense' at all, is that it must be capable of being quoted ('re-iterated') in contexts that the author cannot in principle foresee (see Chapter 2 of this volume). For Derrida, that is, no document or letter is simply 'one': as a text and a piece of writing, it is always, at least potentially, able to mean something *more*.

- *A letter can always not arrive at its destination:* famously, and for reasons close to those just recounted against the idea that there ever could be *one* letter, Derrida disputes Lacan's conclusion that what Poe's story shows us is that 'the letter always arrives at its destination'. A letter can always not arrive at its destination, Derrida insists. 'Common sense' seems to be on Derrida's side here. You would have to be a fool to have absolute faith in the efficiency of any national or international postal service. However, Derrida's philosophical point is a different and stronger one. Derrida argues that for any letter at all to exist as such, whether factually it is mislaid or not, it must be possible for it not to arrive at any proper destination. Without this possibility, no letters, no writing, no sense. This is because letters are made up of signifiers (words, usually), and signifiers – as suggested above – are indefinitely repeatable (iterable). Derrida's deep point here, or the point that puts an end to all hidden depth beneath the fabric of (written) texts, is that *no letter can ever have a single 'proper' place.*

FREUD'S RESISTANCE TO LOGOCENTRISM

A NOTE ON DERRIDA'S WRITING PAD

We have already seen that Derrida is preoccupied in his texts on psychoanalysis with the 'scene of writing', especially in literature. However, what interests Derrida in 'Freud and the Scene of Writing', is a different philosophical point: that Freud, from the time of his first attempts to formalize psychoanalysis as a positive science (in the 1895 *Project for a Scientific Psychology*), continued to use metaphors of writing to describe the psyche. In the introduction to this essay, we saw that it was not only Freud's way of (mis)reading literature that is in need of deconstruction, according to Derrida. Rather, Freud's concepts remain at decisive points betrothed to the founding valuations of Western phonocentrism. What does it mean then, Derrida asks, that Freud continually felt it necessary to describe the 'living psyche', at first indirectly but increasingly directly, as a (dead) writing apparatus?

Freud's dilemma, put most sharply, is that in trying to describe how the psyche works in his so-called metapsychological texts, he needed to describe an apparatus that had two capabilities, which are seemingly irrevocably in tension. First, in what he called the system perception-consciousness, our minds are perpetually open to new experiences (or 'inscriptions', as Freud says). Nevertheless, what dreams and symptoms give testimony to, Freud argues, is that our minds are capable of storing memories for an indefinite period of time. There is no time in the unconscious, Freud stipulates. How then can the mind have at once 'a potential for indefinite preservation and an unlimited capacity for reception' (WD 222)? There are, for Derrida, three stages in Freud's evolution towards an equation of the psyche with a writing machine, in the light of this dilemma.

Even in Freud's earliest attempts at a 'scientific psychology', Derrida notes, the psyche's capacity to receive and retain stimuli is described by Freud in terms of 'spacing, a topography of traces, a map of breaches' (WD 200). This is what Derrida is referring to in '*Différance*' when he says that Freud's theory is already a theory of the trace (MP 18). Memory 'traces' (Freud's word) are retained by the mind only insofar as they repeat, and their repetition is the 'living psyche's' attempt to ward off – defer, delay, suspend, *différer* – any excessive expenditure or build up of energy (like in writing, which we trace out only when the supposed 'living present' that we could have talked about is past, gone, absent).

Secondly, in Freud's *The Interpretation of Dreams*, the dreamwork is compared to different systems of writing: Chinese writing, hieroglyphics, and rebuses.

Finally, there is the 'Note on a Mystic Writing Pad', where the difference Freud has maintained between the 'living psyche' and the 'metaphoric' of writing is wholly collapsed. Here, Freud describes the psyche by considering the functioning of the *Wunderbloch*. This is a children's toy with a wax surface upon which writing can be traced, but which can always be renewed through lifting it off its base. Beneath the surface, however, is a layer of wax – 'like' the unconscious – that permanently retains whatever has been written on the surface.

SPECULATIONS: BEYOND (?) THE PLEASURE PRINCIPLE

Derrida's longest and most difficult piece on Freud is in *The Postcard:* To Speculate – On Freud (PC 259–409). It is here that what is arguably Derrida's key 'deconstructive' argument about Freud is most extensively charted. The text involves a very close, sequential reading of Freud's 1923 book *Beyond the Pleasure Principle*.

Beyond the Pleasure Principle is the text when Freud suggests that a further drive – in addition to the pleasure principle – operates in the psyche: the death drive. The pleasure principle orients the psyche towards a maximization of its pleasure (which involves releasing or lowering levels of excitation), and the minimising of pain. Yet, in his opening chapter, Freud intimates that while everything he has written has affirmed the sovereignty of the pleasure principle within the mind, he is now drawn to a speculation, and to posit a beyond to the pleasure principle. The problem is that Freud does not ever really arrive at a single definition of what this death drive might be, and how it might operate. Derrida's argument about this is multi-faceted, and we will soon see what he thinks of the content of Freud's death drive.

A first key level of Derrida's response, however, is to insist again that what is most interesting about Freud's text is its 'scene of writing'. The point of the text of *Beyond the Pleasure Principle*, for Derrida, is also the text itself. To speculate, in the ordinary and/or financial sense(s) of the word, is to invest something now, with an eye to the future. One does not know whether things will pay off. For Derrida, the point is that *Beyond the Pleasure Principle* is only too true to what Freud announces at its start. He *is* speculating and the speculative step(s) beyond are not beyond at all.

RESISTANCES: BEYOND THE PLEASURE PRINCIPLE

As Derrida avows (PC), all of his engagements with psychoanalysis turn around his reading of *Beyond the Pleasure Principle*, and the issue of the death drive. Why does Freud feel it necessary to speculate in this way, and what is speculated upon? In his discussion on these topics in *Resistances of Psychoanalysis* (RP), Derrida focuses on the notion of resistance in Freud.

Freud observed that, on a very basic level, the patient doesn't always like what the analyst has to say. They may resist psychoanalysis, in what Freud called 'negative transference'. The analyst should not be dissuaded: even the patient's resistance to the analyst has a meaning that can be analysed. It just becomes a question of analysing the resistance. Yet, later in his career, precisely at the time when he felt the need to speculate about a beyond to the pleasure principle, Freud posited what he called a resistance of the id. Even when everything that can be interpreted has been interpreted, people evince a compulsion to repeat that resists analysis (RP 23). This compulsion, as *Beyond the Pleasure Principle* tries to detail, is testimony to the operation of the death drive in the psyche.

Derrida's interest in the death drive is that it represents precisely a resistance that *has no meaning*. The death drive resists analysis. Yet, if it resists analysis, as Derrida specifies, it is because it is *itself* analytic. The word 'analysis', he notes, condenses two meanings. The first is an idea about returning to the origin or founding principle of a thing (an *archaeological motif*). The second is a motif of dissolution. To analyse something is to take it apart, piece by piece. Now, to the extent that Freud's speculation 'paid off', the death drive represents precisely a drive to dissolve or unbind complex unities, including the unity of the organism itself (oneself or another). At the heart of psychoanalysis, Derrida thus observes, we find the hypothesis of a drive that precisely resists psychoanalysis: that insistently and without purpose repeats.

This is also why Derrida's later collection of essays on Freud is called *Resistances of Psychoanalysis*. It is not that the book stages Derrida's resistance to psychoanalysis. In typical deconstructive manner, Derrida is interested to show throughout all his works on psychoanalysis that there is not one 'psychoanalysis'. There is not one psychoanalysis because psychoanalysis *resists itself*. It resists itself in Freud's later speculation on the death drive: a drive that resists analysis, committed only to blindly repeating and reiterating itself – like, Derrida says, the written signifier – continuing without end (RP 24).

CONCLUSION: TO BE CONTINUED...

Here, the undergirding reason that Derrida opposes those who have devoted them-selves to securing Freud's legacy becomes manifest (cf. 'Fors'). If Derrida is right, then Freud's legacy is precisely one that calls into question the possibility of any closed archival system, resistant to contamination. Derrida's point is not just that Freud's legacy can never be secured, after the father has perished. It is that this 'legacy' is itself already divided from within. It points towards the possibility and the necessity that all conceptual systems – and this includes, first of all, the philosophies – cannot close themselves over. This is because they – and us all – are always haunted by a certain drive to repeat, which Derrida, in his texts, aligns with the iterability of the written signifier. As Derrida concludes To Speculate – On Freud by saying, once there is the Freudian speculation on the death drive, the practice of reading, thinking, writing (psychoanalysis) will always have to be (or not to be) 'to be continued'.

FURTHER READING ON PSYCHOANALYSIS

'Me – Psychoanalysis: An Introduction to the Translation of 'The Shell and the Kernel' by Nicholas Abraham' (1979)

Fors: the Anglish Words of Nicolas Abraham and Maria Torok (1986) *
This essay examines the Freudian distinction between introjective (normal) mourn-ing and incorporative (pathological) mourning. Derrida undermines the normative component of this distinction and attests that there is a sense in which incorporative mourning, which preserves the other as 'other', or as a foreign entity within the psyche, might be considered more respectful of the dead other's difference. Related material: *Memoires for Paul de Man* (MPM) 1986, *The Work of Mourning* (WM) 2001.

'Let us not forget psychoanalysis' (1990) *
In a short improvised address before a paper by René Major, Derrida criticizes the various discourses that suggest that psychoanalysis is no longer relevant to discus-sions of the contemporary theoretical and socio-political situation – on the con-trary, he insists on its continuing importance.

'Psychoanalysis Searches the State of its Soul: The Impossible Beyond of a Sover-eign Cruelty' (WA 238–80) 2002 *
In this essay, Derrida argues that psychoanalysis, along with the institution of the university, offers a privileged site from which to resist the phantasm of sovereignty.

'And say the animal responded?' *Zoo-ontologies* (2003) *

In 1997, Derrida presented a week of lectures concerning the role of the animal in Descartes, Kant, Heidegger, Lévinas and Lacan. This article concerns the latter of these, and closely examines the ways that Lacan distinguishes the human from the animal, particularly with regard to the ability to deceive.

CHAPTER 9

Literature

Claire Colebrook

INTRODUCTION

There is a common understanding of the relationship between Derrida and literature, held alike by some of his admirers and critics: Derrida collapses the relationship between philosophy and literature. Nothing could be further from the truth, and this is because Derrida's engagement with literature maintains the necessity of truth, and the necessity of the opposition between truth in its philosophical form, on the one hand, and literary writing on the other. Indeed, according to Derrida, the experience and reading of literature must force us to address the limits of the concepts of truth and, possibly, allow for a 'truth beyond truth'.

Philosophical truth, as it has been determined in the history of Western metaphysics, is opposed to falsity and fiction; it is also designated as primary and originary. On this understanding, there are truths – for example, the fact that the world exists – and then fictions, falsehoods and errors. Derrida, however, wants to think a truth beyond philosophical truth, a 'not true' that is more than, or in excess of, the opposition between true and false (DFT 89) – it is here that his encounter with literature is most significant. The literary work allows for a thought of that which is neither true nor false in the conventional sense, but which is not a lack of truth. If a text displays the way in which an opposition is inscribed – if, say, a story itself comments on its own telling, or remarks on its own fictiveness, or if it bears a title that complicates just where the fiction begins or ends – then it re-traces the border between opposing terms. For example, if a novel opens with some mark such as 'This is a novel', then this statement both places the work within fiction, but in so doing must itself not be fictive.

For Derrida this bordering or marking, while played upon in the explicit literary corpus of fictions and literary genres, is also essential to all texts that present themselves as other than fictive or literary. There must be some inscribing term that inaugurates the series or set within which the text operates (AL 43). Literature will, for example, take a mark or word – such as 'shibboleth' (AL 404), 'demeure'

(DFT 79–88), or 'hymen' (D 173–226) – and show the ways in which a sound and series of letters, a given history of traces, can institute a space or range of terms (LOB 137). The word 'demeure', for example, has a series of resonances both unique to French (including abiding, remaining, permanence, living) and singular to Blanchot's remarking of the term's possible connections, which include French literature's use of 'demeure' to rhyme with meurt (meaning 'die'; DFT 78).

Literature therefore affirms singularity, or that which happens to thought, before decision, conceptuality or law – 'before' anything like philosophical thought can be said to be. These ambiguities or undecidable terms are not accidents or ornaments; literature exposes that these are essential condition of thought and experience as such. On the one hand such literary events are singular: it is unique to a specific language or text that a word can function in this double or undecidable sense. On the other hand, such a singularity, accident, chance or contingency is what makes all thought possible: singularity in general (DFT 91). There is always a border or band, a term that must mark off or organize the differences within which we think. Literature marks and remarks these bordering terms, and thereby exposes a condition of truth – what must have already taken place or been traced in order for any truthful statement to be possible.

For Derrida the experience of the literary, if not the institution of literature (LOB 88), is the experience of a singularity (AL 66, 382) that truth aims to render present but that also disrupts any sense of truth as general, repeatable, meaningful and ideal. Without the singularity of literature – the unique trace, mark or inscriptive event that resists any general reading – there could be no philosophical truth. The possibility of literature, fiction and distance from truth – the possibility of a mark devoid of sense or content – is what both enables and precludes a foundational and original truth. Moreover, it is literature that calls us to read that which, in its singularity, resists reading. In this regard, literature gives us the affirmative dimension of deconstruction. Whereas philosophy and the striving for truth, sense and meaning must always be deferred and remain 'to-come' and thus would seem to present negative and critical projects, the literary text remains or strives to remain unreadable, irreducible to sense and open to an otherness not to be incorporated, translated or understood (LOB 102).

It hence becomes apparent that the simple opposition between a primary philosophical truth and a derivative, imitative or mimetic literature, is deconstructed by Derrida, but it is certainly not dissolved or abandoned. Rather, both terms – philosophy and literature – are transformed and rendered different through Derrida's insistence on their distinction. This then allows Derrida to approach literature not as the representation of some external (or 'transcendent') truth, but as a positive or affirmative 'call' to read that which cannot be placed simply outside the text. It also allows Derrida to read philosophy deconstructively, as dependent on a scene of writing or tracing that it disavows, or places in abeyance. So Derrida is certainly not a 'literary' philosopher if we take literature in its usual 'philosophical' sense as fictive, liberated from truth or mere writing and syntax without sense. Even so, we need to confront the common misreading of Derrida as a 'literary' philosopher for two reasons. Firstly, by understanding what Derrida is not saying, but seems to be saying, we can arrive at a more nuanced reading, aware of the subtleties of Derrida's position. Secondly, Derrida himself has acknowledged that if a misreading, or any supposed accident, is possible, then there must be something in the text itself – something intrinsic or essential – which allows that text not to be faithful to itself.

DERRIDA LE MAL: DECONSTRUCTION AS DISSOLUTION OF ALL THINGS GOOD AND TRUE

According to one of his commentators Richard Rorty, Derrida's great achievement has been the recognition of philosophy as a 'kind of writing'. Rorty's larger project is to demonstrate that there can be no truth outside language, where language is understood as a context of conventions and expectations that is historically, culturally and socially specific. 'Normal' philosophers strive to justify their pictures of the world, and they do this from within the context and language of their time; they play according to the rules. 'Abnormal' philosophers, like Derrida, refuse the established criteria of what counts as a correct or right picture of the world (Rorty 106). Instead, of pretending that writing, or our established ways of writing, represent a picture of some external reality, philosophers like Derrida play with writing, produce new ways of talking, and refuse the idea that we can have a philosophy of language – some true account of language's relation to the world (Rorty 108).

Jürgen Habermas, who is as critical of Derrida as Rorty is celebratory, accepts two of Rorty's main assumptions: firstly, that we are 'postmetaphysical' and cannot intuit some truth outside language; secondly, like Rorty, Habermas argues that Derrida also accepts this linguistic condition and abandons truth criteria and judgement for the sake of purely literary, aesthetic or ungrounded decisions. While Derrida is right, Habermas insists, to criticize a Western reason that would aim to step outside contexts and communicative conventions and offer some pristine pre-textual truth, he is wrong in thinking that this means abandoning truth and reason as such in order to remain within the trivially literary – Derrida's 'writing' – at the expense of 'living contexts' (Habermas 166). For Habermas, Derrida's collapse of the distinction between literature and philosophy constitutes a failure to recognize truths of communication and it means that Derrida abandons any criteria of truth or reason beyond style. For both Rorty and Habermas, Derrida dissolves the distinction between philosophical reason and literary style.

In what follows I want to mark out Derrida's more complex deconstructive relation between philosophy and literature by way of three arguments:

- Derrida does not abandon philosophy in favour of literature or writing; he deconstructs the relation between the two.

- The deconstructed concept of writing or textuality does not preclude or suspend discussions of truth or life but opens up a new way of thinking about all experience, not merely literary experience.

- Far from collapsing the distinction between philosophy and literature, deconstruction places new demands on literary reading, which can no longer be merely literary. Writing is no longer what separates us from life; nor is it what allows us to communicate within life; there is a structure of writing, textuality or literariness in life.

DECONSTRUCTING THE PHILOSOPHY/LITERATURE BINARY: BETWEEN PLATO AND MALLARMÉ

To deconstruct a binary, one does not merely reverse the opposition (OG 24; WD 280); rather, the supposed purity and hierarchy of the terms is altered. The opposition between philosophy and literature is neither symmetrical nor innocent. According to Derrida, philosophy establishes its truth and priority through a certain mimetic understanding of literature, where writing is either the reflection or copy of truth, or where there are true appearances that are then belied by, doubled or mediated in textual appearance (D 193). 'Until Mallarmé' literature has also been understood in relation to philosophy and philosophical truth (D 185), so that we read a text according to some 'transcendent' (or extra-textual) truth, which it represents (AL 104).

Any celebration of literature that asserted that the world was mere text, that we cannot get to truth because we are always within language, or that life transcends any form or concept of truth that we give to it – that is, any simple reversal of the opposition between truth and writing – would leave the opposition in place and would still be metaphysical (D 206). What Derridean deconstruction tries to do is to dismantle the secondary, mimetic, or merely fictive concept of literature. Philosophical truth already and essentially bears all the structures we usually associate with the literary. Further, the literary, as it is usually understood, remains tied up with a logic of truth which, for the sake of truth, needs to be rethought.

As long as we understand literary texts as mere play or language, or as systems of signs that establish closed systems without any reference to reality or truth, we allow the concept of reality or presence – what is – to remain unchanged. Indeed, without a notion of writing as a system of marks or differences that is other than reality, without the secondariness of literature as mere mimesis, philosophy would not be able to think a pure experience or presence that then required communication through writing (see Chapter 2 of this volume). We could say that as long as one is speaking philosophy and using concepts, one must appeal to a truth that is repeatable, justifiable and capable of reiteration beyond the singular present from which it emerges; this law governs the philosophical work. It inheres not only in the very concept of truth, but in concepts as such (LI). Literature's potential to say anything does not lie in the fact that it is secondary, unimportant or mere play. On the contrary, because it does not assume a presence, truth or ground that is already given and there to be represented, it inscribes its own context, remarks or institutes its own scene. What it says – the utterances, descriptions, avowals and promises – are not meant so much as used. And in this quoted or narrative quality of literature – its reference only within its own scene – writing can both disrupt and re-mark the scene of truth.

THE DECONSTRUCTED CONCEPT OF LITERATURE: MALLARMÉ'S MIMIQUE

Derrida's extended essay on Mallarmé, 'The Double Session', first published in French in 1970, takes as its object a brief text by Mallarmé, which itself has a complex textual history. Mallarmé refers to a mime where Pierrot – the character of the mime – discovers his wife Columbine to be unfaithful and so he tickles her to death. Mallarmé's own text describes finding the description of this mime in a booklet; the booklet purports to be by the author of the mime, written after the event (we do not know whether Mallarmé himself saw the 'original' mime). The mime itself was already dependent on a number of sources, including a stylised pantomime where Pierrot 'recalls' a literary figure having tickled his wife to death; Pierrot decides to quote or repeat this action in order to kill his own wife. Mallarmé's 'Mimique' includes a quotation from this earlier pantomime as the epigraph to his own text. So Mallarmé's text, which describes a booklet that describes a mime, is preceded by a quotation from a pantomime where Pierrot recalls the very action that Mallarmé will describe as being acted out.

   Now there is a very obvious, albeit giddying, play of textual mirrors that disturbs what Derrida refers to as the mimetic logic of metaphysics: that there is a being or presence that either presents itself in its own image or requires supplementary images in order to appear as true (D 193). By writing about an event described after the event of its occurrence, an event which already drew on a series of disparate texts that referred to memories, fictions and anticipations, Mallarmé's text has no clear object or referent. The mime described is the acting out of a murder that never took place, inspired by a recollection that 'took place' within another fictive text, and that did not follow or act out any text or script – the mime itself producing the stage or action that will then be described.

Now, Derrida does not oppose Mallarmé's writing to truth; rather, in writing and by way of a series of figures, such as the motifs of the hymen, the mime, light, silence and the whiteness of the page, Mallarmé's 'Mimique' tries to write about the effects produced by writing in such a way that the process of writing produces its before and after, its cause and effect, its space.

What interests us here is less these propositions of a philosophical type than the mode of their reinscription in the text of Mimique. What is marked there is the fact that, this imitator having in the last instance no imitated, this signifier having in the last instance no signified, this sign in the last instance having no referent, their operation is no longer comprehended within the process of truth but on the contrary comprehends it (D 207).

For Derrida, then, Mallarmé's writing 'about' this event displaces the logic of metaphysics, mimesis and truth. Mallarmé's style does not just describe the mime as an object; his own style is itself a mime – acting out or staging the scene, ground or fold upon which it takes place. So, instead of the literary being the inscription or representation of a space or scene, literature displays the borders, bands, and folds that maintain a scene, that open up a space. Mallarmé does not step outside or abandon presence, the 'there is' or truth to inhabit a pure text; rather truth and reference are displaced; the origin or place of truth is outside the scene of metaphysics, outside the logic of before and after, inside and outside – beyond being:

> . . . this reference is discreetly but absolutely displaced in the workings of a certain syntax, wherever any writing both marks and goes back over its mark with an undecidable stroke. This double mark escapes the pertinence or authority of truth: it does not overturn it but rather inscribes it within its play as one of its functions or parts. (D 193)

WRITING, LITERATURE AND LIFE

When Blanchot, in 'The Instant of My Death', places an 'originally' autobiographical event that befell him in a literary narration – being placed before a firing squad towards the end of the war, but at the last minute being freed – we become, Derrida argues, aware of a possibility that haunts all writing (DFT). A text can present itself as true, as a witness of the unique, only if it takes on a form or linguistic scene that allows that instant to be read, repeated, quoted and simulated. Literary texts, far from leaving what they say in the form of reference, place this saying within the scene and in a certain sense 'say nothing' or, alternatively, allow for the saying of anything. That is, if I write that I am writing a story then what is said in the story is removed from its status as referring or representing. What is then said is the saying itself, so literature gives us or calls us to think a 'being without being', a presence without presence or a truth without truth.

The possibility of literature – of quoting, departing from presence, repeating and folding back on itself – not only 'haunts' all life; one might say that this haunting 'is' life (DFT 30). There is not a life on the one hand, fully present and adequate to itself, which may or may not then relate to what is not itself or not present. For we can only say that there is life, that there is anything at all, once what 'is' appears or departs from itself in some form of text or relation. This means that before the relation between one thing and another – say, the relation between truth and appearance – some marking out of relations, some appearance must have already been. We can say that 'There is mimicry' – doubling, copying, appearing, dissimulating; but this troubles the very logic of saying that something 'is'. Life itself – experience, presence or what is – could not be thought and could not be, without some event of tracing, marking or inscription. As Derrida suggests:

> We are faced then with mimicry imitating nothing; faced, so to speak, with a double that doubles no simple, a double that nothing anticipates, nothing at least that is not itself already double. There is no simple reference . . . This speculum reflects no reality; it produces 'reality-effects' . . . Mallarmé thus preserves the differential structure of mimicry or mimesis, but without its Platonic or metaphysical interpretation . . . (D 206)

CONCLUSION

If Derrida does not collapse the distinction between philosophy and literature, if he does not, as Habermas and Rorty claim, argue that philosophical truths are merely effects of writing or fiction, what does literature offer or give to the deconstruction of the philosophical opposition between truth and writing? Derrida suggests that literature offers the gift as such, that the singularity of a text in both its call to be read, and in its resistance to any single or univocal understanding of its meaning, exposes an originary but affirmative passivity (DFT) and indebtedness (AL) beyond the oppositions between active and passive, and beyond any calculable economy. In his readings of literature Derrida does not – as he does in his philosophical writings – expose the border or band that the text inhabits but does not name; he repeats, remarks, recites and affirms that which each text makes possible, its specific and singular event of naming. By reciting names, dates, words or aphorisms, literature remarks itself, and in citing its singularity or calling attention to its 'only once' allows us to think of truth's limit and the necessary inability to think the 'unreplaceable' outside this limit: 'The drama that activates and constructs every signature is this insistent, unwearying, potentially infinite repetition of something that remains, every time, unreplaceable' (S 20).

MAJOR TEXTS ON LITERATURE

Writing and Difference (WD) 1978 *
The literary texts of Edmond Jabès (64–78; 295–300) and Antonin Artaud (232–94) are used by Derrida here to put into question some of the key assumptions of Western metaphysics about writing, the sovereignty of the author, the voice, and the book.

'Living On/Borderlines' (LOB) 1979 *
In this essay, Derrida reads P. B. Shelley's late unfinished poem *The Triumph of Life* through and alongside Maurice Blanchot's *Death Sentence [Arrêt de mort]* and *The Madness of Day*. The text is divided into two bands, the lower referring to problems of translation, readability and the framing of literary texts, including a text's necessary power to live beyond or survive its author. The upper band concerns narration, translation, and survival (*sur-vivre*, which connotes not just living-on but overcoming) not just of texts themselves (through translation and rereading), but also considered as the nature of life itself.

Margins of Philosophy (MP) 1982 *
Margins contains two essays concerned with literary themes: 'White Mythology', which is an analysis of the role that metaphor plays in philosophy, and is thus closely related to the content of this chapter, and 'Qual Quelle' on Paul Válery's relation to everything that could be considered a 'source' to his writing (tradition, languages, cultural and historical backgrounds and so forth), and in turn is an analysis of the 'meaning' of his work (in a similar fashion to the analysis of Nietzsche's meaning in *Spurs*).

Signéponge/Signsponge (S) 1984
Discusses the writing of Francis Ponge through the concepts of name and signature. On the one hand there is the problem of confronting the singular event of Ponge's work, marked by the signature of Ponge. On the other, a signature only works and can be read as singular if something of the event of the text is already lost in repetition and iterability.

'My Chances/Mes Chances: A rendezvous with some Epicurean stereophonies' 1984 * Among other things, this text deals with the psychoanalytic perspective on literature.

Glas (G) 1986 *
One of Derrida's most notorious texts, this book that juxtaposes, in separate columns on each page, a reading of Hegel on the one hand and the writer Jean Genet

on the other. Texts by Genet especially, but also Bataille and Mallarmé and some others, are used as a means to disrupt the all-consuming Hegelian system deconstructively, by insinuating remainders, supplements and interruptions through 'literary' texts that cannot simply be dialectically subsumed (see the section on Hegel in Chapter 13).

'Aphorism Countertime' (AL 414–33) 1992
Derrida looks at the concepts of 'contretemps' and 'aphorism' in relation to Shakespeare's *Romeo and Juliet*. Derrida links the aphorism or marking word to the 'name', which in Romeo and Juliet provides the scene for the tragic relation between the Montagues and Capulets. Even here, when not reading a modernist or typically self-reflexive text, Derrida locates essential literary motifs in Shakespeare's language – the singular name, the temporal accident, 'the letter which does not arrive at its destination' (AL 419).

'Shibboleth: For Paul Celan' (AL 373–413) 1992, also in: *Word Traces* 1994 *
This extract of Derrida's book of the same name discusses some central moments in Paul Celan's poetry: the singularity of dating, the nature of witnessing, and the ethical and political consequences of translation.

'Two Words for Joyce' (AL) 1992
Meditates on 'and He war' from *Finnegans Wake*, which, according to Derrida, affirms the 'call' to read beyond the closure of any single language at the same time as English functions as the point from which Joyce's textual memory and encyclopaedic equivocity emerge (see Chapter 12 of this volume).

Points (P) 1995 *
This valuable collection of interviews includes discussions on a number of writers and literary themes with which Derrida engages: Jean Genet (5–29; 51–67), Francis Ponge (365–71), Paul Celan (372–80), poetry (289–99), and on the relation between philosophy and literature in general (216–19).

Demeure – Fiction and Testimony (DFT) 2002 *
Published in a volume with the short story by Blanchot (The Instant of My Death) that it comments upon, Derrida's text meditates on the themes of the witness, of testimony, and of the singular relation that one has to one's death.

CHAPTER 10

Art

Julian Wolfreys

INTRODUCTION

Throughout his career, Jacques Derrida has returned to the subjects of art and aesthetics on a number of occasions. His writings on these matters frequently address aspects of art and visual representation that might best be termed marginal to what have been understood, traditionally and canonically, as the principal concerns of writing on art. At the same time, however, while Derrida's orientation towards such issues emerges not from some central point of departure but rather from some apparent periphery, his writing patiently and attentively unfolds how the marginal, or liminal, is of crucial, if overlooked, importance to any attempt to read representation, the work of art, or the issue of aesthetics.

Given the limited space available to me here, this chapter will treat of a few 'subjects' to which Derrida has been drawn and from which he draws certain threads in the attempt to open the reading of art to other concerns. These subjects are: subjectile, parergon or frame (and processes of framing), and trait.

In the case of each of these very singular motifs, Derrida's interest has to do with the certain demarcation or erasure of borders, boundaries, and limits – in short, with those marks that determine representation and the work of art, while becoming invisible in the process of making the work appear. Another way to speak of these figures is to suggest that each is a form of writing in a broader sense – an inscription that, while being largely unread, makes possible the signification of the work of art as art. Moreover, in yet another manner, one might say that such figures speak, albeit indirectly, of an acknowledgement of narrative or, to put this another way, acts of spacing which take place within the apparent totality and immediacy of representation and the visual. It should not be thought that these are Derrida's only concerns, nor that one can separate such figures from the interests into which these are interwoven and by which other discourses are traced; indeed, as Derrida himself admits in the jacket 'blurb' from *The Truth in Painting*, such issues also touch upon matters of title, signature, discourse, museum, archive, and so on. However, in order to keep within the frame, I shall write here solely around the three figures to which I have already alluded, beginning with the subjectile.

SUBJECTILE

What exactly is a 'subjectile'? Narrowly defined, it is the material or material support on which a painting or engraving is made. More generally, it is, writes Mary Ann Caws, 'the underlying support of canvas, paper, text' (Caws, SAA xi), or that which makes the image, the text, the representation possible. It is that which makes the text, whether one speaks of words or pictures, appear and yet which, despite its materiality, is immaterial to most conventional discourses on art. We might suggest that the subjectile is therefore a ghost of sorts (cf. SM). Hovering in the background of any text, neither there nor not there, neither completely inside nor outside any text, yet at the border between word and world, the subjectile haunts that to which it gives a place of appearance. Derrida's interest in the subjectile is focused through the work of Antonin Artaud, and in what 'underlies both language and art like a support . . . and which is not to be translated' (Caws, SAA xii).

Thus, the subjectile cannot be assumed; that it '*is something* is not yet a given . . . it does not constitute an object of any knowing' (SAA 63). Neither something nor nothing, an apparent neologism in the text of Artaud not yet having been received into dictionaries in the 1930s, *subjectile* arrives; or rather, it returns, as Derrida shows from older sources in both French and Italian (SAA 64). The subjectile is both 'a substance, [and] a subject', which, as Derrida suggests 'belongs to the code of painting and designates what is in some way below (*subjectum*)', occupying a liminal place or, more accurately, a taking place, a becoming of the *between*, which it both is and is not: 'between the beneath and the above, it is at once a support and a surface . . . everything distinct from form, as well as from meaning and representation, not representable' (SAA 64). The term marks and remarks a certain crossing and recrossing of borders, instituting the very borders that it crosses, while having 'no consistency apart from that of the between' (SAA 71). One might therefore be tempted to write there is no subjectile as such. Such apparent paradoxes speak of the subjectile's power to mark a text, to inform and make possible its taking place, while, in being marked by both a lack and excess, as well as being both excess and lack, the subjectile is irreducible to any stable location or meaning, other than to its own surface and support: 'the word "subjectile" is itself a subjectile' (SAA 65).

Hence, ghost, neither 'a subject . . . nor . . . the object either' (SAA 71): any address to the subjectile cannot be given in terms of a definition that is merely negative or positive, and therefore partaking of some ontological determination. The subjectile belongs to the order of that which leaves its mark in having retreated from the scene of what it makes appear. That there are remains, that the term remains as some untranslatable, undecidable, even unknowable remains, and this remains all that we can say of 'it'; here is the alterity, the spectral condition of the subjectile, a spectral motion akin to the work of writing, which supports meaning and places meaning on its surfaces, and yet which is never that meaning, never what is indirectly represented.

But we should not rush to understand the subjectile merely as the motion, the rhythm of inscription, which traces the opening and revelation of that becoming which is also a between. It should also be remembered that the subjectile is that on which the subjectile comes to remark, though never as itself of course. It is, as Derrida says, both words and page (SAA 114). Words, traces, brush strokes, pencil lines: all are projections and supports, movements and elements in a structure allowing for representation, all the while not being that. At the same time, such marks, performing the representation, the image, the visual that they neither are nor are reducible to, require themselves a support, such as the page, the canvas, the photographic paper. Any image, any representation is only ever possible through such support, and through the violence of appearance and penetration, the weaving motion that is figured through the motif of writing.

Art 'always implies representation, reappropriation, reintegration, transposition, or figurative translation of the same' (SAA 116). Yet the excess of that which makes art and its implications possible is, in its force, its violence, not of art. Art is thus haunted by a writing, by a performative event that is not those elements defining art. The mark named the subjectile, being a constant motion between the representation and its other, betrays the very art that it upholds; it announces that 'Being is not, it is not present, it remains to be born' (SAA 128). The subjectile figures the Other (SAA 137) that we name spectre, ghost, phantom, phantasm – if it is anything it is a 'figure of the unfigurable' (SAA 134). Being 'never literally what it is' (SAA 139), the subjectile bears the trace(s) of the constant un-sensing of meaning, of stable representation, and thus gives the lie to the promise of presence, and of full meaning that representational art would appear to guarantee.

TRAIT

If it is the movement of the *trait* or trace that undoes such stability, what else can be said, what does Derrida have to say of the trait, apropos of art? As Peter Brunette and David Wills point out in their introduction to *Deconstruction and the Visual Arts*, 'much of Derrida's writing on the visual arts has concentrated on the *trait* ... a word that is itself synonymous ... with the term "writing"'. They suggest that:

> It is through the idea of the trait, referring to whatever is drawn, as well as more specifically in French to the brush stroke, that the graphic [as opposed to the

phonic] emerges ... there can be no purely pictorial line, any more than a purely verbal line – because the trait is always already a *retrait*, necessarily subject to repetition and subdivision (Brunette and Wills 1994, 4).

As might be apparent here, the *trait* treats of both feature and mark, drawn line or brush stroke. That the *trait* is a mark, that is to say transmissible and available to reading (at least in principle) means that it is always already remarkable, even though within the work of art it is usually taken as unremarkable, unless recuperable within the architectonics of form and content, and therefore subservient to representation and ontology. The appearance of a *trait* is therefore always a *retrait*. Never appearing for a first time simply, any *trait* always implies repetition, of withdrawal or retreat, and return or re-markability. Its graphic condition thus attests to the *trait*'s identity as a writing, whether the *trait* is a pencil line or brush stroke. Thus, never itself but not nothing, the *trait* is, in its iterability, always already supplementary. Derrida insists on the supplementarity of the *trait* in both 'The *Retrait* of Metaphor' (1998), and also in *Memoirs of the Blind* (MB 3). In both replacement and addition, the *trait* figures, even as it registers, 'an indiscreet and overflowing insistence ... an over-abundant remanence ... an intrusive repetition' (Retrait, 1998, 104). An interruption and an excess beyond identity, the *trait* is that graphic reminder *and* remainder, which, irreducible to either form or content, representation or meaning, marks a passage *between* (to recall the discussion of the subjectile) the visible and invisibility (cf. MB), and thus has to do with the gaze, with vision.

Vision is thus central to all of Derrida's writings on art, even though it is not the only subject. Vision, for Derrida, is based on reading, it is 'about looking and the right to it', which in turn 'becomes solely a matter of lines of demarcation, marks or boundaries, limits, frames, and borders that leave traces of having overstepped the mark' (RI xv). I am tempted to hear in this remark what amounts to a virtual thesis on how to read the visual arts, how to see the difference by which art is made possible, without falling prey to a kind of readerly blindness. Such blindness is called by Derrida the desire for restitution, to which, in their analysis of a painting by Vincent Van Gogh (*Old Shoes with Laces*) Derrida reads Martin Heidegger and Meyer Schapiro succumbing, in the final essay of *The Truth in Painting* (TP 255–382). The interest in what one sees, but which is understood as remaining mute in any conventional analytical construction of the visual, concerns the graphic, as I have already argued.

How the graphic *trait* relates to sight and blindness, visibility and invisibility appears very early on in the discussion between two voices in *Memoirs of the Blind* (MB 2–3). This text considers the structural dislocation or disjunction, the disorder or difference that must take place in any act of self-portraiture. There is a structural displacement between the making of the self-portrait and the necessary blindness that accompanies the production of the work. Put simply, if one looks at the line or stroke – the *trait* – one is making in the act or performance of self-portraiture, one has to draw from memory, from a place that is blind. Conversely, if one looks at one's reflection in order to commit the image to paper or canvas, one cannot observe the making of the line or stroke, which must proceed blindly. In ghostly fashion, the line read and the line to be drawn hovers as the phantasmic trace of memory. It appears and retreats, it is the *trait* and *retrait* by which one sees without eyes. Nothing is seen as such, but a certain revelation takes place in the temporal disjunction of the *trait* and its iterability, whereby there occurs 'an unveiling that renders visible' (MB 122). In this respect, the *trait* is 'not then paralysed in a taut-ology that folds the same onto the same. On the contrary, it becomes prey to *allegory* [or analogy] . . . given over to the speech and gaze of the other' (MB 2–3). Compre-hending the *trait* and its relation to seeing as thinking or reading (one says 'I see' when one means 'I understand'), rather than to what blinds one to comprehension in being seen (arguably, in their receptions of the 'text' of Van Gogh, Schapiro and Heidegger see before seeing and therefore do not 'see'), do not interrupt what James Joyce calls in *Ulysses* the 'ineluctable modality of the visible' (Joyce, 1993, 31). As Derrida remarks, 'in losing his sight man does not lose his eyes. On the contrary. Only then does man begin to *think* the eyes . . . he sees *between* and catches a glimpse of the difference . . .' (MB 128; cf. *Veils*, 2001); to fold back upon our-selves, and to unfold again this point from another perspective: this difference we might name on this occasion the *trait*.

PARERGON

The *trait* leaves a mark, but one that returns never as itself. Whether one is speaking of *trait* or *subjectile*, one is therefore concerned with 'lines of demarcation, marks or boundaries, limits, frames, and borders that leave traces of having overstepped the mark'. Such an act of overstepping dismantles the most reassuring conceptual oppositions (TP), such as presence and representation, visibility and invisibility, text and context, representation and reality, and so on. Thus we are brought to a border, which is not fixed but rather which unfixes any stability in its articulation, every time it takes place. This border is named by Derrida the *parergon* in *The Truth in Painting*. In the deceptively titled first section, 'Passe-Partout', Derrida situates what he calls the 'insistent atopics of the *parergon*' which appears in an enfolded and intimate relation with the 'great philosophical question[s]'. What is art? The beau-tiful? Representation? The origin of the work of art (TP 9)? Before speaking of the *parergon* however, it is important to acknowledge the *passe-partout* as *trait* and *subjectile*.

The dictionary tells us that the *passe-partout* is both a master-key, a shibboleth (AL 373–413) allowing access anywhere or to any encrypted secret, and also a frame composed of two sheets of transparent material mounted back to back; moreover, it is also the adhesive tape holding the two sheets together. The figure of the *passe-partout* is thus an excessive *trait* in its own right, having no single identity but providing the function of *techne* by opening the possibility for decryption and framing the reading to come. At the same time, this *trait* is also a double border. Of course, as Derrida has made clear, all borders are double in that, neither simply an outside nor an inside edge, they touch on both inside and outside, thereby doubling – and dividing – themselves by the mark that takes place. This provides support in a manner similar to that of the subjectile for that which is framed. Derrida ups the ante however in choosing the figure of the *passe-partout*, because it is a double border, and because, used specifically in photography, it is transparent. It is therefore a condition of possibility for both the visible and the invisible, a *trait* neither completely there or not there, not simply a border but doubled in and of itself.

The *passe-partout* is thus a particular example of the *parergon*, which is an 'atopic' as Derrida puts it, because it is:

neither work (*ergon*) nor outside the work (*hors d'oeuvre*), neither inside nor outside … it disconcerts any opposition but does not remain indeterminate and it *gives rise* to the work. It is no longer merely around the work … it puts in place … the instances of the frame, the title, the signature, the legend, etc. (TP 9)

Thus Derrida's *passe-partout* does not merely describe or speak about his project, it becomes the mark or *trait* on the text, neither inside nor outside the book (as with any introduction or preface) that, in supporting the text, also doubles itself by performing the function about which it speaks. Once this is recognized, we cannot go back to seeing the border or frame as merely a delimitation. Derrida's articulation marks an irreversible doubling, appropriate to the figure of the border as an act of inscription, whereby the artwork is transformed, translated from within itself, to become what Derrida unveils it as always already being – a performative gesture without which no work, no text is possible. The border, the *parergon*, which includes but exceeds the idea of the actual frame, and of framing in general, thus partakes of the condition of both *trait* and *subjectile*, in all their possible, excessive significations, as well as in their ruination of stable signification, ontology, representation. Seeing through the key that is also a lens, the *passe-partout*, which is also a passport, seeing becomes translated, vision transformed, as the support and the mark become visible in all their destabilizing yet necessary functions that allow the work of art to appear. Coming to terms with the work of writing within and other than the work of art, as *parergon*, *subjectile*, *trait*, we come to see how problematic the implication is that 'art – the word, the concept, the thing – has a unity and, what is more, an originary meaning' (TP 20). We also come to recognize how '*there is* frame, but the frame *does not exist*' (TP 81). Once more, a phantom effect, the trace of a ghost disorganizing all ontologies, exceeding in its hauntological energy, as the other's signature, an otherwise unreadable graffiti of the apparition.

CONCLUSION

The idiom in painting: this is a fragment of a phrase on and around which Derrida plays at the beginning of *The Truth in Painting*. First and foremost, idiom has to do specifically with expression, with specific characters or properties by which language is identified as one's own; as well as being articulation's singularity (see Chapter 2 of this volume), it is also the form that singularity takes, by which it is manifested. It is thus akin to, analogous with, the subjectile. We might therefore propose the following statement: painting, drawing – both are writing, and writing remains to be read.

This appears to be a rather bald summary, aspiring to the condition of aphorism or two (hardly any idiom to be detected). Another summary of sorts might be risked, although this is not of course to have the last word concerning Derrida's writings on art; no such thing is possible, there being many more strands to tease out, many other equally justifiable locations from which to begin. In summary, however, I would suggest, somewhat provisionally, that Derrida's writing on art is also a writing concerned with vision, with a restitution of the other within, and other than, the visual or what are called the visual arts. If his writing on philosophy has frequently opposed the graphic trace to the phonic, then his writings on art situate the graphic as the place of motion, of rhythm, oscillation, and textile weave within the static, fixable presence assumed in particular forms of representation. Derrida pulls at the loose thread that unravels the certainties of mimetic adequacy. In doing so, he unveils the ways in which the mimetic functions through an often brutal suppression of the heterogeneous, of the mark, the ruin, the trace, in favour of the image without remainder, or what Derrida, in an interview with Peter Brunette and David Wills has described as the 'effect of full silence' and 'mutism' of the work of art (Brunette and Wills 1994, 12). As Derrida reminds us in the same interview, the work of art cannot be without the trace, the graphic remainder in excess of representation and irreducible to any mere matter of form or content: 'the thereness, the being there [of presence in the work of art], only exists on the basis of this work of traces that dislocates itself' (Brunette and Wills 1994, 16). The graphic (whether one is speaking of the line or mark, the trace or subjectile, and, it has to be said the border or margin in its power to articulate location), in its iterability, its seriality, its discontinuous movement, its spatial and temporal work, makes presence possible even as it dislocates it.

So, if Derrida's writing on art addresses vision in different ways, it is also an exploration of what vision does not see, what is both a secret and yet in full view everywhere (cf. TS), what is materially there and yet which is, in a particular way, invisible. Or, to put this another way, we are blind to its dislocating work until our attention is drawn to it, until we redraw our focus, learning to see differently. Thus haunted and structured by the mark, by the spatial play of the visible/invisible within and yet other than representation, art appears only by virtue of the ghost in the machine, by the 'functioning of a *techne*' (RI xxxvi). Subjectile, trait, parergon, all make possible the assignment of the condition of art to art, even though they are in excess of and incommensurate with that condition, that identity. Paying attention to this functioning of the *techne*, where the work of making is also, already, a making appear (thereby placing in plain view everywhere the secret that *techne* and *poiesis* are not as dissimilar as some might believe), 'revelation is seen revealed, exposure exposed, presentation presented, and so on' (RI xxxvi). Yet, acknowledging this writing within art, if we now 'see' the truth in painting (drawing, photography, the so-called 'visual arts'), then we are also called to bear witness to the fact that 'we can no longer discern the limit' (RI xxxvi).

MAJOR TEXTS ON ART

Truth and Painting (TP) 1987 *
This long book contains four of Derrida's most important essays on art: on Kant's aesthetics and the problems of framing (the *parergon*), the drawings of French artist Valerio Adami, Gérard Titus-Carmel's miniature sculptures of coffins, and Heidegger. Regarding the latter, Derrida's discussion centres around the role of misrecognition in Heidegger's use of Van Gogh's painting of shoes in 'The Origin of the Work of Art'. As Derrida points out, one cannot even assume that the painting is of a *pair* of shoes, just because there happen to be two shoes, let alone remark that the shoes belong to a peasant, as Heidegger does (TP 258–60). Seeing clear and true in the reading of the work of art for Derrida involves the suspension of attribution, an impossible interruption of one's desire, and thus to engage in the task of seeing what one does not see by habit.

Memoirs of the Blind (MB) 1993 *
As well as arguing that artist's perspective is paradoxically blind (see above), this text also contains one of Derrida's rare meditations on his French predecessor Maurice Merleau-Ponty, whose later work was also concerned with visibility and invisibility.

Right of Inspection (RI) 1998
Through the motif of the story, Derrida effects the dismantling of the photograph as absolute presentation or representation. There is a phenomenological urge confessed here, to translate and construct out of the apparent immediacy of the image

that which can be deciphered or unravelled, as Derrida says, 'somewhat in the way one speaks of constructions in psychoanalysis or police (re)constructions' (RI 1).

'The *Retrait* of Metaphor' 102–29 ('Retrait') 1998 *
What is ostensibly a critical response to Paul Ricoeur's reading of Derrida's 'White Mythology: Metaphor in the Text of Philosophy' (MP 207–71), is also an extension of this latter piece, developing further his analysis of metaphor, but also the figure of the *trait*, and the relationship between visuality and his concept of general writing or the *trace*.

CHAPTER 11

The Subject

David Roden

INTRODUCTION

There is no single conception of the subject in philosophy but a complex array of 'subjects' satisfying different descriptions and roles in areas like metaphysics, ethics and epistemology. However, it is possible to give some initial characterisations of the concepts of subjectivity most relevant to Derrida's approach to philosophy.

One key notion of the subject is that of a centre of psychological life; a 'self' that remains numerically identical 'beneath' or 'behind' one's actions and experiences. For Descartes, the very act of thinking or experiencing implies the existence of a psychological subject, which he subsequently identifies with an immaterial mind. The act of 'reflection', the monitoring of one's inner life, thus acquires an epistemic privilege famously exemplified in his foundational assertion that the act of thinking (*cogito*) presupposes the existence of the 'I' who thinks.

In his *Critique of Pure Reason*, Kant claims that this reflective 'I think' does not imply the existence of Cartesian mindstuff but is, rather, a 'transcendental subject', a condition of possibility for knowledge. For Kant, I can only represent the world as being a certain way if it is possible for me to be conscious of so representing it. The founder of modern phenomenology, Edmund Husserl – a philosopher who figures extensively in Derrida's early work – asserts, likewise, that the transcendental subject is not *in* the world (like the psychological subject) but is the framework within which *any* world can be thought or experienced. For Husserl, like Descartes, the founding privilege of subjectivity derives from the subjective immediacy or 'self-presence' of mental states. He claims that every experience or thought has an *intentional content* by which it 'refers' to some object that is thought about or experienced. All that is relevant to the content of a thought, however, is the manner in which its 'intentional object' is presented for the subject rather than the empirical existence or non-existence of that object. This self-presence supposedly affords an *a priori* framework in which philosophical questions about the nature of reality or the metaphysical status of a certain kind of entity can be arbitrated independently of the truth or falsity of empirical claims in the natural or social sciences.

As we shall see, Derrida's work seeks to 'deconstruct' the idea of subjectivity as self-presence via two sets of interrelated arguments. (1) The first involves time: Derrida denies that the temporal structure of experience is accessible from a first-person point of view, thus throwing doubt on the metaphysical frameworks of Cartesianism and phenomenology. (2) The second involves meaning or content: Derrida argues that signifying items are characterized by relationships and structures that deprive them of the stability, or 'self-identity', that would enable them to be grasped by a reflecting subject. His commentator Rodolphe Gasché refers to these structures as 'quasi-transcendentals' (Gasché, 1986). As Gasché's coinage implies, quasi-transcendentals are somewhat analogous to 'conditions of possibility' for knowledge or meaning that are posited in transcendental philosophy. However, they are quasi-transcendental because the experiences they make possible problematize or disrupt their own conditions of possibility. Quasi-transcendentals such as trace and *différance* are 'phenomenologically derived' but are not exclusive to the structure of human self-consciousness or awareness because their recalcitrance to reflection deprives them of the privileged role assumed by subjectively accessible conditions. This aspect of Derrida's thought aligns him with modern philosophical naturalists who seek to explicate psychological or epistemic notions in terms which abstract from the supposed data of first-person mental life (the 'functionalist' proposal that psychological terms like 'belief' be defined in terms of causal roles within abstractly defined physical systems being a relevant point of comparison).

However, while Derrida's work deflates the epistemic primacy of the 'first person', it exhibits a concern with the continuity of philosophical concepts that is quite foreign to the spirit of contemporary naturalism. Thus in 'Eating Well or the Calculation of the Subject' Derrida addresses the anti-subjectivism that has characterized much poststructuralist philosophy and Anglophone 'theory' with characteristic reserve (P 256). While conceding that thinkers like Foucault have transformed the role of the subject, he argues that these alterations testify to the necessary possibility of its return – though the revenant need no longer be recognisably 'human' as opposed to 'animal', or 'alive' as opposed to 'non-living' (P 268–9). The 'classical' conception of subjectivity deconstructed in Derrida's work conforms to a certain 'metaphysics of presence' that has been described in Chapter 3. It implies a boundary demarcating what is 'proper' and proximate to a subject (its mental states, its body, its meanings, and so forth) and what inheres in 'other' subjects or non-subjective things. Deconstruction contributes to a philosophical account of a non-classical subject whose 'phenomenology' is contingent upon and 'open' to historical or technical environments that are also its quasi-transcendental conditions. However, as we shall see below, the classical subject exerts a hold on Derrida's thinking where he qualifies this contingency in the most radical manner: as a relation to an 'other' so transcendent that it resists conceptualization through rational methods of belief-fixation.

THE PHENOMENOLOGICAL SUBJECT

Husserlian phenomenology seeks to clarify philosophical concepts by recovering their sources of meaning in intentional experiences. Derrida's early works like *Speech and Phenomena* and *Edmund Husserl's Origin of Geometry* generally seize on some purported feature of phenomenological subjectivity to show that it can only fulfil this sense-bestowing function if it exceeds phenomenological reflection in some way. Derrida attempts to show that phenomenology is afflicted by the very insecurity that Husserl hoped to resolve in areas like the foundations of mathematics, because its language is incapable of determining the field to which it applies (SP 10–12).

The insecurity is exhibited most clearly in Husserl's account of time-consciousness. Its starting point is the transcendental assumption that the content of our experience of objective succession depends upon the organisation of subjective time. This would not be possible if each phase of my experience of (say) a melody were a temporal atom, intending only the present note. Somehow the *successiveness* of the notes must be given as well. Husserl explains this by analysing experience of the 'now' into three indissociable aspects: (1) an intending of the current phase of the object; (2) a 'retention' or primary remembrance of the previous experience; (3) a 'protention' anticipating the experience to come. In retention, Husserl claims, I 'intuit' the pastness of the past; living through the expired consciousness while the current impression is *continuously modified* by the upsurge of a new 'now'.

Derrida locates a tension between this continuist model and Husserl's need to ensure fidelity to phenomenological fact. He claims that Husserl's account implies two 'apparently irreconcilable possibilities': (a) that the temporal present is constituted in relation to an 'non-phenomenologizable' continuum in which retention just shades into ordinary recollection; and (b) that 'the source of [phenomenological] certitude in general is the primordial character of the living now' – thus distinguishing retention radically from the remembering of times not contiguous with the 'now point' in the temporal continuum (SP 67; see the section on Husserl in Chapter 13). The first possibility implies, against Husserl's explicit intent, that the enabling structures of temporality must be phenomenologically inaccessible because the continuum is not a plausible candidate for intuitive consciousness. None of its 'parts' exist as a 'self-identical' object, but each is constituted by relations in continuous flux (SP 65–6). Thus the absence of another now cannot be accounted for in terms of the difference between a determinate 'now point' and a similarly self-identical past 'now' in retention – phenomenologically, they are equally indeterminable. Derrida proposes, instead, that we should account for the representability of conscious life in terms of the essential repetition implied by the 'trace' of a past that inflects each 'instant' of consciousness; a 'bending back' or fold 'irreducible in presence or self-presence' (SP 68; cf. OG 184). Whereas the content of Husserl's retained past tracks the 'now' impression it modifies, the content of the trace – if it is permissible to speak in these terms – is constrained by 'the move-ment of repetition', or by relations within a 'general text' or 'weave' of traces, in which there is no stabilizing centre such as Husserl's notional present.

SCRIPTURAL SUBJECTIVITY

Any analogy between phenomenological time and the trace structure is thus, for Derrida, both provisional and inadequate (SP 68; MP 13). Like all quasi-transcen-dentals, 'trace' is topic neutral. It does not qualify the structure of retention more than, for example, it characterizes the structure of signification. Thus Derrida also describes the system of traces as a 'generalized writing' – a trope drawing on wri-ting's ambiguous status as an external technical medium that insinuates itself in subjective life by emancipating meaning from local contexts of interpretation. Fol-lowing Husserl's lead, Derrida sees the technicization of thought wrought by gra-phic inscription as a condition of historical conceptions of science as a transcultural search for objectivity or axiomatic completeness (EHOG 87). However, *generalized writing* – or the system of traces – is not limited to the activity of writing in the reg-ular sense but is 'the essence and the content of these activities themselves' (OG 9).

Derrida holds that linguistic signs exemplify the trace-structure because their meaning depends on contrastive relationships within linguistic systems (a position he derives initially from Saussurean linguistics but which is arguably developed with greater logical resource in the work of Quine and Davidson). However, he importantly qualifies this 'holism', claiming that this interdependence deprives sys-tems of any closure or finality. There is no referent or 'transcendental signified' that removes the dependence of signs upon other signs, or, as Husserl would say, 'ful-fils' a signifying intention in the thing or state of affairs intended. The experience of a thing, for Derrida, is thus already a 'sign' or text or a 'grapheme' (in the general-ized sense) in so far as its content depends upon a temporal, cognitive and linguistic context that is 'always on the move' (OG 49).

The subject of thought, experience and intentionality is, accordingly, an 'effect' of a mobile network of signifying states structurally open to modification or recontextua-lization. *Différance* captures this essential openness by capitalizing on the homonymy between the French verbs for differing and deferring. The identity or stability of the system of traces is differed-deferred because it is 'vitiated by the mark of its rela-tion to the future element' (MP 13–17). This bears comparison, once again, with Husserl's concept of protention, but it is not a subjective anticipation or synthesis.

MATERIALISM AND NATURALISM

The affiliation between deconstruction and a philosophical naturalism inspired by work in contemporary biology, artificial intelligence and cognitive science is acknowledged in Derrida's frequent discussions of 'cybernetics', computing, and technologies whereby experience is 'archived' in scriptural or digital media (OG 9, 47; WD 228; AF; N 199–214). This 'materialist' tendency in Derridean thought is exemplified early on in 'Freud and the Scene of Writing' where the phenomenologically-derived notion of 'trace' is applied to a reading of Freud's *Project for a Scientific Psychology*.

In the *Project*, Freud sought to apply late nineteenth-century discoveries concerning the structure and function of nervous tissue to a model of the physical realization of mental functions. The explanatory 'atom' of Freud's model is the 'neurone', a nerve cell that can transmit or receive quantities of excitation (Qn). Freud's account of psychological function confronts the problem of how a system composed of interconnected populations of neurones can be receptive to novel stimulations (perceptions) and retain the influence of past excitations – that is, exercise the function of memory. Memory is accounted for by what is now referred to as the 'Hebb rule' in theories of neural networks. Freud proposed that the resistance exhibited by pathways through a special system of 'psychic' or ψ neurones would be *reduced* by the passage of Qn (ψ neurones resist because they are protected by a sheath of perceptual neurones, thus receiving lower doses of stimulation). The 'memory' of past stimulations is represented by the lower resistances associated with frequently stimulated pathways.

For Derrida, the significance of Freud's account of memory lies less in its neurological plausibility than in the way it both applies and 'displaces' a model of mental representation as a kind of 'brain writing' whose inscriptions are unproblematically present or absent like marks on a white sheet (see Chapter 8 of this volume). The scriptural metaphor is warranted in so far as memory is 'incised' by the 'breaching' of paths through the ψ system. However, as Derrida points out, it is impossible to identify the memory trace with a particular pathway or passage since memory *just is* differences: 'an equality of resistance to breaching, or an equivalence of the breaching forces, would eliminate any preference in the choice of itinerary. Memory would be paralysed. It is the difference between breaches which is the true origin of memory, and thus of psyche' (WD 201). In the first instance, then, memory is not represented by absolute quantities in the neural system but – as with the Saussurean sign – by a differential text.

As before, these differences are *deferred* rather than constituting a closed system. The memory trace cannot correspond to a particular ensemble of such differences because its function requires a rebreaching and thus a change in both absolute and relative resistance. Thus there is no original mnemic-inscription that could be stored and self-identically repeated in recollection:

[Repetition] does not happen to an original impression; its possibility is already there, in the resistance offered *the first time* by the psychical neurones. Resistance itself is possible only if the opposition of forces lasts and is repeated at the beginning. It is the very idea of a first time which becomes enigmatic. (WD 202)

Thus as Daniel Dennett has recently suggested with regard to the neural correlates of conscious experience, it is always an 'open question' what the psycho-neural trace 'signifies'; its essence or content depends on how it is subsequently deployed within the system.

TECHNICS

Derrida's use of scriptural idioms to displace the subject does not disavow the need for mental or extra-mental agencies to implement the functions of the psyche. However, by emphasizing the non-local, differential character of the trace, Derrida allows us to think of these 'writing machines' as distributed and inter-connected in a manner irreducible to the time of phenomenology:

> The 'subject' of writing does not exist if we mean by that some sovereign solitude of the author. The subject of writing is a *system* of relations between strata: . . . the psyche, society, the world. Within that scene, on that stage, the punctual simplicity of the classical subject is not to be found. (WD 226–7)

Accordingly, we can no longer think of public media of expression as expressing (more or less inadequately) an inner life whose intrinsic character would be unaffected by social texts. The trace is intrinsically extrinsic: a function of the way in which it is repeated or re-deployed. The importance of repetition is brought out in Derrida's reading of J. L. Austin's *How to do Things with Words*, where he argues that for a sign to function in normal or 'serious' contexts it must be transferable or 'iterable' into 'deviant' contexts, altering its semantic or performative value (LI 12). Iteration is not the repetition of some self-identical attribute, however, because there is nothing to a sign *beyond* rules determining that some mark is a token of a given (semantic, syntactic or performative) type. However a sign being iterable means that its deviant occurrences (the ones that 'break' the rules) are essential to its 'proper' or serious uses. There can thus be no pure form or meaning corresponding to the essence of the sign – a principle that Derrida extends to all contentful states such as pictorial inscriptions or experiences (LI 10).

The principle of iterability can be seen as undermining the very possibility of the subject as conceived in modern epistemology or ethical theory. However, Derrida re-conceptualizes the subject as an 'assemblage' of texts/agencies with no principled boundary. For example, Derrida argues that a distinctly modern form of subjectivity – the authorship and experience of 'literature' – is predicated on technologies and practices which, as in the Freudian psyche, both 'censor' and enable the

dissemination of texts. Thus while Kafka's parable 'Before the Law' is typographi-
cally identical to a passage in the penultimate chapter of *The Trial*, the former is a
distinct 'work' with a kind of legal personhood: 'If someone were to change one
word or alter a single sentence, a judge could always declare him or her to have
infringed upon, violated, or disfigured the text' (AL 211). The 'singularity' of the
work (see Chapter 2) is regulated by conventions *that constitute our experience of a
unique literary object*. These might be thought of as mere adjuncts to the work –
much as Kant regarded *parerga* such as picture frames or the draperies on statues
(TP). However, the 'literariness' of the work is constituted by its legal status. The
border of the *ergon* (work) depends on its 'outside' (*parergon*). By the same token,
framing always involves the disposition and control of iterable marks or 'traits' that
can be iterated in ways that transform the framing/forming of works: 'The frame is
essentially constructed and therefore fragile: such would be the essence or truth of
the frame. If it had any' (TP 73; cf. AF 25–8). New scriptural technologies such as
the Internet may subvert the modern institution of copyright – introduced, after
all, to regulate printed matter – by allowing unregulated distribution and regraft-
ing of texts. Since the character and content of experience is determined by its
modes of repetition, storage or framing, 'what is no longer archived in the same
way is no longer lived in the same way' (AF 18).

For Derrida, experience is technically modifiable through its modes of reproduction because it *already* has the iterative structure of generalized writing. This
position has the virtue of removing certain obstacles to thinking about the subject
naturalistically. By distributing and externalizing the functions of the subject, it
implies that subjectivity is too dependent on the world to be the constitutive
'origin' of it (as in Husserl) and thus is more easily seen as amenable to causal-
scientific explanation. In this sense, at least, the quasi-transcendental must be rigorously distinguished from the transcendental. However, while Derrida is deflationary
in this regard, he has consistently affiliated himself with thinkers who – like Lévinas
and Heidegger – seek to address conditions of thought or experience that are radically indescribable within any ontology or scientific metaphysics. *Différance* and the
other quasi-transcendentals are sometimes viewed as 'pre-ontological' in this sense.

ALTERITY OR OTHERWISE?

In his recent work, Derrida has been especially concerned to show that there are
pre-ontological conditions of thought that are 'ethical', testifying to an encounter
with an 'other' whose nature is indeterminable in principle. This 'alterity' can be
seen as consequent upon the lack of any final context within which competing principles of judgement can be arbitrated. Iterability implies, as we have seen, that the
text is *both* context-bound *and* transcends any *given* context, supposing 'both that

there are only contexts, that nothing exists outside context . . . but also that the limit of the frame or the border of the context always entails a clause of nonclosure. The outside penetrates and thus determines the inside' (LI 152; cf. OG). Thinking, acting, judging, and so forth, are thus always and essentially 'precipitate' or ahead of themselves – not because there are no rules but because rules have no existence beyond their instances in which they are applied and the contexts regulating these applications (AR 230–98; see also Chapter 6 of this volume). Any application of a rule is thus potentially also an act of reinterpretation or invention: 'Each case is other, each decision is different and requires an absolutely unique interpretation, which no existing, coded rule can or ought to guarantee absolutely' (AR 251).

There is a deliberate conflation of the normative and the descriptive in this 'can or ought'. One cannot *not* be precipitate but here – where the case of legal decision is being considered – one *should* in acting, modify or re-institute the context or 'frame'. For Derrida the principle underlying this 'ought' is not, as in Kant, determinable by reason and thus replaces the principle of autonomy – according to which the responsible subject must be the sole author of its action – with a principle of 'heteronomy'. Responsibility is 'excessive' and thus undermines the subject as 'a principle of calculatibility' – even if, Derrida cautions, calculation is *also* an absolute moral and political necessity (P 272; OCF).

In these ethical ruminations Derrida consistently leans on Lévinas' conception of subjectivity as a kind of 'hostage' persecuted by an alterity that – as in the logic of the trace – always precedes any act of consciousness or identification (see Chapter 5 and the section on Lévinas in Chapter 13). This occasionally leads to the inflation of indeterminability to the status of a quasi-mystical transcendence. But it should not be forgotten that Derrida always deconstructs the Lévinasian notion that the other should also be seen as transcending our epistemological capacities (WD 126). Here it is important to bear in mind that a language of absolute 'alterity' or otherness finds its place within the framework of transcendental philosophy where the subject, or some equivalent notion like 'Language' or Heidegger's *Dasein* (which Derrida describes as analogous to a transcendental subject [P 273]) still operates as an organizing principle. It is, arguably, only within the 'super-context' of some such constitutive framework that we can intelligibly speak of an 'other' which transcends it. Thus it remains unclear whether the core arguments developed in Derrida's work on language, mental representation or transcendental subjectivity can ever licence the rhetoric of 'radical transcendence'.

MAJOR TEXTS ON THE SUBJECT

Speech and Phenomena (SP) 1973

Speech and Phenomena problematizes Husserl's attempt to isolate a pure subjective sphere of expression untainted by any involvement with the pragmatic or associative dimensions of language. Related material: *Edmund Husserl's Origin of Geometry* (EHOG); ' "Genesis and Structure" and Phenomenology' (WD).

Writing and Difference (including Cogito and the History of Madness, Violence and Metaphysics, 'Genesis and Structure' and Phenomenology) (WD) 1978
Cogito and the History of Madness deconstructs Foucault's history of the Enlightenment exclusion and medicalization of madness. Derrida argues that Foucault's invocation of madness as the 'other' of reason takes insufficient account of reason's capacity to transcend historical structures – as exemplified in Descartes' use of 'hyperbolic' doubt in *Meditation* I.

Margins of Philosophy (including '*Différance*', 'Signature Event Context') (MP) 1982
Différance is a synoptic piece exploring the interweaving of *différance* in a range of subjectivist and anti-subjectivist philosophies. 'Signature Event Context' articulates Derrida's single best idea – 'iterability' – and is crucial for understanding the interplay between subjectivity, writing, and the social practices and institutions addressed in later work.

The Truth in Painting (including Parergon) (TP) 1987
Parergon explores the peculiar logic of the frame or 'parergonality' in a reading of Kant's Analytic of the Beautiful. As suggested above, we can think of framing practices and technologies as, in various ways, externalizing the formative function of the imagination. Related material: *The Postcard* (PC) 1987; Before the Law (AL) 1992.

The Postcard: From Socrates to Freud and Beyond (including 'Le facteur de la Vérité', 'To Speculate – on Freud') (PC) 1987
'Le facteur de la Vérité' is a critical reading of Lacan's seminar on Poe's 'The Purloined Letter'. Derrida criticizes Lacan for reading the letter in Poe's story as signifying the 'truth' of female sexuality as castration. 'To Speculate – On Freud' develops some themes of 'Freud and the Scene of Writing', notably the way the structural delay at the origin of the secondary process accounts for the functional non-specificity of 'pleasure' in *Beyond the Pleasure Principle*. It also examines the role of autobiographical speech acts in inaugurating the 'scientificity' of psychoanalysis (see Chapter 8).

Of Spirit (OS) 1987
Among the broader themes covered here are Heidegger's discussion of the animal and later claims that the hermeneutics of Being requires a pre-ontological 'event' of affirmation or 'pledging'. Related material: 'And Say the Animal Responded?', *Zoo-ontologies*, 2003.

Points: Interviews 1974–1994 (including 'Eating Well or the Calculation of the Subject') (P) 1995
'Eating Well' provides useful and largely accessible introduction to Derrida's views on the subject.

Acts of Literature (including Before the Law) (AL) 1992
'Before the Law' is a reading of Kafka's parable, 'Before the Law'. It lucidly addresses the constitutive effects of framing and the function of authorship. Worth comparing to Foucault's 'What is an Author?'.

Archive Fever (AF) 1995
This book takes up the themes of archiving, inscription and the technically mediated character of subjectivity and links them to the notion of messianic time. Related material: 'Freud and the Scene of Writing' (WD 196–231), *The Postcard*, *Spectres of Marx*.

CHAPTER 12

Translation

Jonathan Roffe

The history of Western philosophy has been characterized by a general lack of attention given to the theme of translation. Despite the unceasing examination that language in general has undergone, and despite the fact that philosophy has always been undertaken *in* language, the movement between languages, translation, has served above all as food for anecdote. For Jacques Derrida, this position is profoundly mistaken. Very much to the contrary, his writings incessantly return to the question of translation, always insisting on its decisive importance. In fact, Derrida frequently puts his name to extremely strong statements on the topic, such as the following:

The question of deconstruction is . . . through and through the question of translation' (Letter 1).

Nothing is more serious than a translation (AR 118).

The problems I wished to formalise above all have an irreducible relationship to the enigma . . . of translation (LOB 89).

To refuse translation is to refuse life (LOB 137).

More recently, Derrida has even spoken of 'an admiration for those men and women who, to my mind, are the only ones who know how to read and write – translators' (WRT 174–5).

These seemingly hyperbolic remarks are only the protruding tips of various icebergs in Derrida's work, for in fact he links the theme of translation to almost all of his main concerns. This chapter will work through four of the more prominent aspects of Derrida's encounter with translation: (1) his initial insistence on *transformation* instead of translation; (2) the relation between a text's translation and its survival; (3) the story of Babel and the question of the proper name; and (4) the crucial link that Derrida finds between translation and philosophy.

TRANSLATION AND LANGUAGE

However, to side for a moment with the philosophical tradition that has for the most part overlooked translation, it isn't hard to see why one might be justified in considering it as marginal or secondary: what real interest does translation have as a primary question for philosophy, since it rests upon knowing first of all how language, meaning and truth work? Once we understand these things, then translation will be able to be explained properly. Consider the following passage from Descartes' response to Hobbes' criticisms of the *Meditations*:

> Moreover, in reasoning, we unite not names but the things signified by names; and I marvel that the opposite can occur to anyone. For who doubts whether a Frenchman and a German are able to reason in exactly the same way about the same things, though they yet conceive the words in an entirely diverse way?

George Berkeley's *Principles of Human Understanding* puts a related point this way:

> In vain do we extend our view into the heavens and pry into the entrails of the earth, in vain do we consult the writings of the learned men and trace the dark footsteps of antiquity – we need only draw the curtain of words, to behold the fairest tree of knowledge, whose fruit is excellent, and within the reach of our hand.

Many other examples could be enumerated from canonical Western philosophy. The common thread here, despite an obvious difference in argument, is of course the idea that words (what Ferdinand de Saussure called *signifiers*), in whatever language, are to be considered as fundamentally separate from the meaning (Saussure's *signifieds*) that they refer to. And in fact, for Derrida, this is a situation *without exception* in the whole history of philosophy (see below). While the physical use of language trades in a number of concrete mediums (like sound and sight), and is conducted in languages that profoundly differ from each other in structure, all language use makes reference to that which *transcends* concrete signifiers, both in particular and more generally.

Derrida refers to this meaning-beyond-language in his first works using the term 'transcendental signified' (OG 20, 23, POS 19; cf. EO 119–20), and it is with this concept that translation first gains focus in Derrida's early work. In a 1968 interview with Julia Kristeva, he formulates the following point:

In the limits to which it is possible, or at least appears possible, translation practices the difference between signifier and signified. But if this difference is never
pure, no more so is translation, and for the notion of translation we would have
to substitute a notion of transformation: a regulated transformation of one language by another, of one text by another. (POS 20)

This quotation condenses a number of arguments that we will need to unpack a
little. In the first sentence, Derrida offers a definition of translation based on the
intrinsic difference between signifier and signified; that is, translation detaches the
word from the meaning and then carries over the meaning into another language
where the appropriate word is reattached to it. In fact, carrying across, or over, is
the etymological sense of the word translation in many languages: for example, the
French (*traduction*) and English words derive from the Latin *translatio*, carrying-
across; in German, translation is *Übersetzung*, crossing or carrying-over. Note that
Derrida is not here rejecting this as a bad concept of translation. His point is rather
that if there is any translation at all, *this is it* – unless meaning is distinguishable
from words, then there could be no translation *tout court*.

The second sentence above draws upon Derrida's understanding of language as
writing, in particular the concepts of *trace* and *context*. Without being able to enter
into great detail on the topic here (see Chapter 2), the *trace* is one of the terms that
Derrida uses to mark his alternative view of language. The basic point, developed
rigorously throughout his earlier texts, is that words, rather than having fixed reference to some kind of transcendental signified, are only transient elements in a general system of other words: words are, for Derrida, traces of other words that rely
upon their differences from each other to be distinguished. The consequence of this
point is simply that we can never extract a single word (and its single meaning) from
such a system of traces, because what gives that word its unity are other words. For
translation, this means that we cannot determine the meaning of *a* word, because
this word and hence its meaning are bound up with the multiplicitous traces of
other words from which it cannot fundamentally be detached, and thus that it is
quite simply an impossible task. Rather than imagining language as a discrete set
of signifiers, Derrida's concept of the trace indicates something like a boundless
sea of shifting, fundamentally interrelated, references.

A question that Derrida has been frequently confronted with now emerges:
if there is no *a priori* guarantee of the meaning of word, due to the shifting sands of
the trace, how can meaning be fixed at all? How do we even understand each other
on this account? More topically, what makes translation in the traditional sense
possible, if the structure of language itself disqualifies it in advance? Derrida's
response is that the play of the trace is fixed and systematized by *context*, that is,
by 'pragmatically determined situations' (LI 150). This concept has a very wide
currency for Derrida, and includes not just grammatical contexts that allow us to

distinguish words in a sentence, but social circumstances that authorise particular ways of using language ('But, beyond . . .'), legal divisions like the inside and outside of a book (see, for example, LOB 87–9) and even whole languages (LI 136). For Derrida, all stability and (more or less) permanent reference of signifiers to signs are guaranteed by context.

A final point needs to be added here: no context can ever be totally closed up. As language for Derrida always has a trace-structure, context can only stop the drift of the trace *relatively* completely, leaving a gap: the entry of alterity onto the scene (see Chapter 5 of this volume), the condition of possibility for all decisions (see Chapter 6), and the ultimate basis for freedom in Derrida's thought.

In sum then, Derrida is at once proclaiming: (1) the impossibility of translation (given the trace structure of language); (2) the possibility nonetheless (given his determination of context) of a pragmatic operation of translation in this traditional sense, so long as certain crucial provisos are taken into account; and (3) the importance of recognizing the impossibility of any context being fully closed up. Thus, in the discussion we have been referring to, Derrida continues: 'That this opposition or difference cannot be radical or absolute does not prevent it from functioning, and even from being indispensable within certain limits – very wide limits' (POS 20). Translation, which always minimally transforms the languages in question through a dislocation of certain contexts of meanings, remains possible, even indispensable – within very wide limits.

LIVING ON: TRANSLATION AND TEXTS

Having seen briefly what Derrida considers translation and language to be, we can now turn to some of the further questions he raises in relation to translation, the first of which will be something he calls the *survival of the text*. The problem would be as follows: if a text (for example, a book) has any kind of singularity or self-consistency of its own, then there must be something about it that resists being reincorporated back into the ceaseless play of language – a text must be minimally untranslatable. On the other hand, this untranslatability is also the text's unreadability, because translation is that procedure of discerning the meaning behind or above the text. In this sense, in order to be readable, it must be translatable, without approaching total translatability, which would risk the text being totally undone as a discrete entity, threatening to dissolve back into the play of the signifier in the trace. Derrida puts the enigma like this:

> A text lives only if it lives on, and it lives on only if it is at once translatable and untranslatable . . . Totally translatable, it disappears as a text, as writing, as a body of language. Totally untranslatable, even within what is believed to be one language, it dies immediately. (LOB 102)

In other words, the closer we get to the edge of the contextual limits that stabilize the transfer of meaning, the more perilous the survival of the text as text becomes. On the one hand, if we approach each text or statement as disconnected, in its singularity, from the context that it finds itself in, it becomes less and less meaningful, because it is with reference to such a context that a meaning can be discerned a step beyond the realm of signifiers. On the other hand, the more universally accessible the meaning of such a text or statement becomes, the more it approaches absolute banality and dissolves into the context that surrounds it (the two 'bands' of text in Derrida's Living On/Borderlines are each written to approach one of these limits). This is the logic behind claims Derrida sometimes makes that 'in a sense, nothing is untranslatable; but in another sense, everything is untranslatable; translation is another name for the impossible' (MO 57).

However, as we have seen, both extremes are in fact inaccessible for Derrida, given the universal significance of context on the one hand, and its inability to be totally closed on the other. This allows us to make sense of another type of claim that we find in Derrida's text, apparently contradicting the above (not to mention itself): 'As a matter of fact, I don't believe that anything can ever be untranslatable – or, moreover, translatable' (WRT 178).

Translation is thus, for Derrida, the name of readability in general. The possibility of splitting the signified from the signifier of a text (be it a statement, a book or a whole language), which is precisely the thesis of translation, is the condition of possibility for the survival of the text – that is to say, 'to refuse translation is to refuse life' (LOB 137). And thus every act of language use in general has as its condition of possibility the activity of translation. We can see here the disjunction between Derrida and the canon of philosophy discussed at the beginning of the chapter, which would insist that language has to be able to work *within* a language first before we can start talking about translation. For Derrida, translation *is* language use in the most fundamental sense.

BABEL: TRANSLATION AND THE PROPER NAME

These concerns with the relation between translation and reading, or the survival of texts, lead us directly to another of Derrida's frequent references on this topic, the Biblical story of the tower of Babel. Derrida circles around this story time and time again (for example AR 104–33; AL 256–309; PC 9, 165, 240–1; EO 98–104; Two Words) drawing out a number of different points in relation to several other writers (for example, Walter Benjamin and James Joyce), but above all insisting that 'Babel . . . can provide an epigraph for all discussions of translation' (EO 100). One aspect of this important theme for Derrida will concern us here, a concept that involved a different kind of survival, the survival of identity through the figure of the *proper name*.

The proper name (and, for the same reasons, the signature) are significant for Derrida because they are marks of *propriety*: ownership, for example, legal and otherwise, is bound up with the properness of the proper name. When an author publishes a book, it must be *her* book, and the proper name guarantees this *her-ness*. This propriety is going to be threatened, on Derrida's account, by the nature of language and translation.

Babel, according to Derrida, is the story of God's proper name, and its (mis)fortunes in translation. In this story, a certain tribe called the Shems (a name that means 'name' in Hebrew) begin building a tower that will reach to the heavens, from where they will impose a single tongue (the Hebrew word here is 'lip', which Derrida suggests involves a certain violence) over the whole earth. God sees this, with mounting jealousy according to Derrida, and descends, scattering the builders and imposing a plurality of languages that render the construction permanently unfinishable. What particularly interests Derrida is *how* this imposition and scattering are brought about. In short, God descends, and pronounces his *name*. This name is what has been confusingly translated as Babel ('Bavel' in Hebrew means 'confusion'), and its pronunciation brought about the confusion of tongues. Derrida argues that, in pronouncing his proper name, God imposed a completely unresolvable double-bind on the Shems: on the one hand, hear my name and obey my voice, for I am God, and I am the only one in control (that is, translate my words into your tongue and obey them); but also, on the other hand, do not understand my proper name, understand that I am beyond, and that my rules are total and transcendent (that is, above all, do not translate me, for I exceed your worldly economy of life).

For Derrida, this double bind structures every use of a proper name, which calls out at once for recognition (translatability) and for singularity and a status of absolute non-appropriation (non-translatability). This double bind is also fundamentally ethical: there is a demand, a duty 'to translate and not to translate' (AT 117), to understand, to enter into relation with an other (to translate them into one's own idiom), but at the same time to preserve the otherness of the other (to not translate them).

To take a more straightforward example, we could compare, as Derrida does (AR 109–11) *Pierre* and *pierre*. The former of these is obviously a French name. We can say that the English 'translation' is Peter, but in fact, insofar as it is a proper name, it is untranslatable: Pierre is the word that means *this person here*, and not a general category of things. Pierre is singular, and therefore his name must be uniquely his. The second of these words is the French common noun that we translate into English as 'stone', and like common nouns in general, it is very easily translated; perhaps we could say 'universally' so. The problem for Derrida, as we have seen, is that at the point where the proper name becomes totally untranslatable, it can no longer mean anything. In order to work at all (to *mean* Pierre), it must at a certain point be improper, and enter the world of translatability (see here Derrida's problematization of Heidegger's search for the proper name of Being [MP 25]).

TRANSLATION AND PHILOSOPHY

I would like to turn now to one of Derrida's well-known earlier works to tease out a further point relating to translation, the analysis Derrida offers of Plato's *Phaedrus* in Plato's Pharmacy (D 63–171). This text discusses, among other things, a particularly problematic term in the translation of Plato's Greek, *pharmakon* and, during the course of this discussion, the following phrase is introduced: ' . . . with this problem of translation we will thus be dealing with nothing less than the problem of the very passage into philosophy' (D 72).

What does this mean? Recall again the analysis of the transcendental signifier that we discussed at the opening of this chapter, which we have seen Derrida complicating in certain ways. His point was that translation, insofar as it occurs, works by separating the signifier from the signified. Now, Derrida wants to remind us that this is not only the thesis of translation, but that of philosophy too. Ironically enough, we find Derrida insisting on a division that other people have mistakenly suggested that he dissolves: if there is any philosophy, then it must be the case that it is not simply restricted to one language, but metalinguistic. The word 'truth' is not the truth (and neither are *'verité'*, *'Warheit'*, and so forth), and it is truth or meaning or value that philosophy and its practice is oriented towards. In short, translation and philosophy share the fundamental assumption that something exists beyond language – the transcendental signified. Derrida sums up this homology as follows:

> What does the philosopher say when he is being a philosopher? He says: What matters is truth or meaning, and since meaning is before or beyond language, it follows that it is translatable . . . The origin of philosophy is translation or the thesis of translatability, so that wherever translation in this sense has failed, it is nothing less than philosophy that finds itself defeated. (EO 120)

This point is particularly problematic for philosophy, according to Derrida, because the context of philosophy has always been, and will continue to be, that of certain concrete languages. We must 'recognize that philosophy does not take place outside of a natural language' (P 348). While this might be nothing peculiar or problematic for most uses of language, philosophy's claim for Derrida is that the particular language in question is radically irrelevant, since what is above all important is what escapes language. In the face of this puritanism of philosophy, Derrida emphasizes that it is in fact the case that:

> The entirety of philosophy is conceived on the basis of its Greek source . . . The
> founding concepts are primarily Greek, and it would not be possible to philo-
> sophise, or to speak philosophically, outside this medium. (WD 81)

Historically speaking

> the so-called fundamental concepts of philosophy were tied to the history of
> certain languages, the Greek language, the German language, the Latin lan-
> guage; and there comes a moment in which one can no longer dissociate the
> concept from the word in some way. (P 347)

This is a crippling double bind. On the one hand, philosophy is committed to the
existence and superior importance of everything that is beyond language. On the
other, unfortunately, philosophy is always done within a language, and is marked
by those languages that have constituted it historically. Moreover, without the support or 'subjectile' (see Chapter 10 of this volume) of a natural language, philosophy would be impossible, it would 'die immediately' (LOB 102). We might call this
the necessary idiomaticity of philosophy, which deals with universals but always
expresses them through the supplement of natural language.

Let's turn now to Plato's Pharmacy for some more detail on these issues, and the
problem that emerges in the course of translation for philosophy, no less for translation itself. The problematic word that Derrida isolates, as I have said, is *pharmakon*. Like many words in every language, it contains a reserve of undecidability
(LI 136) – that is, it can mean (signify) more than one thing. It is important to
insist on this, because Derrida is not making any sort of claim that it is a magical
word, or somehow 'naturally speculative', a privilege Hegel claimed for *Aufheben*
(and the German language more generally). Nonetheless, *pharmakon* and its cog-
nates are a particularly spectacular example of the perils of translation, because,
among its various senses are included the opposing pair *poison* and *remedy*.

In the course of the *Phaedrus*, Plato creates a myth concerning the origin of writing, allowing him to distinguish between good and bad writing (a figure that Derrida finds to be all-pervasive in Western philosophy), using in the course of his
story-telling, this word *pharmakon* on many occasions, and of course translators,
guided by the *meaning* of Plato's argument, have rendered it here as *remedy* and
there as *poison*. However, Derrida argues, even the most assiduous and careful translation is going to be derailed by the reserve of undecidability that the *pharmakon*
presents (and, to go one step further, not even Plato himself could have control
over the *pharmakon*, because there is always the possibility for it to signify otherwise). Regardless of exactly how the word is translated in any particular instance,
the translator 'nonetheless erases, in going outside the Greek language, the other
pole of the word *pharmakon*' (D 97). Derrida is not suggesting here that there have

not been any good translations *yet*, but that '*without mistranslation*' (D 71, my emphasis), the text has been 'rendered almost unreadable ... first and foremost by the redoubtable, irreducible difficulty of translation' (D 72).

The problem, in other words, is that in order to have access to the 'truth' or 'meaning' of Plato's text, we need to have reference to the words that he used, but these offer as much betrayal as fidelity to his 'original intentions' (see the section on Husserl in Chapter 13 of this volume). The *pharmakon*, and the intrinsic undecidability in language *per se*, is literally a poison to philosophy and translation traditionally understood. In terms of translation more generally, Derrida's point is that the split between word and meaning can never be guaranteed in advance, and there will always need to be difficult and unguided decisions whenever translation is involved (see Chapter 6). For philosophy, its founding orientation (towards truth, meaning, value and so forth) is always bound to be tangled up in language, which perpetually muddies the water, and makes pure and unmediated access to the transcendental signifier simply unattainable. Philosophy will always be translating, even at the points where it seems most immediately in touch with Truth, the Good, everything that it believes is beyond language.

CONCLUSION – TRANSLATION AND POLITICS

The discussions I have described in this chapter are only the very tips of a large number of icebergs, and I have perhaps excluded two of the most important sites of discussion of the theme of translation in Derrida's work: *politics* and *ethics*. We can at least say, very briefly, that since context is the stabilizing force that makes translation possible, there is a certain political meaning, broadly speaking, that we can ascribe to it: context is always a non-natural (LI 133), imposed 'homo-homogeneity' (MO 39–40; cf. OG 123), and this means that it always favours some rather than others. Furthermore, it always excludes certain things, in particular, everything which disturbs the tranquillity of this imposed homogeneity. The term that Derrida uses to describe this disturbance, and which is borne witness to by the 'gap' that no context can ever completely close up, is *alterity*. Therefore translation, which is the activity of one context opening itself up to what lies beyond it, immediately concerns ethics (see Chapter 5).

FURTHER READING ON TRANSLATION

'But beyond ...' 1986
A response to a criticism of Derrida's essay, 'Racism's Last Word' (1985), which discusses his understanding of contextual requirements (here, genres of writing) in language use.

'Fors' 1986
'Freud and the Scene of Writing' (WD 196–231)
Positions (POS) 1981
These texts deal in part with certain aspects of the way the concept of translation is put to work in psychoanalysis, whether in Freud, Nicholas Abraham, or by the nature of its concepts themselves.

'Letter to a Japanese Friend' 1988
In response to a query by a Japanese translator of his work, Derrida offers some ruminations on the meanings, positive and negative, of the word 'deconstruction', and its possible translation.

'Living On/Borderlines' (LOB) 1979
'Schibboleth' (AL) 1992
Signéponge/Signsponge (S)
'Two Words for Joyce' (1984)
'Ulysses Gramophone' (AL 253–309)
Each of these texts deals with aspects of translation as they relate to particular literary writers (respectively, Maurice Blanchot, Paul Celan, Francis Ponge, and James Joyce). The first of these also contains the most exemplary discussion of the translation-ethics relationship that is very important for Derrida's work.

Monolingualism of the Other, or the Prosthesis of Origin (MO) 1998
In the course of this discussion of the relationship between colonialism, language and culture, Derrida frequently turns to discuss the role of translation in both maintaining and disturbing hegemony. This is the most significant text linking the fortunes of translation to those of politics.

'Roundtable on Translation' (EO 93–161)
This discussion is one of the most accessible texts on Derrida's interest in translation, which ranges over topics including Babel, the proper name, and Derrida's readings of Freud, Blanchot, Heidegger and Benjamin's The Task of the Translator.

'What counts as a good translation?' (2001)
Derrida's best discussion of the practice of translation itself, and what kind of criteria we can bring to bear on the topic. Ostensibly based around a discussion of the French word *relever*, which Derrida translates here as 'to season', but which he had earlier used as a French translation for the notorious Hegelian *aufheben* (MP 69–108).

CHAPTER 13

Encounters with Other Philosophers

*David Allison, Robert Bernasconi, Simon Critchley,
David Rathbone and Fiona Jenkins*

HUSSERL

David Allison

Most of Husserl's commentators have insisted on the rigorously systematic character of his writings. Despite the modifications that his avowed 'new beginnings'
continually introduced, most critics have sought to explain the development of
Husserl's work by appealing to a principal theme or problematic. Most often, however, this approach resulted in the elevation of particular doctrines, each valued
according to the interest of the respective scholar. Thus, Husserl's task of genuine
philosophical thinking became transformed into what Eugene Fink has called a
series of 'symptoms' and the complete work was judged according to Husserl's
so-called 'doctrine' of the moment. Moreover, the number of historical 'influences'
to which his thought was claimed to have been indebted also assumed epidemic
proportions. Critical access to Husserl's thought therefore focused upon the explicit
themes or doctrines of cognition, the ego, intersubjectivity, ontology, constitution,
logic, reduction, ideality, and embodiment – not to speak of Husserl's Cartesianism, empiricism, or his indebtedness to Frege and Wundt. With the publication of
Jacques Derrida's *Speech and Phenomena*, however, Husserlian scholarship underwent
a dramatic revision. In that and several adjoining texts (including *The Origin of
Geometry* and the essay ' "Genesis and Structure" and Phenomenology' that is
found in *Writing and Difference*), Derrida argued that the development of Husserl's
phenomenology was best demonstrated not in terms of a particular problem, but by
the examination of a certain prejudice – namely, the epistemological and metaphysical value of presence (see Chapter 3) – a prejudice that guided the formulation of
Husserl's entire work. Derrida contends that Husserl's account of consciousness,
subjectivity, objectivity, constitution, evidence, and logic, implicitly or explicitly

draws massively upon this unexamined emphasis upon presence – the term 'presence' referring to that which *is*, or that which is self-contained and internally stable.

For Derrida, the coherence of Husserlian phenomenology arises not from the reduction to a particular 'doctrine' but rather, from the demands imposed – both epistemological and metaphysical – by this emphasis upon presence. Precisely what this value of presence consists in, how it operates as an ongoing prejudice within his philosophical system, and what consequences it entails for Husserlian phenomenology, are the subject matter of Derrida's general critique.

Derrida makes three basic claims in *Speech and Phenomena*, each of which this chapter will examine.

- The first is that temporal presence serves as the underlying axiom in Husserl's doctrine of signification, as set forth in his *Logical Investigations*, Investigation 1: Expression and Meaning.
- Derrida's second claim is that Husserl's subsequent reflections on ideality, consciousness, and objectivity, continually draw upon the 'essential distinctions' that he established for signification in this First Logical Investigation – hence the necessity for Derrida's stress upon this early text of Husserl's.
- Third, and more generally, Derrida maintains that this emphasis upon presence has in one way or another determined the various accounts of being, truth, and language, not only for Husserl and phenomenology, but for the broader tradition of Western philosophy as such, which he frequently describes as perpetuating a 'metaphysics of presence'.

In choosing to begin with a critique of the *Logical Investigations*, Derrida has selected the most important, if not the most influential, of Husserl's writings on language. Derrida's interpretation is striking because he claims that the whole of phenomenology is implied in a reflection on language, and that a discussion of meaning, expression, grammar, and logic – the themes of the *Investigations* – will anticipate and prove pivotal for Husserl's more 'transcendental' problems regarding consciousness. The value of Derrida focusing his analysis here, lies in the fact that Husserl begins the *Investigations* with a set of 'essential distinctions', a group of operative concepts that will guide his thought to the end. As will become apparent, Derrida's deconstruction gradually undermines these distinctions, or more aptly, highlights that they were always already undermined.

Derrida stresses the importance of these 'essential distinctions' to Husserl's work, not only because they dictate the course of his work, but because they repeat, in an explicit and cogent way, the very basis of traditional metaphysics. But this is only one stage of the argument, however, for he does not mean to portray Husserl and phenomenology as just another example in the history of metaphysics. Derrida will argue even more emphatically that Husserl's thought is precisely the paradigm of this tradition. And it is ultimately the claims and pretensions of phenomenology – the parameters of which are admittedly vast – that Derrida wants to contest.

Derrida asserts that Husserl continually invokes the most traditional concepts of Western metaphysics to serve as the foundation for phenomenology, and this is evident from the first 'essential distinction'. By this procedure, Husserl makes a decision to interpret the sense of being in a particular way. For Husserl and the tradition, Derrida argues, the sense of being has always been interpreted as presence, and this interpretation assumes two forms: firstly, something *is* insofar as it presents itself, or is capable of presenting itself to a subject – as the present object (ob-jectum) of a sensible intuition, or as an objectivity presented to thought. Secondly, we say that a subject (sub-jectum), or self in general, *is* only insofar as it is self-present, present to itself in the immediacy of a conscious act. Derrida will contest this emphasis upon immediacy, but for the moment it is enough to recognize that the former sense marks the interpretation of being as objectivity (ousia, physis, and so forth), the latter as subjectivity (parousia, nous, and so forth). The interpretation of being as presence and self-presence entails a series of philosophical consequences and conceptual oppositions that persists to the present day, and nowhere are these consequences more strikingly evident than in the thought of Husserl.

As part of his project of deconstruction, Derrida discusses how these oppositions and dualisms continue to function in phenomenology. Among the many conceptual oppositions to be found there are those of matter (hyle) and form (eidos, idea), corporeal and incorporeal, body and soul, animate and inanimate, signifier and signified. Phenomenology is hence found to retain many of the dualisms of the Western philosophical tradition. Far from being a 'presuppositionless' method (as phenomenologists often claim), the interpretation of being as presence provides phenomenology with all of its fundamental concepts. The highest principle of phenomenology, apodictic evidence, is precisely a call for the bringing forth of objects to an immediate and self-present intuition. The notion of transcendental consciousness, as well, is nothing more than the immediate self-presence of this waking life, the realm of what is primordially 'my own'. By contrast, the concepts of empirical, worldly, corporeal, and so forth, stand opposed to this realm of self-present ownness. They constitute the sphere of otherness, the mediated, what is different from, for example, self-present conscious life. All these concepts find their systematic unity in Husserl's account of language.

Language, for Husserl, serves scientific thought and finds its model in the highest degree of scientific objectivity, the form of logical predication. We should not forget that it is through language that meaningful statements can be recorded and transmitted, that a body of doctrine can be set down and verified, that a community of scientists can communicate, and that science itself becomes possible. Meaningful language, consequently, has its own rules and purpose; it is a 'pure logical grammar', and it expresses meanings in predicative form – in the form of a possible reference to an object.

This is where Husserl makes the first 'essential distinction' of the *Logical Investigations*. He argues that in language there are two fundamentally different sorts of signification: indication and expression. For Husserl, however, only one of these – expression – is meaningful. Expression alone, properly speaking, bears sense. It is important to understand why Derrida seizes upon this distinction. Meaningful language is limited to expression. But how does expression differ from indication? Husserl understands indication to be a movement of empirical association. One sensible sign stands for something else: it is a mark, a note, an object, that makes us pass from something present-to-thought to something that is only anticipated or expected. There is no meaning content present in indication, there is only an empty signifier and nothing that is signified. That is yet to come, and yet to be presented. For Husserl, however, an expression carries a meaning content with it. Meaning is present as the signified content of expression. Derrida argues not only that this account of language and meaning is impossible, but that it is essentially contradictory, given the conceptual framework of the metaphysics of presence that Husserl is tacitly using.

For Husserl, the meaning content of expression is ideal. An expression is composed of an explicit and willed intention that 'animates' a non-sensible signifier, for example, the 'thought' or 'imagined' word, the mere 'form' of the actually uttered or written sign. In animating this purely formal signifier, the sign becomes invested with meaning, and meaning is ultimately the content of an interpretation, while the sign or signifier in general is always a sign of, or for, something else. Now, for Husserl, all these elements of expression are non-real because they all take place within the immediacy of a self-present consciousness – what in the *Logical Investigations* he calls the sphere of 'solitary mental life', and what he will later call transcendental consciousness.

The difficulty in such a conception, and Husserl realizes this, is that actual communication always involves an abandonment of this privileged sphere. It involves the going-out into a world, and into a realm of empirical fact. For this reason he maintains that expression is necessarily 'interwoven' with indication in every case of effective communication. Husserl must preserve the distinction between the two kinds of sign, however, if he is to retain the ideal status of meaning, the possibility of a purely present and complete meaning. The original distinction is possible, in turn, only if expression can effectively take place within the purity of 'solitary mental life'. Communication with others, then, would be a re-presentation of what primordially occurs in this inner sphere. What is 'meant' in communication is merely 'indicated' by means of sensible signs, by the actually spoken or written signs. The problem for Husserl lies in the relation between expression and indication. What is the nature of this 'interweaving'? If there is to be pure expression at all – and, consequently, pure meaning – it must take place wholly within the internal sphere, independently of indication: it would be a 'silent' monologue. There could be no meaningful communication per se in such a case, and following Husserl's account, communication would come at the expense of meaning. But if indication were not merely 'interwoven' with expression, if it were shown to be absolutely necessary to the very concept of expression, then the initial possibility of their distinction itself becomes suspect. And it is just this very distinction between expression and indication that Derrida contests, together with the terms it rests upon: 'solitary mental life' and purely ideal, self-present meaning.

Derrida first devotes a long critique to Husserl's account of ideality. He insists that an ideal meaning is never a pure presentation to begin with; rather, it is already a re-presentation to consciousness, it is a product that is constituted across a series of discrete acts. What constitutes the ideality of meaning for Husserl is the possibility of its being repeated an infinite number of times. Clearly, this is never completed; its completion would demand our disappearance as finite subjects. In any event, the ideal involves a relation of identity between acts, between a present act and an act that lies outside present consciousness. Moreover, the very form of the signifier, the sensory contour of a word or sign, is itself a constituted historical product. The signifier is neither accidental nor idiomatic; it always reflects a definite linguistic origin and heritage. In addition, each occasion of its use represents only one instance of its many possible uses; each use selectively repeats a pre-existent convention. And what is it, finally, that really happens in this 'interior monologue', in this expression of 'solitary mental life'? The expression is not a communication, for there is nothing to communicate: for Husserl, meaning is immediately self-present to the subject so there is no need to communicate. What kind of expression is this if there is no need to communicate anything to anyone? Husserl says this pure expression takes place entirely in the imagination. The interior monologue, then, is a phantasy representation. But Derrida reminds us that, for Husserl, the imagination can never be purely 'neutral' or 'presuppositionless' (as phenomenology aims to be); it is always the modification of a prior experience, and its positional character always testifies to some kind of origin in empirical reality (SP 55). No matter how it is modified, reality becomes represented in the imagination. To sum up, the imagination, and consequently the expressive monologue, is fraught with all those elements Husserl sought to exclude from it, all those empirical references which enter in under the various headings of repetition and representation. From the very start then, language must be just this: a structure of repetition and representation. There can be no refuge from empirical determination in such a structure, and there is no pure expression outside of indication.

Derrida's critique entails two consequences for Husserl's theory of language: there can be no purely 'ideal' meaning, no pure presence of ideality, for at every moment ideality would have to depend on precisely what is non-present, what is only repeated and represented in another presence. There can be no sphere of pure self-presence either, for in the simplest act of signifying, 'solitary mental life' would be fractured by all that lies outside it, namely, the world. Once this occurs, the distinction between indication and expression can no longer be maintained. There is no presence or self-presence for signification, there is only an endless series of reverberations. What 'presents' itself in language is the representation of non-presence, what Derrida calls 'otherness', 'difference', or 'alterity'.

The distinction between indication and expression seems to be of questionable worth, Derrida contends, once the important function of representation and repetition is made clear. In carrying out his deconstruction, Derrida shows how Husserl's whole theory of language is undermined by a still more fundamental problem – one that leads back to the phenomenological form of experience itself – the problem of time. Husserl claimed there was no need for communication in the 'interior monologue' because, among other reasons, it took place in an 'instant', in the 'blink of an eye'. Following this account, meaning would be immediately present in the self-same moment. There would be no need to mediate its presentation by means of indicative signs. There would be no temporal distention in this process because signifier and signified are united in what is often termed a 'now' moment.

By Husserl's own premises, however, such an argument must again fail. His theory of time dictates against any 'punctually isolated' moment, for he claims elsewhere that time is a 'phasing', a continual movement of protentional and retentional traces. In *The Phenomenology of Internal Time-Consciousness*, Husserl argues that the present necessarily includes the phases of past and future under the heading of retention and protention. The present is hence internally divided and this conception of time denies the possiblity of a temporally isolated 'moment' or 'instant'. The very presence of the present is conditioned by what is absent or not yet realized. Far from being the point of origin for constitution, the 'present' is itself constituted, produced, and derived from a more primordial source of non-presence. Again, Derrida finds no arche of presence or self-presence. What he does find is a groundless play of differences that reflects an 'outside and beyond' of past and future (SP 82–7).

Derrida invokes the later account of temporality not merely to play upon an inconsistency within Husserl's own thought, but rather to exhibit something far more important. In the *Logical Investigations* and elsewhere, the very concept of life had been understood as immediate self-presence, as the 'living presence' of self-conscious thought. The historical importance of this concept cannot be overstated; for Derrida it characterizes the modern thought of subjectivity since Descartes. Husserl, however, became increasingly sceptical of this view, as can be seen in his arguments against Brentano in *The Phenomenology of Internal Time-Consciousness*, against Hume in *Erste Philosophie*, and all throughout his later works, up to and including *The Origin of Geometry*. He came to see that if the present 'now' were conceived as a punctual instant, there could be no coherent account of experience as such. One would paradoxically end in denying the identity of one's own experience, one's own self, as did Hume. There could be no self-relation in such a case, and in short, there could be no life, understood as absolute subjectivity.

Derrida concludes that the whole problem and history of language must be entirely rethought. Instead of trying to capture and retain a pure presence, we must conceive signification from the start as a movement away from self-presence, a movement away from the pure presence of a discrete origin and the ideal presence of an identical meaning content (WD 278–93). As a movement of *différance* (see Chapter 3), signification precedes and gives rise to the very concepts of self, presence, and meaning. The proper account of signification begins not with the present and fulfilled meaning content (expression), but with the sense that remains to be assembled and built up across the itinerary of convention and practice. Following the work of Ferdinand de Saussure, Derrida maintains that linguistic meaning is not so much the product of an explicit meaning intention as it is the arbitrary configuration of differences between signs (OG). Meaning derives from the distance that extends between one particular sign and the system of other signs in linguistic use. It is this differential character of signs that must first be reckoned with, and this results from conventions existing within language – it is not a matter of meaning intentions that supervene from without. There is no meaning, no signified content, that stands above and is free from this play of differences, and this includes the 'transcendental subject' (See Chapters 2, 11 and 12 in this volume). Nor could meaning withstand the continuous shifting of differences, the continuous sedimenting of traces, as some ideal identity. For Derrida, there is only a likeness or sameness to meaning, which is constituted across the history of ever-changing usage. Absolute objectivity, therefore, could never be claimed for meaning yet for Husserl, the highest degree of objectivity is that of absolute ideality: the perfect identity of an omnitemporal meaning (cf. MP 207–71).

What is striking in Derrida's claim is the objection that linguistic meaning can never be completely present, either in itself or as the content of consciousness. There can never be an absolutely signified content, an absolutely identical or univocal meaning in language. All these values are denied to meaning once we admit its dependence upon non-present elements. Meaning can never be isolated or held in abstraction from its context, for example, its linguistic, semiotic, or historical context. Each such context is itself a system of reference, a system of signifiers, whose function and reality point beyond the present. What is signified in the present, then, necessarily refers to the differentiating and non-present system of signifiers in its very meaning. We can only assemble and recall the traces of what went before: we stand within language, not outside it.

Starting out with the metaphor of 'presence', philosophy has generated a system of concepts whose import can be seen as essentially theological, what Heidegger has called the tradition of 'onto-theo-logy' (see Chapter 7 and the section on Heidegger in this chapter). Ontology and theology are fundamentally united in their insistence upon a common ground and universal account of being, a first cause and final reason to things. For the tradition of Western metaphysics, this unity has always been asserted under the title of an absolute and non-empirical reality, a transcendent being or principle that would subtend the empirical order by virtue of its role as cause and form, arche or telos. What was traditionally held to invest the world with order and substance is ultimately something transcendent to that order: the Divine, the One, the principle of intelligibility, the unconditioned.

Now it is precisely this kind of theological status that the concept of meaning – interpreted as absolute identity – has enjoyed in the history of Western thought, and particularly when the account turns to problems of knowledge and signification. Despite the impurity of language and communication (signs are arbitrary), the possibility of an ideal and identical meaning has always been held out, whether as pure 'form', 'eidos', 'idea', 'ideal', or as absolute referent in the form of an ideal content of signification, what Derrida elsewhere calls the 'transcendental signified' (POS 14–36; OG 27–73; see Chapter 12 in this volume).

Thus, for Husserl, what is 'impure' in language is 'the sensory or so to speak bodily' aspect – the factually uttered phrase, the actually written complex. The 'purity' of language, the very possibility of meaningful language, lies outside this sphere in the non-empirical or ideal realm of meaning, in what can be purely 'meant' or 'intended' by language, in what can be 'expressed' by language, in the 'now' moment of transcendental consciousness. Thus, Derrida's reflection on Husserl's project leads us to conclude that these distinctions can no longer be claimed for language for the precise reason that there can be no expression without indication, no signified without the signifier, no meaning or sense without the factually constituted complex of signifiers. To conclude that expression can never be 'reduced' to an absolutely objective core of meaning, to conclude that meaning itself is no longer conceivable as a purely ideal presence, is also to conclude, for Derrida, that a certain period of metaphysical thought has come to a close.

FURTHER READING ON HUSSERL

Edmund Husserl's The Origin of Geometry: An Introduction (EHOG) 1978
Following Husserl's late essay 'The Origin of Geometry', *Edmund Husserl's Origin of Geometry* argues that phenomenology cannot restrict itself to a 'static' description of intentional experiences, but must also consider the role of language and technology in constituting ideal meanings.

HEIDEGGER

Robert Bernasconi

When Jacques Derrida introduced the word 'déconstruction' in 1967, he presented it as a translation of Heidegger's terms *Destruktion* and *Abbau*, but he soon made it clear that it was introduced to initiate a radical confrontation with Heidegger's thought. Like Heideggerian *Destruktion*, Derridean deconstruction is neither a method nor a negative critique, but they are in other respects strikingly different. Heidegger employed the term *Destruktion* in *Being and Time* in 1927 as part of his attempt to combat the degeneration of tradition into a series of dogmas. This was to be accomplished by returning to the primordial experiences on the basis of which the Greeks first articulated the fundamental determinations of Being that have guided the Western philosophical tradition ever since. By contrast, deconstruction addresses a different problem and offers a different solution. The starting point of deconstruction is the widespread diagnosis that the tradition of Western metaphysics was in some sense at an end. This diagnosis raised certain theoretical problems that Derrida explored exhaustively with his procedure of double reading. Subsequently, Derrida broadened his conception of deconstruction to address certain aporias of thought – for example, the aporias of the gift, of hospitality, and of the duty to go beyond one's duty – which he approached independently of any explicit claims about the history of Western metaphysics. This shift is itself to be seen as part of Derrida's attempt to distance himself from Heidegger. In both cases Derrida tries to uncover the structures that organize and to that extent transcend conventional reason, but in his earlier works Heidegger had a centrality that to a certain extent he has lost, now that Derrida has turned more to ethical and political themes.

The idea that Western metaphysics was at an end is associated with Heidegger, among others, but Heidegger explored it only after *Being and Time*, when he identified the task of thinking as the overcoming (*Überwindung*) of metaphysics or, more cautiously, a coming to terms (*Verwindung*) with metaphysics. Derrida's response was to introduce the worry that any attempt to pass beyond metaphysics could not be separated from metaphysics and thus was doomed to fail. His conviction that Heidegger's understanding of the end of philosophy was problematic was already clear from the opening of Violence and Metaphysics in 1964 (French publication), where he described it as a problem put to philosophy that philosophy cannot itself resolve (WD 79). There Derrida judged the idea of the end of philosophy to be ultimately metaphysical on the grounds that it reinscribes classically metaphysical notions of unity and teleology, as well as reinstating the classical opposition between inside and outside in terms of a distinction between what is inside and what is outside Western metaphysics. For this reason Derrida preferred to write of the closure of metaphysics, rather than its end, and to insist that the closure had always been in play within metaphysics from the outset.

One reason, therefore, why Derrida's relation to Heidegger has not always been well understood is that he borrowed and then transformed a term from *Being and Time*, *Destruktion*, to describe an approach that was in fact both inspired by and a response to the later Heidegger's account of the overcoming of metaphysics that emerged a full decade later. This is not a small matter. Apart from the differences between early and late Heidegger, the fact that Derrida was responding to the later Heidegger, that is to say, Heidegger's thinking from the mid-1930s on, helps to explain the initial impact of Derrida's thought: he was one of the first French thinkers to develop a penetrating understanding of Heidegger's later works. It has to be remembered that Heidegger published relatively little between 1929 and 1952, and, furthermore, it was only with the publication of Heidegger's two-volume *Nietzsche* in 1961 that the fundamental basis of his later thought was apparent to his readers. Derrida was among the first to take advantage of that. Many of Derrida's readings of Heidegger are for that reason directed against the standard readings of the time. For example, 'The Ends of Man' (MP 109–36) addressed the anthropological (mis)reading of Heidegger that focused on the human being rather than the question of Being, just as 'Restitutions' addressed Meyer Shapiro's reductive reading of Heidegger's famous essay, 'The Origins of the Work of Art' (TP 257–382). Both texts also involve deconstructions of Heidegger's own philosophy (see Chapter 10 of this volume).

That Heidegger's reading of Nietzsche was especially important for Derrida becomes apparent if one examines Derrida's strategy of what has come to be known as 'double reading'. The procedure is, on the one hand, to find within so-called metaphysical texts a rupture that transcends metaphysics and, on the other hand, to find within texts that claim to surpass metaphysics that which is not entirely free of it. Rather than opt for one reading over another by choosing a metaphysical or a non-metaphysical reading (see Chapter 3 of this volume), Derrida considers both readings indispensable. There is no decision as to whether a text is metaphysical or not: this is found to be undecidable (WD 84). Nevertheless, even if Derrida does not identify with one reading or another, Derrida will not simply juxtapose two already available readings. At least one of them is new and is directed to 'a blind-spot' in the text (OG 163). Furthermore, this additional reading, insofar as it is persuasive, comes to belong to the history of the text at hand, that is to say, to the text not as a thing in itself but as the history of its readings (OG 159). Derridean double reading can be said to have formalized the ambiguity that marks Heidegger's relation to Nietzsche. Some commentators try to resolve that ambiguity by concluding that Heidegger moved from a more sympathetic to a more critical stance toward him, but Derrida considers all such attempts, whether by Heidegger or his commentators, to be themselves metaphysical gestures, as is clear from

Interpreting Signatures (1989). It is in this spirit that Derrida writes in *Of Grammatology*, already in 1967, that Heidegger is at once contained within the metaphysics of presence and transgresses it, and that it is impossible to separate the two (OG 22). Derrida always reads Heidegger with one eye directed to what exceeded Western metaphysics and another for what remained enclosed within it: 'We are not going to emprison all of Heidegger's text in a closure that this text has delimited better than any other' (MP 123). Hence the need for double reading, but also the difficulty of sustaining it. Double reading arises out of necessity because there is no straightforward exit from metaphysics and no simple adherence to it either. Derrida often proclaims the extraordinary resilience of the metaphysical tradition, but this is balanced by his attention to those moments within the tradition, often at its margins, where one can encounter what exceeds the tradition.

In 1968, in 'The Ends of Man', Derrida made another effort to outline the strategies at work in deconstruction and again he did so with reference to Heidegger. He began by identifying two dominant strategies among philosophers that attempt to exceed metaphysics. The first, which is undertaken at the risk of merely confirming what one sets out to deconstruct, is 'to attempt an exit and a deconstruction without changing terrain, by repeating what is implicit in the founding and the original problematic, by using against the edifice the instruments or stones available in the house, that is, equally in language' (MP 135). Derrida associates this strategy with Heidegger, a point he had underlined in the contemporaneous piece, '*Ousia* and *Gramme*', where he highlighted in Heidegger's reading of Aristotle a point at which 'the destruction of metaphysics remains within metaphysics' (MP 48). However, Derrida grants that Heidegger sometimes also employs a second strategy, one that Derrida considers more characteristic of Emmanuel Lévinas (see the section on Lévinas in this chapter). The second strategy is to try to change terrain in a discontinuous fashion by placing oneself outside. Derrida believes that neither strategy works on its own and one must interweave them both in 'a new writing': 'one must speak several languages and produce several texts at once' (MP 135). The strategy of double reading therefore is governed by the need to evade the alternatives and set up another relation between the text and the history of metaphysics. It is also on the basis of such differences that the confrontation between Derrida and Heidegger remains very much a live issue among many philosophers.

There have been significant changes in emphasis in Derrida's reading of Heidegger. For example, in *Of Grammatology*, Derrida accepts Heidegger's reading of Western philosophy as perpetuating a metaphysics of presence, even though the Heideggerian insistence upon the epochality of this is subsequently challenged (OG 74–93). Derrida turns away from Heidegger as his successive deconstruction of metaphysical texts leads him to the conclusion that there never was one single, over-arching metaphysics. One sees this perhaps most clearly in 'Sending: On Representation', where Derrida's questioning addresses specifically the unity of a destiny of Being in the light of the dissension of the sending, leading him to ask 'wherever this being together or with itself of the *envoi* of being divides itself, defies the *legein*, frustrates the destination of the *envoi*, is not the whole schema of Heidegger's reading challengeable in principle, deconstructed from a historical point of view?' (Sending, 1982, 322). In other words, for Derrida the tradition of metaphysics is not unified but plural: there is not a single 'letter' (*envoi*) coming from the philosophical tradition, but many.

There are three great strengths to Derrida's early reading of Heidegger, which are characteristic of almost all his readings. Firstly, there is the repeated application of the formal strategies elucidated above, which provides this form of thinking with a certain rigour. Secondly, Derrida's deconstructive readings of Heidegger are powerful because he so often enriches our understanding of the texts he reads by his attention to detail. Thirdly, there is the parasitic nature of Derrida's readings, whereby Derrida almost never argues for a position on his own terms. This means that his readings have the character of an internal reading, in spite of the fact that external influences are also always brought to bear. That is to say, he initially borrows the resources with which he works initially from the text or texts whose possibilities he is exploring but proceeds by a process of cross-fertilization to juxtapose these resources with others drawn from elsewhere. So, if Heidegger is almost omnipresent throughout Derrida's works, then so are, for example, Nietzsche and Freud. Notwithstanding the impression of eclecticism, the advantage of this approach is that he can draw on certain assumptions without unequivocally committing himself to them.

However, the parasitic character of Derrida's early thought also gives rise to what has subsequently seemed to his critics to be its greatest weakness. That is to say, what appeared as a strength in the context of theoretical issues and the need to evade certain argumentative traps threatens to be a liability now that he has turned more to ethical and political issues, where one is constantly called upon to judge and to decide the matters at hand (see Chapter 6). For some, the combination of the parasitic and formalistic aspects of Derrida's thought gives the impression that deconstruction can neutralize offensive phrases and be put to the service of almost any cause. Although the criticism is not altogether fair, Derrida's *Of Spirit* is sometimes read in this light as an apology for Heidegger's politics. This places a burden on the decision as to which texts are to be deconstructed. But there is no procedure for making these decisions. In principle any text can be deconstructed.

Derrida's *Of Spirit* is a meditation on the relation between Heidegger's political discourse and his metaphysical commitments. Derrida finds that it is a metaphysical gesture that in part leads Heidegger astray: specifically, Heidegger in the 1930s embraces the philosophical language of spirit (*Geist*), as well as a number of metaphysical presuppositions concerning technology and animality, even after announcing in *Being and Time* that it should be avoided. Derrida in this work once again succeeds in persuading us to reread Heidegger with fresh eyes, although there is the question of whether Derrida employs the strategies of deconstruction to make a somewhat arbitrary division between a 'good' and a 'bad' Heidegger that is supposed to salvage something from the 'wreckage' but on terms that have not been fully articulated. It seems to be in response to such concerns that Derrida has given increased attention to Lévinas at the expense of Heidegger in his work during the 1990s and beyond (VR 17).

MAJOR TEXTS ON HEIDEGGER

'Violence and Metaphysics', *Writing and Difference* (WD 79–153) 1978
This well-known essay defends Heidegger's ontology against Lévinas' critique of it, but at the same time it also starts the process of putting in question Heidegger's account of the history of Western metaphysics.

'The Ends of Man', *Margins of Philosophy* (MP 109–36) 1982
This lecture, first delivered in New York in 1968, contested the anthropologistic readings of Hegel, Hussel, and Heidegger still prevalent at that time. It retains its value for the clear elucidation at the end of the essay of the formal necessities governing deconstructive double reading.

'*Ousia* and *Gramme*', *Margins of Philosophy* (MP 29–67) 1982
First published in 1968 in a *Festschrift* saluting Jean Beaufret, one of the first French Heideggerians, this *tour de force*, focused on a single footnote in *Being and Time*. Unknown to Derrida, he raised questions about Heidegger's reading of Aristotle on time, that Heidegger to a certain extent had himself anticipated in *Basic Problems of Phenomenology*, a lecture course form 1927–8.

'Sending: On Representation' 294–326 (Sending) 1982
Although largely overlooked, this is one of the most important of Derrida's essays on Heidegger, not so much for its examination of the notion of representation, important though that is, but because it addresses most directly the sense of sending (*schicken*) within the idea of destiny (*Geschick*) that governs the later Heidegger's account of the history of Being (*Seinsgeschichte*).

'*Geschlecht*. Sexual Difference, Ontological Difference' 65–83, 1983
The first of a series of four essays entitled *Geschlecht*, albeit the third essay in the series, which continued the elucidation of Heidegger's reading of Trakl begun in the second, has not yet been published. The focus of this first essay was a few remarks on sexual neutrality by Heidegger in his 1928 lecture course *Metaphysical*

Foundations of Logic. It is important as one of Derrida's first forays into the question of sexual difference, but it also raised issues about the ambiguity of dispersion (*Zerstreuung*) in Heidegger – both as a universal structure and a mode of inauthenticity – that helped to reopen in a new way the question of the relation of the ontological to the ontic.

'*Geschlect II*: Heidegger's Hand' 161–96, 1987

Whereas the first *Geschlecht* essay focused on its meaning as sexual difference, in this lecture, delivered in Chicago in 1985, Derrida focused on its sense as racial difference, albeit he also questioned the translation of *Geschlecht* as 'race'. The lecture had its origins in Derrida's course on Philosophical Nationality and Nationalism. This wide-ranging essay also touched on a number of issues that would recur in subsequent texts in more depth, such as animality and Heidegger's politics, but the highpoint was a reading of part of Heidegger's essay on Trakl, 'Language in the Poem'.

'Interpreting Signatures (Nietzsche/Heidegger): Two Questions' 58–71, 1989

This text, which belongs to the Gadamer-Derrida debate, offers directives for a future reading of Heidegger's *Nietzsche* (see section on Nietzsche in this chapter).

Of Spirit (OS) 1989

Because it appeared at roughly the same time as Farias's notorious *Heidegger and National Socialism*, this text immediately found itself in the midst of a ferocious controversy on Heidegger's politics that it was perhaps not well suited to address. It has been subjected to as much hostile scrutiny as almost any of Derrida's texts and has been presented as symptomatic of deconstruction's inability to address political issues. By juxtaposing Heidegger's attempt in *Being and Time* to avoid talking about 'spirit' and its return in the 'Rectoral Address', this essay elevated sensitivity to Heidegger's language.

'Heidegger's Ear: Geschlect IV – Philopolemology' 163–218, 1993

Although it begins with a discussion of friendship that anticipates *The Politics of Friendship*, this lecture delivered in Chicago in 1989, continued the exploration of political resonances in Heidegger's thinking that had been highlighted by *Of Spirit*. A brief evocation of Heidegger's discussion of dike in 'The Anaximander Fragment' is particularly significant given Derrida's subsequent privileging of the term justice, as, for example, in *Spectres of Marx*.

Aporias 1993 *

This book is an engagement with one of the most central concepts in Heidegger's *Being and Time*, being-towards-death, which forms the guarantee of my unity as a subject. Derrida, in meditating on the theme of the aporia, deconstructs this unity, with further reference to Lévinas.

The Villanova Roundtable: Conversation with Jacques Derrida (VR 1–28) 1997 *
In this interview, Derrida suggests that his fundamental discontent with Heidegger revolves around the emphasis that Heidegger accords to gathering compared with his own insistence upon disassociation, which Derrida argues is the condition for community (VR 15). See also TS 246; SM.

LÉVINAS

Simon Critchley

Derridian deconstruction can, and indeed should, be understood as an ethical demand, provided that ethics is understood in the particular sense given to it in the work of Emmanuel Lévinas. Lévinas' work, whose full philosophical importance is only now beginning to be recognized, exerted a powerful and continuous influence on the development of Derrida's thinking. By following the intricate textual dialogue between Lévinas and Derrida, one can see how the question of ethics can be compellingly raised within deconstruction.

This section will proceed by way of a brief introduction to Lévinasian ethics, before then showing why Lévinas' work should occupy a privileged place in discussions of deconstruction, as well as discussing some of the general convergences and dissonances between him and Derrida. In the final two sections, I examine Derrida's two main texts on Lévinas: 'Violence and Metaphysics' and 'At This Very Moment in This Work Here I Am'.

LÉVINASIAN ETHICS

Before considering Derrida's take on Lévinas, it is necessary to consider Lévinas' fundamental ethical project, which can be schematically exemplified in his famous statement that 'ethics is first philosophy'. One might sketch the movement of Lévinas' thinking – a movement that Derrida compares with the crashing of a wave on a beach, always the same wave returning and repeating its movement with deeper insistence (WD 312) – by saying that ethics occurs as the putting into question of the ego, the knowing subject, self-consciousness, or what Lévinas, following Plato, calls the Same. It is important to note that the Same refers not only to the intentional acts of consciousness, but also to the intentional objects that give meaning to those acts and which are constituted by consciousness. Thus, the domain of the Same maintains a relationship with otherness, but it is a relation in which the 'I', or ego, reduces the distance between the Same and the other, and in which their opposition fades. Now, the Same is called into question by the other; or, to use Lévinas' words, it is called into question by the alterity of that which cannot be reduced to the Same, that which escapes the cognitive powers of the knowing subject. When Lévinas uses the term ethics in his first major work, *Totality and Infinity*, he defines it as 'the putting into question of my spontaneity by the presence of the Other' (Totality, 43). Ethics hence describes the non-totalizable relation with the other, the placing in question of the ego, or consciousness, by the alterity of the other.

Ethics, for Lévinas, then, is also critique; it is critical of the liberty, spontaneity, and cognitive emprise of the ego that seeks to reduce all otherness to itself. The ethical is the location of a point of alterity, or what Lévinas calls 'exteriority', that cannot be reduced to the Same. Thus moral consciousness is not an experience of values, but 'an access to exterior being' (*Difficile Liberté*, 409). This exterior being is named 'face' by Lévinas, and is defined as 'the way in which the other presents himself, exceeding the *idea of the other in me*'. In the language of transcendental philosophy, the face is the condition of possibility for ethics. For Lévinas, then, the ethical relation is one in which I am related to the face of the other, whom I cannot evade, comprehend, or kill, and before whom I am called to justice, to justify myself.

The meaning of ethics is found in the relation that I have with the other and in the unique demand that is placed upon me by him or her. The other who approaches me is a singular other who does not lose himself or herself in a crowd of others. Similarly, the subject who is faced with an obligation, and who is prepared to expiate or substitute himself or herself for the other, is an entity not immediately subsumable under a universal concept of the ego, or as something belonging in common to all human beings. Rather, at the moment of obligation, of responsibility, it is I, a singular self, who am obliged to respond to a particular other (Otherwise, 84). What Lévinas means by ethics maintains at best an oblique and perhaps even a critical relation to the philosophical tradition as a whole. Lévinasian ethics does not tell us how we ought to act, nor does it even claim a normative system or procedure for formulating and testing the acceptability of certain maxims, judgements or values. Rather, Lévinasian ethics bears a critical relation to the philosophical tradition (both ontological and ethical) that has reduced otherness to the sameness of subjectivity; to an ontology within which otherness is subsumed.

DERRIDA AND LÉVINAS: HOMOLOGY OR HETEROGENEITY?

Somewhat famously, Derridian deconstruction attempts to locate a 'nonsite, or a non-philosophical site, from which to question philosophy' (Deconstruction and the other, 1984, 108). It seeks a place of exteriority, alterity, or marginality, that is irreducible to philosophy. Deconstruction is the writing of a margin that cannot be represented by philosophy. In question is an other to philosophy that has never been and cannot become philosophy's other, but an other within which philosophy becomes inscribed. The proximity of such sentiments to Lévinas' own resistance to the Western philosophical tradition is immediately apparent.

However, the paradox that haunts Derrida's deconstructive discourse is that the only language that is available to deconstruction is that of philosophy, or logocentrism. Thus to take up a position exterior to logocentrism, if such a thing were possible, would be to risk starving oneself of the very linguistic resources with which one might deconstruct logocentrism (OG 14). Deconstruction is hence always a double reading. It is suspicious about simply adopting a point exterior to Western metaphysics, and this is one of the main points of contestation in Derrida's first essay on Lévinas – 'Violence and Metaphysics' – which will be considered shortly.

But why should Lévinas be given a privileged place in this book on Derrida and deconstruction? Consider some remarkably candid comments that Derrida made about Lévinas during a discussion transcribed in *Altérités* (p. 74) that was published in French in 1986. In responding to the charge that he rarely speaks on ethics, as well as a request to comment on his relationship to Lévinas, Derrida suggests:

> Faced with a thinking like that of Lévinas, I never have an objection. I am ready to subscribe to everything that he says. That does not mean that I think the same thing in the same way, but in this respect the difficulties are very difficult to determine; in this case what do differences of idiom, language or writing mean?

Derrida also disagrees with the suggestion put to him that he does not acquiesce in sharing the traditions of phenomenology and Judaism to the same extent as Lévinas (*Altérités*, 75). Such remarks were admittedly transcribed from an oral, improvised debate, but they make the point that a privilege accorded to Lévinas in this discussion of Derrida's work is not without foundation, even if the work of these two thinkers is evidently not identical.

There are also other, ultimately more powerful reasons for privileging Lévinas, which will be demonstrated in the course of this chapter. Firstly, Derrida's 1964 essay on Lévinas, 'Violence and Metaphysics', shows the problematic of deconstructive reading preparing itself through a dialogue with Lévinasian ethics. This essay hence provides clues as to the genesis of Derrida's general deconstructive problematic; more specifically it also shows how that problematic arises primarily out of a confrontation with the ethical thinking of Lévinas, and in particular with his text *Totality and Infinity* (see Chapter 5 of this volume).

Secondly, Derrida's 1980 essay on Lévinas, 'At This Very Moment in This Work Here I Am', allows one to judge whether Derrida's deconstructive problematic has developed as a whole, and in particular *vis-à-vis* the question of ethics. This text ana-lyses Lévinas' later work, *Otherwise than Being or Beyond Essence*, which might itself actually be read as a response to Derrida's 'Violence and Metaphysics'. It will be these two texts that are explored in what follows below. Derrida's and Lévinas' succession of textual encounters calls the work of both of these two thinkers into question, and leads them to a deeper level than the ontology of questioning (what is x?) that dominated the Western philosophical tradition – namely, responsibility for the other.

VIOLENCE AND METAPHYSICS

In *Totality and Infinity*, Lévinas defines metaphysics as the desire for the absolutely other (Totality, 33). Derrida sees Lévinas' philosophical project as inaugurating something 'new, quite new, a metaphysics of radical separation and exteriority' (WD 88). On one level, Derrida agrees that Lévinas' ethical metaphysics consti-tutes a transgression, or dislocation, of classical ontology and of the Greek thinking of Being that Husserlian phenomenology and Heideggerian ontology repeat. On Derrida's reading, this new metaphysics seeks to found itself upon the datum, or evidence, of an experience that has been dissimulated by the Graeco-German tradition: namely, the encounter with the other person, the buried nudity of experi-ence that continually denies the attempts of the Greek *logos* to comprehend and reduce its radical alterity. Understood in this way, Lévinasian metaphysics is a 'return to the things themselves' (WD 107–8) that seeks to undermine phenomen-ology and ontology.

However – and here we approach the dominant gesture of 'Violence and Meta-physics' – the transgression of phenomenology and ontology that is effected by Lévinas' empirical metaphysics in fact presupposes the very things that it seeks to transgress. As has been shown, for Derrida, the Husserlian project is suspended between the authentic metaphysics it sought to promote and the degenerate meta-physics it sought to reject (see the section on Husserl in this chapter). Adopting a similar argument, Derrida claims that Lévinas' metaphysical overcoming of trans-cendental phenomenology presupposes that which it seeks to overcome (WD 121, 133), which does not negate the legitimacy of the attempt, although it leaves the Lévinasian text suspended and hesitant in the space between metaphysics and its outside.

Without going into detail regarding Lévinas' criticisms of Husserl and Heideg-ger – roughly for perpetuating an imperialism of the same – and without consider-ing Derrida's qualified support for these two theorists under attack, it is important to take note of the 'two origins' (WD 82) and two historical configurations that Derrida establishes in the opening pages of this essay: (1) the Greek *logos*, whose conceptual totality encloses the field within which philosophy is possible, a field within which Hegel, Husserl, and Heidegger tirelessly labour; (2) non-philosophy as the attempt to escape the nets of the Greek *logos*. On Derrida's reading, Lévinas attempts to escape Greek logocentrism through recourse to a Hebraic origin and a messianic eschatology that are opened from within an experience of alterity that the Greek philosophical tradition can neither reduce, nor comprehend.

Although Derrida is respectful of the autonomy of each origin, his claim in 'Violence and Metaphysics' is that the only conceptual language available is that of the Greek *logos*. The attempt to articulate conceptually an experience that has been forgotten or exiled from philosophy can only be stated within philosophical conceptuality, which entails that the experience succumbs to, and is destroyed by, philosophy. This is the necessity that echoes throughout Derrida's essay (WD 152): the necessity of lodging oneself within the philosophical conceptuality in order to destroy it (WD 112), the necessity of being destroyed by philosophical conceptuality – a double necessity. 'Violence and Metaphysics' is suspended between these two origins (WD 84) in such a way as to maintain a dialogue between the Jew and the Greek, and which also postpones the decision of choosing between them. Derrida's reading also reveals that Lévinas' work is itself between these two origins, despite his efforts to be free of *logos*, ontology, and the 'imperialism of the same' that he associates with the Western philosophical tradition. But 'Violence and Metaphysics' is a double reading that is not simply against Lévinas. Derrida is not denouncing an incoherence in Lévinas, but wondering about the *necessity* that provokes such an incoherence, not only in the work of Lévinas, but also in the tradition more generally. That said, Derrida does highlight that Lévinas' ethical overcoming is conceptually dependent on those very traditional resources that it sought to overcome, and Derrida offers a double refusal of both remaining with the limits of the tradition and of the possibility of transgressing those limits. He is between philosophy and its other, and there is a suggestion that this relationality is itself ethical. In this respect, however, Derrida argues that Lévinas' language betrays him. The dream of pure empiricism, of the radical otherness of the other, evaporates when language awakens. And this is something that Lévinas' later work explicitly takes into account.

AT THIS VERY MOMENT IN THIS WORK HERE I AM

As mentioned, Lévinas' later work incorporates many of the lessons learned from Derrida's 'Violence and Metaphysics'. If there is an under-determination and a certain philosophical naïveté in *Totality and Infinity*, then this is completely transformed in *Otherwise than Being or Beyond Essence*, where the aporia entailed in the attempted expression of the ethical in the language of ontology (Greek language) become arguably the central preoccupation. Lévinas' real innovation in *Otherwise than Being* is the model of the Saying and the Said as a way of explaining how the ethical signifies within ontological language. To explain this distinction briefly, the Saying is my exposure – corporeal, sensible – to the other, my inability to refuse the Other's approach. It is the performative stating, proposing or expressive position of myself facing the other whose essence cannot be caught in constative propositions. On the other hand, the Said is a statement, an assertion or constative proposition, about which the truth or falsity can be ascertained.

That 'At This Very Moment' was written as a homage to Lévinas' work submits Derrida to a number of performative problems. To create a work that maintains the other in its otherness, entails that the text or the work must not be given back to Lévinas' name, his proper name, which would be to perpetuate an imperialism of the same and of subjectivity. To write a text for Emmanuel Lévinas is to write a text that is not *for* him, but for the other. Consequently it is ethically necessary, for the moment, to be ungrateful, faulty, and, to recall a word from Derrida's first essay on Lévinas, *violent*.

Yet it is important to recognize that ingratitude, faultiness, and violence are not directed against Lévinas; they are not moments of an external critique which would naïvely oppose itself to the supposed generosity, flawlessness, and peace of Lévinasian ethics. Ingratitude, faultiness, and violence are the necessary conditions of a fidelity to Lévinas' work, a work that works precisely to the extent that it cannot be returned to the proper name of Emmanuel Lévinas. To schematize this, one might say that it is only in ingratitude and violence that the ethical Saying is maintained. To write a text for Lévinas, is to create a work that is neither for him, nor against him, but one in which the modalities of for and against become inseparable yet inassemblable conditions for the possibility of ethical Saying. Given that Lévinas' text is directed toward the wholly other, then surprisingly, perhaps, what is at stake here is nothing less than the success or failure of Lévinasian ethics.

'At This Very Moment' can be said to move between three formulations of an ethical imperative or performative: 'He will have obliged [*Il aura obligé*]', 'E. L. will have obliged [*E. L. aura obligé*]', and 'She will have obliged [*Elle aura obligé*]'. The transition from the pronoun 'Il' to the pronoun 'Elle' is mediated by the initialled proper name of Lévinas, E. L. The deconstructive fabric of Derrida's reading of Lévinas is stretched across these two pronouns, where the threshold that divides both the masculine Pro-nom from the feminine Pro-nom and the pronominal from the proper name is continually transgressed.

We can sketch briefly the movement of Derrida's reading in two moments. First, Derrida tries to find out how Lévinas' work works; second, he tries to show how, Lévinas' work does not work. The first moment of reading shows how Lévinas' text resists the economy of the Same, or logocentrism, and goes generously unto the other: briefly '*Il aura obligé*. Conversely, the second moment of reading is the ingratitude and violence required to maintain the alterity of the first moment. The second moment is performed by showing how Lévinas subordinates sexual difference to ethical difference and thereby encloses both the 'Il' and the 'Elle' in the economy of the Same. The work is not returned to E. L. but to the other of the wholly other: *Elle aura obligé*.

Derrida's work is governed by a similar necessity: the work of Derrida's work is one that must not be returned to and circumscribed by Derrida's proper name. 'At This Very Moment' is possessed of a 'dehiscence' that allows it to resonate with an alterity that must not be reduced to ontology and propriety. Derrida's work works in so far as it returns the text to 'Elle' and lets the voice of feminine alterity interrupt Lévinas' work. To reduce the textuality of 'At This Very Moment' to the proper name of Jacques Derrida (by saying, for example, 'In this essay, Derrida says . . .', 'Derrida's final word is . . .', and so on), as I have often been obliged to do, is to foreclose the opening announced by ethical alterity and to cover over the ethical interruption the text seeks to maintain.

This point can be reinforced by an examination of the narrative structure of 'At This Very Moment'. The text is not a monologue spoken by the signatory, Jacques Derrida; it is at the very least a dialogue for two voices, and one might even call it a 'polylogue' (P 393–4). The horizontal dash that precedes the first word of the essay indicates that somebody is speaking; the quotation marks denote a voice that is not necessarily that of the text's signatory. Turning the pages of the essay, one finds nine more of these dashes, each denoting a change in the persona of the textual voice. Furthermore, 'At This Very Moment' is spoken, or written, by a number of voices that are sexually differentiated into masculine, neutral (sic), or feminine.

It has already been established that if Lévinas' work works, then it is precisely to the extent that it allows the trace of the wholly other. Now, if this 'Il' is sexually neutral, how can it be marked with a masculine pronoun? The sexual indifference of ethical difference treats masculinity and neutrality as synonyms. Does not the supposed sexual neutrality of ethical difference lead ineluctably to a mastery of sexual difference and, synonymously, a mastery of the masculine over the feminine? If this is the case, then how can Lévinasian ethics be considered ethical?

These questions take us right to the heart of the second moment of reading. The claim is that Lévinas makes sexual difference secondary with respect to the sexually neutral wholly other. To mark the neutrality of the wholly other with a masculine pronoun is to make sexual difference secondary as femininity. One might say that sexual difference is Lévinas' 'blind spot' (see MB). How does Lévinas remain blind to sexual difference? Two enclosures can be detected in Lévinas' work: first, by making sexual difference secondary and by seeking to master the un-said alterity of the feminine, the 'Il' of the wholly other risks enclosing itself within the economy of the Same; second, by seeking to enclose sexual difference within ethical difference, Lévinas encloses the feminine within the economy of the Same, and thus remains enclosed within the economy of the Same that he has continually striven to exceed.

By making sexual difference secondary to ethical difference and by equating sexuality with the feminine, as Lévinas does, does not the feminine, then, become wholly-other to the Saying of the wholly other? If 'She [*Elle*]' is the other to 'He', and if 'He' is the wholly other, then 'She' is the other to the wholly other. The question then becomes: as the other to the wholly other, as a being that possesses greater alterity than the wholly other, does 'She' not demand greater ethical respect and priority than 'He'? 'The other as feminine (me), far from being derived or secondary, would become the other of the Saying of the wholly-other' (ATM 46).

FURTHER READING ON LÉVINAS

Adieu to Emmanuel Lévinas (AEL) 1997 *
This second homage to Lévinas' work, this time in the form of a eulogy, returns to the problem of the feminine and also raises a theme that will be prominent in most of Derrida's work between 1997 and now: hospitality. This term almost never appears in Lévinas' writings, but Derrida highlights the paradoxical way in which this is actually highly hospitable. In this text, Derrida also ruminates on the '*adieu*', the goodbye, and mourning more generally. Related material: *Of Hospitality* (OH) 2000, *The Work of Mourning* (WM) 2001.

HEGEL

David Rathbone

Nietzsche lamented readers who approach texts like plundering troops, aiming to get in, grab what they can, and get out again as quickly as possible (*Human All Too Human*, § 137). Hegel is such a reader's worst nightmare. His writing is voluminous, dense and complicated, his style demanding that the reader share the author's work ethic by toiling over the text. But if Hegel is the opportunist's nightmare, he is also the grammatologist's dream, 'the last philosopher of the book and the first thinker of writing' (OG 26). In following Derrida's reading of Hegel, we shall be dwelling upon both the ways in which Hegel cannot actually achieve all that he thinks he can, as well as the ways in which he cannot think all that he actually achieves.

Derrida's interest in Hegel, first announced in *Of Grammatology* (OG 24–6) and in the essay 'Différance' (MP 1–28), is introduced in detail in the two essays 'From a Restricted to General Economy: A Hegelianism Without Reserve' (WD 251–78) and 'The Pit and the Pyramid' (MP 69–108). This interest is explored in most depth in *Glas*, but *Glas*'s investigations in turn echo out through 'The Age of Hegel' (in *Who's Afraid of Philosophy*), through the quarter of *The Truth in Painting* devoted to Valerio Adami's drawings, called '+R (Into the Bargain)' (TP 151–81), and through the interviews in *Points* – 'Between Brackets I' (P 5–29) and '*Ja*, or the Faux-bond' (P 30–77). The encounter with Hegel thus forms a relatively compact site in Derrida's *oeuvre*, the above texts all appearing between 1967 and 1975.

In his article Différance, Derrida tells us that his thought, 'although maintaining relations of profound affinity with Hegelian discourse, is also, up to a certain point, unable to break with that discourse; but it can operate a kind of infinitesimal and radical displacement of it' (MP 14). In order to understand this displacing operation of Derrida's, which is both an affinity and a break, Hegel's writings must be tackled and his ideas grasped.

HEGEL BOOT CAMP

Hegel sees history as a story with a moral. To tell the story properly Hegel has to tell it three times, from three different points of view: the subjective point of view, the objective point of view, and the absolute point of view.

The first telling of Hegel's story is the narrative told from the subjective point of view, called *The Phenomenology of Spirit*. That book tells the story of the unfolding diversity of the forms of consciousness – not a random diversity but, rather, one systematically organized through a process of successive contradiction and synthesis called *dialectic*. That's three technical terms: contradiction (when concepts oppose each other), synthesis (when concepts overcome opposition), and dialectic (the name of the conceptual process). Each of these three terms relies on the word *concept*, our fourth technical term. A 'concept' is whatever can be posed in thought. Forms of consciousness are immediately real to those concepts undergoing them, but to talk about them we must represent them. *Representation* connects the conceptual with the real by enabling us to picture an instance of a concept – it is a figurative or 'picture-thinking'. The story about the history of the forms of consciousness is a story of representation, both in the sense that each form of consciousness is characterized by a way of representing the world, but also in the sense that the story itself is a representation of what has been happening to consciousness in its myriad forms.

The last and most important technical word can now be added. The problem is this term poses a translation difficulty. The German word is '*Aufhebung*', which is the process of the synthesis of new concepts that resolves the contradictions between oppositions without destroying them, but rather raising them up to a higher perspective in which the identity in all difference becomes apparent. The standard convention is to use the neologism 'sublate', which has the disadvantage of representing the German word as odder than it really is, for *Aufhebung* is an ordinary German word from everyday speech. We need an English word that means: raise/lift/remove/abolish/cancel/nullify/suspend/annul(marriage)/separate repeal/terminate/adjourn/reverse.

'Uplift', 'overcome', 'surmount', 'sublimate', 'transcend' and 'transform' have all also been tried, along with others. 'Boot' is a more prosaic word that has gained a new connotation in the computer age, and I shall use it in this essay to indicate that double sense of *Aufhebung* as a process which both stamps itself out, and lifts itself up by its own shoelaces. Derrida's suggestion of the French word *relève* is convenient for English speakers, for it has a cousin in English with a strong family resemblance: 'relieve'. We will come back to this in section two.

With these technical terms now introduced, we can give the bare bones of Hegel's system. The first major insight of speculative thinking (which is what Hegel calls his philosophy) is that upon specification, all concepts fall apart into contradictions, not haphazardly, but rather in a systematic way. 'In the beginning' of this first, subjective story, there was an ineffable unity: fully implicit, fully immediate, fully abstract, fully 'in-itself'. The story of the *Phenomenology* is the story of spirit (or *Geist* as mind) making itself fully explicit, fully mediated, fully concrete, 'in-and-for itself'. In order to begin this process, the specification of 'the one' falls apart into the first contradiction: sensory perception. I am not what I perceive, and what I perceive is not me. This emergence of understanding, the first moment in the child's consciousness, just as it was in our remote ancestors, is the first *Aufhebung* which boots the perceptual process itself into being (*Phenomenology*, section A: Consciousness). Then consciousness falls apart into self and other, the most primitive form of which is for Hegel slavery and mastery (*Phenomenology*, section B: Self-Consciousness). This is a deeper contradiction: the master is free but dependent on the slave, whereas slaves, although able to look after themselves, are not free. The eventual *Aufhebung* of this contradiction comes when a thinking arises that is able to master itself and serve its own ends. The modern individual emerges as master-and-servant in one form of self-consciousness, and this mediation boots consciousness up another level, in which understanding and thinking can confront one another in the next dialectical show-down (or up), in the contradiction between individuality and freedom (*Phenomenology*, section C: Free Concrete Mind). Since each mediation is a recapitulation of the whole dialectic up to that point, the mediations grow progressively more convoluted as the book progresses along its systematically recursive path, until finally we reach the form of consciousness able to tell itself the story which the *Phenomenology* contains. The children's book *The Never-Ending Story* tries to present the story of someone reading a book, upon whom it gradually dawns that they themselves are a character in the story they are reading. This is the aim of the *Phenomenology*: to have you come to realize that the form of consciousness able to read and comprehend that very book thereby recognizes that the process it has understood is none other than the very process that has culminated in yourself. And *that* realization is supposed to be the *Aufhebung* that boots the reader out of self-consciousness and into absolute consciousness, resulting in fully mediated, fully explicit, fully concrete freedom of mind. For free concrete mind, the dialectic is apprehended on the level of representation, but it is its conceptual significance that is the main thing. The history of the forms of consciousness reveals ways of thinking (and so seeing) which have run like trains on the tracks of conceptual connection. Dialectical mediation reveals a systematic backbone of concepts that have worked themselves out in the forms of consciousness and self-consciousness, which we are able to represent in order to express their implicit conceptual content.

Hegel's first telling of his story has been the story from the inside, so to speak – the subjective story, the story of what it has been *like* to experience consciousness in its many and varied forms. The second story, the story from the objective viewpoint, is the story from the outside. The history of what the undergoing of these forms *looked* like, rather than what they felt like, is the history of the institutional forms they took. The history of institutions is this objective viewpoint, and in the lectures on the history of art, the history of religion and the history of philosophy, as well as in *The Philosophy of Right*, Hegel recounts the stories of the religions, movements, schools and societies which have given outward expression to the inner lives of their members.

The third and final telling of Hegel's story is in his work *The Encyclopedia of the Philosophical Sciences* (1990). Having heard the subjective and objective stories of spirit's quest to find a form adequate to its infinite content, spirit has already realized at the end of the *Phenomenology* that the sequence of objective and of subjective forms of manifestation of spirit are representations whose conceptual content is being traced out in these empirical histories. The concepts so revealed are themselves all related through an ordering that is not dependent upon a sequence in time. To retell the whole of the previous two stories using not the temporal sequence of history but rather the absolute sequence of logic is the task of the *Encyclopedia*. It is the story of the concepts themselves, of how they unfold out of and into each other, not in representation in time, but in the non-temporal order of thinking itself. So their sequence is not in the lived time of the subjective story, nor in the world time of the objective story, but in the conceptual sequence of the absolute order, which is logical, not temporal.

So the beginning of the third and final story is not some hazy prehistory of proto-perception or prehistoric cultures, but the absolute starting point of the absolutely simplest concept: *being*, the very concept of there being something at all. As soon as we try to specify this concept, it splits into two: being in general (indeterminate being), and being something (determinate being). The contradiction of these two concepts boot the concept of 'quality', or as Hegel put it 'being for-itself'. And so begins the dialectical engine upon its third and final rearrangement of the whole story, which according to Hegel achieves the synthesis of the subjective and the objective perspectives in the absolute idea: the concept of concept, or the concept of free concrete mind understanding the process that culminates in itself. This concept of free concrete mind is seen to emerge through the dialectical consequences of the concepts of art and of religion, the contradiction that boots the concept of philosophy. Having fully realized that its own understanding is the protagonist of the *Encyclopedia*, the mind is thus *transparent* to itself, concrete, and free. All is revealed. So the story goes.

WHAT A RELIEF! DERRIDA AT LAST

In the spirit of Nietzsche's aphorism abhorring looting readers, we have been abiding by Derrida's motto: 'Let us proceed slowly' (G 22a). Like playing a conjuring trick back in slow motion, Derrida finds a sleight of hand concealed in the Hegelian system by way of his meticulous examination of various moments of the dialectic. 'There is an undue haste – let us call it *motivationist* to save time – that *Glas* parodies, puts on stage (and in trouble) in order to make way for a general re-elaboration' (P 56). The re-elaboration of the reading of Hegel that Derrida pursues is organized by the thought that *Aufhebung* always actually happens in writing, and so is inseparable from representation. Derrida suggests that: 'the *Aufhebung* – *la relève* – is constrained into writing itself otherwise. Or perhaps simply into writing itself. Or better, into taking account of its consumption in writing'.

This brings us back to Derrida's proposal for a translation of *Aufhebung*: *relève*, more or less the English word 'relieve', although its primary French connotation – 'to point out' – is only captured in the English phrase 'to throw into relief' (MP 121). In Derrida's idiom, we can say that contradictions are relieved of their conceptual content in synthesis by throwing their differences into relief, as the dialectic progressively relieves the pressure of the implicit through writing itself down.

Derrida's two articles 'From Restricted to General Economy' and 'The Pit and the Pyramid', form a kind of dual portal into *Glas*. The former approaches Hegel by gathering up George Bataille's various engagements with Hegel, which leads into the latter's investigation of the question of Hegel's theory of the sign.

Bataille forms one of the crucial influences on Derrida's reading of Hegel. From his associations with the surrealists in the 1920s to his post-war *Summa Atheologica*, Bataille challenged the assumption that the economy is actually about wealth and its accumulation. Bataille points out that this is so only from a sufficiently restricted point of view. As our perspective becomes more general, we see that industry in general actually amounts to the highly organized manufacture of waste, and that the most general question of economy is not how to save more, but how to waste more, so as to increase demand and so growth. This has always been manifest, Bataille points out, in the religious phenomenon of the sacrifice, in the political phenomenon of torture, and in the inextricability of mortality and sexuality. But this realization is met not with despair but with a 'sovereign laughter' (WD 255–6).

To laugh at philosophy (at Hegelianism) – such, in effect, is the form of the awakening – henceforth calls for an entire 'discipline', an entire 'method of meditation' that acknowledges the philosopher's byways, understands his techniques, makes use of his ruses, manipulates his cards, lets him deploy his strategy, appropriates his texts (WD 252).

Through Bataille's lens, Hegel's works resolve into a double story. On the one hand is Hegel's own story, the official story of what's going on in the dialectic, how it converges on the whole because it converges in every detail, with the negative cancelling itself out in every mediation and being wholly transformed into a positivity which compounds accumulatively. But shadowing this sanctioned mainstream is a counter-culture proliferating in the background that, although invisible from the official perspective, is in fact the source of its momentum. It is the failures of the official dialectic that preoccupy Bataille, not as errors on Hegel's behalf to be corrected, but rather as systematically located and meticulously documented lapses, locating unacceptable yet indispensable mediations which escape the scrutiny of the official 'Hegel' but are essential to the 'counter-Hegel'. Thus what Bataille calls for example 'the sovereign' and 'the servile' are related to the official dialectic of the master and the slave but always fail to perform their ritual functions in the orthodox manner. The restricted form of sovereignty is lordship, but the sovereign individual laughs at the lord who is wholly enmeshed in what from the sovereign perspective is the imaginary reality of the system. The sovereign is freed by the joyful wisdom that he finds in 'the knowledge that we have of our own nothingness'. Sovereignty, or inner experience, answers to communication, but is not fully part of it: as Bataille says, inner experience can be expressed, but it cannot be betrayed. He thus recognizes that 'the Hegelian *Aufhebung* is produced entirely from within discourse, from within the system or the work of signification' (WD 275).

It is to Hegel's semiology that Derrida turns to further interrogate Hegel's official line on what he means, and what meaning itself is. The sign is for Hegel the fluid medium of spirit, its element. The concept of representation *is* the concept of the sign. The official story is that the sign is a kind of bridge or transition that independently self-present subjects use in order to exchange meanings. Its dialectical treatment begins at *Encyclopedia* §379, the point at which the concepts of logic and of nature have overcome their contradiction in the concept of spirit (that point in the system exactly parallel to the location of the family in the story from the objective viewpoint, which Derrida examines in depth in *Glas*, and to the odd section in the *Phenomenology* on phrenology, which also gives Derrida pause for thought). Hegel treats of the sign under the moment of the *Aufhebung* of memory and imagination in psychology, the outward manifestation of intelligence: 'the sign is any immediate intuition, but representing a totally different content from what it has for itself'. This is a pivotal point for Hegel, because he wants to say that all of reality as experienced in time is symbolic, composed only of representations which must be reiterated to yield up their conceptual content. Experience must be read 'like a book' to find its meaning. The official story is that there is *only one* coherent story to be read out of history; the counter-story, that there is *never just one* counter-story, and the unity dreamt of by the official story is imaginary, not real. This is because representation can never decide if it has entirely captured the reality it is standing for, just as concepts can never decide if they have entirely captured every subtlety of representation. The dream of the official story is for Hegel inseparable from the fundamental assumption that there is only one true intelligence, expressed most fully in alphabetic writing. This leads Hegel to denigrate other indigenous forms of representation such as Chinese characters or Egyptian hieroglyphics as not just different but inferior. Derrida traces the tangles Hegel gets himself in as he tries to make the official story hang together: 'The Chinese language is both too differentiated and insufficiently differentiated, too accentuated and insufficiently articulated' (MP 103).

These considerations of Bataille, and of Hegel's account of the sign, leave Derrida wondering: could an activation of Hegel be possible that is not beholden to the official story?

> What might be a 'negative' that could not be *relevé*? And which, in sum, as negative, but without appearing as such, without *presenting* itself, that is, without working in the service of meaning, would work? but would work then as pure loss? Quite simply, a machine, perhaps, and one which would function. A machine defined in its pure functioning, and not in its final utility, its meaning, its result, its work (MP 107).

Glas is just such a device and Derrida sets its parameters accordingly: 'I am interested in the experience, not the success or the failure' (G 19a). The extra-dialectical contradictions that drive this machine proliferate wherever reality misbehaves and refuses submission to systematic booting.

GLAS

Glas is built in two columns, as if the 'book', like you, had a left brain and a right brain, and was written in stereo: left channel on Hegel, right channel on Jean Genet, a French novelist, playwright and uncompromising non-conformist. Here we are listening in mono, so keep in mind that this is only the Hegel half of the story. I hang the word 'book' on tenterhooks because it is stretching it a bit to call *Glas* a book in any traditional sense. Derrida has said of *Glas*: 'It is just that I really no longer know what one "means to say" today with the word "produce", in general and *a fortiori* for this type of "product" or "produced effect" that is called a

book, all the more so for a writing that is no longer altogether a book, that is, *Glas*.'
What Derrida says of the complications of Hegel's writing applies all the more so to
Glas itself: 'The rigorous and subtle corridors ... cannot be summarised without
being mistreated' (WD 254).

Derrida wrote a new preface to the English translation (in *Glassary*, 1986, 17–20).
He suggests that *Glas* '*presents itself* as a volume *of* cylindric columns, writes *on*
pierced, incrusted, breached, tattooed cylindric columns, on them then, but also
around them, *against* them, *between* them that are, through and through, tongue and
text' ('Proverb', 1986, 17).

In French, *glas* is what bells do: knell, sound, toll, or ring. In German, *Glas* is
glass – the transparent concrete, so to speak. Both meanings resonate throughout
this text. Page one opens abruptly, as if we have walked in on a conversation already
underway: if you turn to the last page, you will see that not only does the text end
equally abruptly, but that the end of the Genet column flows into the start of the
Hegel one, and vice versa. But Derrida has warned that this link is interrupted, and
should be called a hiccup rather than a continuity: 'a caesura or hiatus prevents
what in effect resembles such a band or strip turning back on itself' (P 51). The
reader undergoes more or less utter disorientation for three complex pages before
realizing on page four that experience was calculated to illustrate Derrida's point
of departure.

There have been many introductions to Hegel for sale and generally available.
And the problem of the introduction in/to Hegel's philosophy is *all* of Hegel's
philosophy: (the) *already* posed throughout, especially in his prefaces and fore-
words, introductions and preliminary concepts. So, already, one would be found
entrained in the circle of the Hegelian beginning, sliding off endlessly (G 4a).

The slippage of the dialectic examined most closely by Derrida is that around the
moment of the family as that form of objective spirit that is synthesized in the *Aufhebung* of the contradiction between the abstract right of private property and the
concrete right of morality (*Moralitat*) in ethical life (*Sittlichkeit*). Derrida suggests
that 'what remains irresoluble, impracticable, nonnormal, or nonnormalizable, is
what interests and constrains us here' (G 5a). Derrida makes Genet play Hegel's
heckler as he teases unintended contradictions out of the text, setting solid chunks
of it to soak in a sceptical solution of disruptive spirit, unwilling to ignore the endless distractions of excess connotations. The tidy negation that clings to Hegel's key
concept ('ab-solute' spirit means *insoluble* spirit) is thereby shaken off as spirit gets
rethought as thoroughly soluble. Derrida does not connect his quotes into the flow
of the text in the conventional manner, but rather juxtaposes them as sub-columns
and text-boxes not interrupted by referencing (to figure out where he's quoting
from, you need to look up the *Glassary*, 137–81). Why separate and disjoin a text
like this? To remind the reader that the unifying effect that the text generates is
not actually the whole story to its meaning, and that the exclusive attention to this

effect's operations, which constitutes what we usually mean by 'reading', obscures the text's depths to the point of eclipse. Derrida's text flows around dissolving chunks of Hegel, releasing what they meant to say, along with what they didn't, back into the contexts out of which they first crystallized. Dissolved spirit concentrates and gels in varying ways around the concepts of family, wo/man and reproduction. Chunks of objective, subjective and absolute spirit fizz with meanings stretched into resonators like musical strings. The 're' of 'relieve' is the key to the concept of vibration: in the general fluidity of soluble spirit, the crucial thing is not to be too hasty in assuming we know the answer to the question: 'What is happening?' (*Glassary*, 1986, 150). For, 'if there were a decidable response to this question, it could not be said in a word' (*Glassary*, 1986, 122), but only by following the imperative to 'be always doing several things at once' (TP 174). Derrida says in *Positions*: 'It is still a question of elucidating the relationship to Hegel – a difficult labour, which for the most part remains before us, and which in a certain way is interminable' . . . (POS 43). Hegel: still before us (for *the most part*), still interminable (in a *certain* way).

FURTHER READING ON HEGEL

'This is Not an Oral Footnote' 1991 *
Includes a short and easy-to-follow three-page discussion (203–5) of some of the textual strategies that Derrida uses in *Glas*.

NIETZSCHE

Fiona Jenkins

At a conference on 'Nietzsche Today' held at Cerissy-la-Salle in 1972, the speakers included Jacques Derrida, Jean-Luc Nancy, Jean-François Lyotard, Phillipe Lacoue-Labarthe and Sarah Kofman. Coming at the peak of a wave of interest in Nietzsche's work on the French scene, inspired by Georges Bataille's *Sur Nietzsche* (1945), the publication of Martin Heidegger's two-volume *Nietzsche* (1961), Gilles Deleuze's *Nietzsche and Philosophy* (1962), and Pierre Klossowski's *Nietzsche and the Vicious Circle* (1969), the conference presented readings of Nietzsche's texts that for the first time posed seriously the question of how they might be read in a fashion attentive to their curious and demanding style. Reading Nietzsche *today* demands, as Derrida puts it in *Of Grammatology*, 'a different type of reading, more faithful to his type of writing' (OG 19). Nietzsche's writing throws off philosophy's subordination to logos and to truth and it demands the deconstruction of the meaning of the tradition in which such subordination has been rendered imperative. As inspiration and model for a deconstruction of metaphysics, Nietzsche's importance for

Derrida cannot be underestimated. Yet there are comparatively few texts in which Derrida directly writes *on* Nietzsche. In responding to a question posed to him in interview about this, Derrida highlights how precisely what is important to him in the Nietzschean text is what makes it resist any systematization and hence any adequate account of 'what Nietzsche said (or meant)'. He calls this quality of the text its 'singular and irreducible multiplicity' (N 216). Yet clearly these are the qualities that Derrida finds in all the philosophical texts he reads, whether they be by Plato, Hegel, Husserl, Freud or Blanchot, the very character of deconstruction being such as to refuse to allow the voices of a text to be reduced to a 'monology' or single meaning. What then is the privilege of Nietzsche in this respect? To this Derrida replies: 'I don't know: he is perhaps, of them all, the most mad!' It follows that in a special sense, with Nietzsche 'above all', the freedom and suffering of his madness must not be forced 'into the straightjacket of an interpretation' (N 217). This chapter will proceed by engaging with the three main texts in which Derrida writes on Nietzsche.

SPURS: NIETZSCHE'S STYLES

The popular image of Nietzsche as *master* of suspicion, able to lead us out of the coiling maze that morality, modernity and Christianity have trapped us in, is one that Derrida hints we should be wary of. Charting a wayward course through Nietzsche's texts in *Spurs* he remarks that, 'Nietzsche too is a little lost there, lost much as a spider who finds he is unequal to the web he has spun' (SNS 101). In this reading of Nietzsche, Derrida seeks to do justice to the labyrinthine quality of a text that he will later refer to as a logic of the 'perhaps'.

The key to such a logic here is the emphasis placed upon Nietzsche's 'style'. Style is initially articulated as the 'pointed' aspect of writing, as its 'spur' and hence as that which makes writing a weapon or a defence: 'In the question of style there is always the weight or *examen* of some pointed object. At times this might only be a quill or a stylus. But it could just as easily be a stiletto or even a rapier' (SNS 37). Likewise, in the undecidability of *attack upon* or *defence against* the 'matrix' of philosophy, Derrida discerns the subtle operation of Nietzschean thought, at once a motion of inscription, engagement and of 'recoiling' – the latter a means of keeping at a distance and repelling. Thus the 'spur' of the title at once evokes the fashion in which the prow of a boat cuts into the water, but also, how a spur of land jutting into the ocean is the point on which the waves break. The opposition of active and passive at first appears determinative of such metaphors. Yet this antithesis, like that of the masculine versus the feminine (cf. AEL, ATM, P 89–108), will be one crucial 'point' (spur) of a deconstruction intent on mocking the figure of the masculine philosopher who, with his incisive 'phallic' instruments of thought, pursues a quest to subdue the feminine 'matrix' – which, however, always turns back to engulf him.

SUPPOSING TRUTH TO BE A WOMAN

In the opening paragraphs of *Spurs*, Derrida announces that the 'question of style' amounts to taking 'woman' as a subject (SNS 37). Ruminations on women, in a 'style' that has seemed to many readers simply misogynist, are rife in Nietzsche's texts. Yet Derrida is surely right to point out the complexity and importance of such references. A rather infamous remark from the preface of Nietzsche's *Beyond Good and Evil* reads:

> Supposing truth to be a woman – what then? Are there not grounds for the suspicion that all philosophers, insofar as they were dogmatists, have been inexpert about women? That the gruesome seriousness, the clumsy obtrusiveness with which they have usually approached truth so far have been awkward and very improper methods for winning a woman's heart? For certainly, she has not allowed herself to be won – and today every kind of dogmatism is left standing dispirited and discouraged . . .

In the matrix of philosophy truth is the object of desire and especially a desire for possession, a desire Nietzsche insists is eternally thwarted as the woman 'truth', repulsed by her suitors, withdraws. Truth also repels and abhors woman in her other aspect as a lover of 'mere appearance'. With the pointed weapon of the figure of woman *as* truth, however, Nietzsche paradoxically evokes woman's 'artistry' to which his texts also constantly refer; the 'love of appearance', the feminine skill of 'seeming to be', he holds to be a creative power that slides into a philosophically inadmissible confusion of appearance and reality (*Gay Science* §58).

For Derrida, the power of woman to engage desire on the borders of a never-decidable 'reality' becomes a complementary figure to the question of style in relation to the 'serious', logocentric discourse of philosophy. A 'truth-as-untruth', the truth of dissimulation that 'makes real' what it creates, troubles desire itself, making it uncertain of what it wants. Hence the importance Derrida draws attention to and amplifies in his own text of the figure of 'veiling' (see *Veils* 2001, 49–62), which instead of connoting female passivity becomes a dynamic operation linked to the image of the sail's engagement with the force of the wind (its ability to cut through the sea by fleeing before the wind). The French term *les voiles*, which plays through Derrida's reading, signifies both veil and sail, concealing, alluring, displacing and acting 'at a distance'. Such 'action at a distance' is a form of power Nietzsche treats as 'feminine'; it constitutes the 'lure' of woman. At the heart of this 'lure', however, lies a masculine imperative, the *necessity of maintaining distance* that is constitutive of the possibility of *sustaining the stability* of desire. Hence what Derrida says might be the 'advice' of one man to another:

> A woman seduces from a distance. In fact distance is the very element of her power. Yet one must beware to keep one's distance from her beguiling song

of enchantment. A distance from distance must be maintained ... *Il faut* la distance (qui faut). It is necessary to keep one's distance (*Distanz*!). (SNS 49)

It is necessary; and yet the 'seduction' of philosophy entails forgetting the imperative of distance in pursuit of possession, wanting to know the truth. In pursuit of the truth, however, closing in on the object of desire, all that will be encountered is the 'averted' veiled face of woman. Crucially echoing the moment of crisis that Nietzsche discerned in modernity when the pursuit of knowledge encounters its own impossibility of justification (*Gay Science* §344), here:

> The philosophical discourse, blinded, founders on these shoals and is hurled down to these depthless depths to its ruin. There is no such thing as the truth of woman, but it is because of that abyssal divergence of truth, because that untruth is a 'truth'. Woman is but one name for that untruth of truth. (SNS 51)

As in Nietzsche's text, there is thus for Derrida a certain privilege attached to the figure of the feminine (which we are warned not to equate with a woman's femininity or female sexuality or any other 'essentializing fetish') such that woman can be presented as 'writing' (see Chapter 2), playing the same role of suspending the ultimate referent of self-identity and 'undoing' philosophical desire (see Chapter 8).

DERRIDA, NIETZSCHE AND FEMINISM

Hostile questions have been raised about *Spurs* by feminist critics concerned at Derrida's deployment of the 'figure' of woman as the 'untruth of truth' and the apparently uncritical repetition of motifs of the seducing woman, gaudy in her finery, lacking any reality of her own. According to Derrida, however, in reading the figure of 'woman' we must encompass both Nietzsche's appreciation of the feminine *and* his anti-feminism. Thus, for Nietzsche, and perhaps for Derrida, too:

> Feminism is nothing but the operation of a woman who aspires to be like a man. And in order to resemble the masculine dogmatic philosopher this woman lays claim just as much as he – to truth, science, objectivity in all their castrated delusions of virility. It wants a castrated woman. *Gone the style.* (SNS 65 – referring to *Beyond Good and Evil* §232)

'Nothing', retorts Michelle Le Doueff, 'will give a clearer idea of how French colleagues welcome feminism than this statement by Derrida' and she goes on to remark that here, in speaking of women, Derrida is uncharacteristically allowing himself to be for once 'straightforward', to *say* what he really *means*. Turning the tables on the question of the philosopher's desire, she declares that 'the pleasure derived from speaking ill of feminists, and indeed from vilifying us, is so great that Derrida does not mind bluntness and abruptness for once' (Le Doueff).

This irritated response does little, however, to engage with the problematic question of the 'proper voice' in this as in other deconstructive texts. Is Derrida indeed particularly '*blunt*' here concerning women and feminism? Is Nietzsche? When Derrida insists upon an affirmative 'excess', an 'active' dimension of artist-dissimulator 'woman', it is an excess that inhabits both the 'distance' constitutive of sexual difference and the self-affirmative play of dissimulation, as well as the polyphony (many voices) of the text. According to Derrida, it is crucial that in Nietzsche's text this excess implies that 'woman' cannot be resolved into a single position or placed within the constraints of an oppositional structure such as that of activity versus passivity. Positions *change places constantly*. Nietzsche's own complex investment in this figure of woman is rendered by Derrida as more than doubled:

> He was, he dreaded this castrated woman.
> He was, he dreaded this castrating woman.
> He was, he loved, this affirming woman. (SNS 101)

Such a comment speaks less of '*bluntness*' than of what Derrida calls the necessity of 'traversing the undecidable' – the heterogenous text – as well as the rupturing potential (the *point?*) of an 'excessive' affirmative moment breaking a dialectical prison of antitheses (SNS 95). It is, indeed, this 'affirmative excess' that has become crucial to a new generation of feminists – best represented in the influential work of Judith Butler – who have sought to break out of a feminism doubly constrained by the opposed motifs of woman-oppressed-by-her-masculinist-construction and woman-as-radically-free. By deconstructing the opposition of artistry and truth both Derrida and Nietzsche open the way to an articulation of identity as performative and of a certain stylistic 'parody' at the site of affirmative excess appearing as a gesture of freedom. Yet we also must allow that such freedom is less *rationally* generated than linked to what Derrida elsewhere speaks of as the '*madness*' of the decision (see Chapter 6), a madness that is never far away when he is writing 'on' Nietzsche and in/through Nietzsche's voices. And so it is never quite the freedom *of* a man or a woman that is at stake in 'grand style', never the freedom of a *proper* subject, but rather the freedom of a way of moving, of distancing and approaching, of dancing perhaps, irreducible to its choreography.

HISTORY OF AN ERROR: CONTESTING HEIDEGGER

We have not yet begun to engage with what for many readers might appear the main point of Derrida's *Spurs* – its dispute with Heidegger's attempt to systematize Nietzsche's thought. Yet in another sense all the ground has been prepared already, for neglect of the figure of woman – and hence of the question of style in the Nietzschean text – again appears as the elusive point of undoing of the Heideggerian 'frame'. Much is at stake here; first, Heidegger's claim that Nietzsche is the 'Last metaphysician', that he represents an inverted Platonism in undoing the privilege accorded to 'true reality' by affirming the irreducibility of appearance; and, second, the very style of Heidegger's reading – or lack of it – which attempts to impose a system and identity on a text that Derrida will characterize, conversely, in terms of its 'contradictory mobility' and indelible *resistance* to system.

Derrida, rereading Heidegger's reading begins from the latter's indifference to the figure of woman in a key, highly condensed chapter of Nietzsche's *Twilight of the Idols*, 'How the "Real World" at Last became a Myth: History of an Error'. This tragi-comic text begins from the formulation of self-identity proper to the assured masculine philosopher, 'I Plato *am* the truth', but pronounces in the second era of the idea of a 'true world' that now, the idea *'becomes a woman'*. If, in the first epoch of this narrative, truth is a way of being – an ethos that aims at *being unchanging*, with the second era, the idea has (impossibly!) *become something*, it has become woman by becoming a 'form of truth's self-presentation' (SNS 87). As such, it takes on all the seductive tropes of action-at-a distance that we have already seen attach to the figure of woman. Heidegger's detailed and intricate reading of the 'History', however, neatly *skirts* this 'inscription of woman' (SNS 85) failing to mention it, let alone make anything of it, as though it were *improper* to the text.

Derrida's 'deconstruction' of Heidegger's way of positioning Nietzsche as the 'last metaphysician' therefore turns upon a further elaboration of the figure of woman in terms of 'the question of the *propre*', that is, of the values of propriety, property, and appropriation. The logic of truth's self-presentation is to be undone by woman herself, insofar as she exists only in excess of what is 'proper'. For in relations of desire it is never entirely clear what is given and what appropriated, where self-possession is undone or how it is maintained. Derrida's proposal is that Nietzschean undecidability, here traced through the figure of woman, disturbs Heidegger's own reliance upon a logic of the proper in seeking a 'genuine' apprehension of Being. Heidegger wishes to show that Nietzsche forgets Being and must be a metaphysician. Derrida, however, claims that this very opposition metaphysical/non-metaphysical is traversed by the question of the *propre* and that in a sense Heidegger too *knows* this (SNS 117–21). Yet in evading the question of style, Heidegger proves unable to *acknowledge* what he *knows* about Nietzsche.

In seeking to establish the systematicity, the coherence and wholeness of Nietzsche's thought – which, he claims, is in the end, but *one* thought, the thought of eternal return – Heidegger remains seduced by faith in an underlying meaning. But what, asks Derrida is the underlying meaning of a 'fragment'? *Spurs* concludes with a playful meditation on a fragment found among Nietzsche's posthumous notes: 'I have forgotten my umbrella'. What is the ultimate meaning of this enigmatic remark? How might it be decoded? This phrase could as Derrida suggests equally be a fragment of overheard conversation, a note for a concept, or a citation of something else (SNS 123). Its undecidability, our inability in the end to definitively say what it means, is unfurled by Derrida as an allegory of the general undecidability of Nietzsche's text that is of the same status. The very nature of language, its style, makes it impossible to point to a single meaning that is supposedly hidden behind the veils of these texts.

OTOBIOGRAPHIES

If Nietzsche's texts are 'undecidable' might anything be made of them? Does Heidegger 'appropriate' Nietzsche to his own ends, making Nietzsche the last metaphysician so that he, Heidegger, might become the first non-metaphysical thinker? And is there something about these *especially* undecidable texts that makes them especially vulnerable to being taken over, seized and turned to unanticipated ends? In 'Otobiographies' Derrida takes on one of the most controversial aspects of Nietzsche's work, the appropriation of his texts to various social and political ends, most notoriously, by Nazi ideologues.

We might ask whether this mis/appropriation was somehow foreseen by Nietzsche himself. In *Ecce Homo*, a text which begins in speculation on the necessity of his 'being misunderstood', he writes:

> I know my fate. One day my name will be associated with the memory of something monstrous – a crisis without equal on earth, the most profound collision of conscience, a decision that was conjured up against everything that had been believed, demanded, hallowed so far. I am no man, I am dynamite . . . (Why I am a Destiny, I)

Yet in posing the question of Nietzsche's 'foresight', we must at once also ask what would be the importance we could give to such a self-projection into the future. In approaching these questions, Derrida is careful to give a wide berth to the redemptive as well as the culpable potential of ascribing to Nietzsche some clear anticipation of his 'uses'. His interest lies rather with the 'text' as subject of an unassumable responsibility, for:

> If one refuses the distinction between unconscious and deliberate programs as an absolute criterion, if one no longer considers only intent – whether conscious or not – when reading a text, then the law that makes the perverting simplifications possible must lie in the structure of the text 'remaining' . . . (EO 30)

This form of responsibility to the text is integral to the kind of reading Derrida develops in *Spurs* and it follows from the articulations of deconstruction developed earlier that what counts as 'falsification' and 'appropriation' of a text is never clear cut. Playing with questions about the undoing of the machine/life divide that he shows to also haunt Nietzsche's 'autobiographical' statement, *Ecce Homo*, Derrida begins to develop the thought of text as a 'programming machine' bringing opposing forces into relation to one another – those relations of coupling, conjugation or marriage that fascinate Nietzsche as a genealogist – as in the 'coupling' of the Nietzschean discussion of life as ascending, or degenerate, to the Nazi ideology of Aryan purity. The point of identifying such a 'machine' would not, however, simply be to decipher its movements but to intervene in them, on the assumption, perhaps, that this same Nazism that *we do not yet understand* may also be haunting our present. A 'practical rewriting' of the Nietzschean corpus may then be a task of pressing political urgency. He writes:

> It cannot be entirely fortuitious that the discourse bearing his name in society, in accordance with civil laws and editorial norms, has served as a legitimating reference for ideologues. There is absolutely nothing contingent about the fact that the only political regime to have effectively brandished his name as a major and official banner was Nazi . . . (EO 30–1)

Here, however, Derrida warns that he is not saying that Nazi ideology offered either the only or the best reading of Nietzschean politics; rather, that such a reading cannot be dismissed as irrelevant to the text, for the *structure* 'makes it possible'. Nor can we assume that we already know very well what 'Nazism' is. Instead of Nietzsche or Heidegger being 'explained' by their affinities with Nazism, reading the Nietzschean or Heideggerian corpus is a part of the important task of *beginning* to come to some understanding of the meaning of that political configuration.

POLITICS OF THE PERHAPS

This is 'perhaps' the task, or a part of the task, that Derrida takes up in *The Politics of Friendship*. Three key chapters of this work are concerned with Nietzsche and with his logic of the 'perhaps' in which Derrida finds an affirmative philosophy that deconstruction will echo. His concern in offering an affirmative reading is not to save Nietzsche from his associations with relativism, nihilism or Nazism but to point to the *suspensive* moment of the Nietzschean text as a moment of resistance to all reductive gestures and hence an opening onto futurity.

Nietzsche's writings are peppered with the use of the word 'perhaps' – *vielleicht* – of which Derrida remarks that 'the thought of the "perhaps" perhaps engages the only possible thought of the event . . .' (PF 29). The 'perhaps' is, he says, the most *just* category for the future. The 'perhaps' marks the break in a calculable future; it is the point of difference between this futurity and a programme or a 'process without an event' (PF 29). In this way it is linked to friendship, to 'the opening of what comes' and its attendant risk of insecurity, a risk to which Derrida counter-poses Aristotle's or Plato's equation of friendship with what is reliable and sure. Yet this 'counter-posing' of stability and instability is not the same as posing them as opposites. For the other aspect of Nietzsche's 'perhaps' to which Derrida wishes to draw attention is its connection with Nietzsche's refusal of the metaphysician's 'faith in antithetical values'. In *Beyond Good and Evil*, Nietzsche invites, under the sign of the 'perhaps' a non-metaphysical reflection upon the possibility that good things may be entangled, knotted up with, and inextricable from their antithesis, wicked things (#2). The 'perhaps' here seems to suspend the possibility that we would ever decide unequivocally one way or another. Equally, the 'perhaps' opens out a demand for interpretation – it is, writes Derrida;

> The shudder of the sentence, the shudder of an arrow of which it is still not know where and how far it will go, the vibration of a shaft of writing which, alone, promises and calls for a reading, a preponderance to come of the interpretive decision. (PF 31)

The incomplete sentence, another trademark of Nietzschean style, likewise 'strikes home' in outstripping itself, its futurity that of *iterability* and of 'the natural miracle ... that such sentences outlive their author, and each specific reader, him, you and me, all of us, all the living, all the living presents' (PF 32). Nietzsche's incomplete sentences thus, in a sense, 'begin at the end', 'initiated with the signature of the other' (PF 32) instead of bringing to an end, closing or completing.

It is in this sense, then, that Nietzsche's philosophy of the future, his promise *to* and *of* a future is close to Derrida's own. For Derrida, critique and genealogy are 'always made in the name of a future that is promised' (N 225). And it is for this reason that Derrida holds that no one has broken more radically than Nietzsche with 'the Greek or Christian canon of friendship – that is, with a certain politics, a certain type of democracy ...' (PF 40). Famous for his hostility to democracy, Nietzsche speaks only against 'democracy in general'; he says nothing against what Derrida calls 'democracy to come' and, indeed, makes implicit appeal to such a notion (N 234–5). With it, like Derrida, Nietzsche welcomes futurity, affirming messianically (see Chapter 7 of this volume) the other-to-come out of profound dissatisfaction with present times.

MAJOR TEXTS ON NIETZSCHE

Of Grammatology (OG) 1974
Derrida intermittently discusses Nietzsche in his first well-known book (OG 19–20), prefiguring his later reading in *Spurs*.

Spurs – Nietzsche's Styles (SNS) 1979
Spurs is dedicated to the conjunction of a series of questions in Nietzsche's work centering around *style*. The notorious texts in which Nietzsche's apparent misogyny emerges offer Derrida the chance to dwell on the relation between truth, woman and writing; in particular, the ambiguous connections between the figure of woman and truth in Nietzsche are used to discuss the ambiguity of truth itself, and the idea of a 'true meaning' to Nietzsche's work as a whole.

'Choreographies' (P 89–108) 1981; also (EO 163–85) 1982
A correspondence conducted by Christie McDonald with Derrida on feminism, this text originally published in *Diacritics* includes some discussion of the relationship between woman and Nietzsche as it is dealt with in *Spurs*. Related texts: Voice II (P 156–70) and *Geschlecht*: Sexual Difference, Ontological Difference 1983: both on aspects of sexual difference.

'Otobiographies', *Ear of the Other* (EO 1–38) 1986
In this text, Derrida examines the relationship between Nietzsche's writing and the subsequent (political) uses to which it has been put. Related text: Interpreting Signatures, Nietzsche/Heidegger: Two Questions 1986. Also offers a fascinating history of the varieties of 'use' to which Nietzsche has been put, particularly with regard to Heidegger.

The Politics of Friendship (PF) 1997
One way to approach this demanding book would be through its chapters on Nietzsche, especially read in conjunction with the interview Nietzsche and the Machine. This is helpful for understanding how Derrida's ruminations on friendship link into thoughts about democracy as futurity – 'to come'.

'Nietzsche and the Machine' (N 215–256) 2002
This interview with Richard Beardsworth is perhaps one of the most accessible occasions on which Derrida explains how he sees the relation between his own work and Nietzsche's. It sums up and extends themes he touches on elsewhere in his work.

Bibliography

ENGLISH TRANSLATIONS OF DERRIDA'S WORKS

EDITORS' NOTE

The following constitutes an extensive bibliography of Derrida's work in English. Given that numerous translations of Derrida's work have been published more than once, and then sometimes in alternative versions, we have, where possible, attempted to adhere to three criteria. Firstly, we have endeavoured to include the fullest versions of each text, which may have been supplemented by Derrida himself in the course of its publication history, for example, the expanded version of 'Force of Law', contained in the recent *Acts of Religion* (2001, 230–98). Secondly, we have listed only the most easily available versions of texts (assuming that the available translation is of acceptable quality), which are in general their most recent publication. This means that some familiar titles are listed more recently than one might expect, or under different titles, for example, the recent republication of 'Of a Newly Arisen Apocalyptic Tone in Philosophy' (1993), which replaces a number of earlier versions by the same translator. Thirdly, rather than including articles published initially in a journal, we have favoured references to texts available in a collected volume of essays – these are, in any case, almost always easier to find in this latter format. Those texts, finally, which are listed without reference to a translator are originally in English.

1973

Speech and Phenomena, and Other Essays on Husserl's Theory of Signs.
David B. Allison (trans.). Evanston: Northwestern University Press.

1974

Of Grammatology .
Gayatri Chakravorty Spivak (trans.). Baltimore: Johns Hopkins University Press.

1975

Responses to Questions on the Avant-Garde.
Peggy Kamuf (trans.). *Diagraphe* 6, October, 52–3.

1976

Becoming Woman.
Barbara Harlow (trans.). *Semiotext(e)* 3(1), 128–37.

1978

Edmund Husserl's Origin of Geometry: An Introduction.
John P. Leavey, Jr (trans.). New York: Harvester Press.

Speech and Writing according to Hegel.
Alphonso Lingis (trans.). *Man and World* 11, 107–30.

Writing and Difference.
Alan Bass (trans.). Chicago: University of Chicago Press.

1979

Living On: Border Lines.
James Hulbert (trans.) in Hartman (ed.). *Deconstruction and Criticism*. London: Routledge & Kegan Paul, 75–176.

Me – Psychoanalysis: An Introduction to the Translation of 'The Shell and the
Kernel'. by Nicolas Abraham
Richard Klein (trans.). *Diacritics* 9(1), 4–15.

Scribble (Writing/Power).
Cary Plotkin (trans.). *Yale French Studies* 58, 116–47.

Spurs: Nietzsche's Styles/Eperons: Les styles de Nietzsche.
Barbara Harlow (trans.). Chicago: Chicago University Press.

1980

An Interview with J. Kears and K. Newton.
K. Newton (trans.). *The Literary Review* 14(18), 21–2.

The Archeology of the Frivolous: Reading Condillac.
John P. Leavey, Jr (trans.). Pittsburgh: Duquesne University Press.

1981

Dissemination.
Barbara Johnson (trans.). Chicago: University of Chicago Press.

Economimesis.
Richard Klein (trans.). *Diacritics* 11, 3–25.

Positions.
Alan Bass (trans.). London: Athlone.

1982

All Ears: Nietzsche's Otobiography.
Avital Ronell (trans.). *Yale French Studies* 63, 245–50.

Letter to John P. Leavey, Jr.
John P. Leavey, Jr (trans.). *Semeia* 23, 61–2.

Margins of Philosophy.
Alan Bass (trans.). Chicago: University of Chicago Press.

Sending: On Representation.
Peter and Mary Ann Caws (trans.). *Social Research* 49(2), 294–326.

1983

Critical Relation: Peter Szondi's Studies on Celan.
James Hughes (trans.). *Boundary 2* 11(3), 155–67.

'Excuse Me, but I Never said Exactly So': Yet Another Derridean Interview.
Paul Brennan (trans.). *On The Beach* 1, 43.
Available online at http://www.hydra.umn.edu/derrida/so.html (9th September 2003).

Geschlecht: Sexual Difference, Ontological Difference.
David Farrell Krell (trans.). *Research in Phenomenology* 13, 65–83.

The Principle of Reason: The University in the Eyes of its Pupils.
Catherine Porter and Edward P. Morris (trans.). *Diacritics* 13(3), 3–20.

The Time of a Thesis: Punctuations.
Kathleen McLaughlin (trans.) in Alan Montefiore (ed.). *Philosophy in France Today*.
Cambridge: Cambridge University Press, 34–50.

1984

An Idea of Flaubert: Plato's Letter.
Peter Starr (trans.). *Modern Language Notes* 94(4), 748–68.

Deconstruction and the Other: Interview with Richard Kearney in Kearney (trans.
and ed.). *Dialogues with Contemporary Continental Thinkers*. Manchester: Manchester
University Press, 105–26.

Languages and Institutions of Philosophy (IV. Theology of translation).
Joseph Adamson (trans.). *Semiotic Inquiry* 4(2), 139–52.

My Chances/*Mes Chances*: A Rendezvous with Some Epicurean Stereophonies.
Irene Harvey and Avital Ronell (trans.) in Joseph Smith and William Kerrigan
(eds). *Taking Chances: Derrida, Psychoanalysis, and Literature*. London: Johns Hopkins
University Press, 1–32.

No Apocalypse, Not Now (Full Speed Ahead, Seven Missiles, Seven Missives).
Catherine Porter and Philip Lewis (trans.). *Diacritics* 14(2), 20–31.

Signéponge/Signsponge.
Richard Rand (trans.). Columbia: Columbia University Press.

The Unoccupied Chair: Censorship, Mastership and Magistriality.
Peggy Kamuf (trans.). *Semiotic Inquiry* 4(2), 123–36.

Two Words for Joyce.
G. Bennington (trans.) in Daniel Ferrer and Derek Attridge (eds). *Post-structuralist
Joyce: Essays from the French*. Cambridge: Cambridge University Press, 148–58.

1985

Deconstruction in America: An Interview with Jacques Derrida.
Peggy Kamuf (trans.). *Critical Exchange 17*, Winter, 1–33.

Letter to a Japanese Friend.
David Wood and Andrew Benjamin (trans.) in Robert Bernasconi and David
Wood (eds). *Derrida and Difference*. Warwick: Parousia Press, 1–8.

Racism's Last Word.
Peggy Kamuf (trans.). *Critical Inquiry* 12(1), 290–9.

Tribute to Paul de Man.
Kevin Newmark (trans.). *Yale French Studies* 69, 323–6.

1986

The Ear of the Other: Otobiography, Transference, Translation.
Avital Ronell and Peggy Kamuf (trans.), Christie V. McDonald (ed.). New York:
Schocken Books.

But, beyond . . .
Peggy Kamuf (trans.). Critical Inquiry 13 (Autumn), 155–70.

Fors: The Anglish Words of Nicolas Abraham and Maria Torok.
Barbara Johnson (trans.) in Abraham and Torok (eds). *The Wolfman's Magic Word:
A Cryptonomy*. Minneapolis: University of Minnesota Press, xi–xlviii.

Glas.
John P. Leavey, Jr and Richard Rand (trans.). Lincoln: University of Nebraska
Press.

Interpreting Signatures (Nietzsche/Heidegger): Two Questions.
In Diane Michelfelder and Richard Palmer (eds and trans.). *Dialogue and Deconstruction: The Gadamer-Derrida Encounter*. New York: SUNY Press, 57–74.

Literature and Politics.
Noha Khalaf (trans.). *New Political Science* 15, Summer, 5.

Mémoires: For Paul de Man.
Cecile Lindsay, Jonathan Culler and Eduardo Cadava (trans.). New York: Columbia University Press.

Proverb: He that Would Pun . . .
In John P. Leavey (trans. and ed.). *GLASsary*. Lincoln: University of Nebraska
Press, 17–20.

Three Questions to Hans-George Gadamer.
In Diane Michelfelder and Richard Palmer (eds and trans.). *Dialogue and Deconstruction: The Gadamer-Derrida Encounter*. New York: SUNY Press, 52–4.

1987

Cinders.
Ned Lukacher (trans.). Lincoln: University of Nebraska Press.

Geschlecht 2: Heidegger's Hand.
John P. Leavey Jr (trans.) in Sallis (ed.). *Deconstruction and Philosophy*. Chicago: University of Chicago Press, 161–96.

Interview with Imre Saluzinski.
In Saluzinski (ed.) *Criticism in Society*. London: Methuen, 13–24.

The Laws of Reflection: Nelson Mandela, in Admiration.
Mary Ann Caws and Isabelle Lorenz (trans.) in Jacques Derrida and Mustapha Tlili (eds). *For Nelson Mandela*. New York: Seaver Books, 13–42.

The Post Card: From Socrates to Freud and Beyond.
Alan Bass (trans.). Chicago: University of Chicago Press.

The Truth in Painting.
Geoff Bennington and Ian McLeod (trans.). Chicago: University of Chicago Press.

Some Questions and Responses.
In Derek Attridge, Alan Durant, Nigel Fabb, and Colin McCabe (eds). *The Linguistics of Writing*. Manchester: Manchester University Press, 252–64.

1988

A Number of Yes (Nombre de Oui).
Brian Homes (trans.). *Qui Parle* 2(2), 120–33.

Choral Work with Peter Eisenman.
J. Kipnis and T. Lesser (trans. and ed.). London: AA Publications.

Fifty-Two Aphorisms for a Foreword.
In Andrew Benjamin (trans. and ed.) *Deconstruction: Omnibus*. London: Tate Gallery, 67–9.

Jacques Derrida in Discussion with Christopher Norris.
In Andrew Benjamin (trans. and ed.) *Deconstruction: Omnibus*. London: Tate Gallery, 71–5.

Limited Inc.
Samuel Weber and Jeffrey Mehlman (trans.), Gerald Graff (ed.). Evanston: Northwestern University Press.

On Reading Heidegger: An Outline of Remarks to the Essex Colloquium.
David Farrell Krell (trans.). *Research in Phenomenology* 17, 171–88.

Telepathy.
Nicholas Royle (trans.). *Oxford Literary Review* 10, 3–41.

1989

Biodegradables: Seven Diary Fragments.
Peggy Kamuf (trans.). *Critical Inquiry* 15(4), 812–73.

Desistance.
Christopher Fynsk (trans. and ed.) in Lacoue-Labarthe *Typography: Mimesis, Philosophy, Politics*. London: Harvard University Press, 1–42.

The Ghost Dance: An Interview with Jacques Derrida.
Jean-Luc Svoboda (trans.). *Public* 2, 60–74.

How to Avoid Speaking: Denials.
Ken Frieden (trans.) in Harold Coward and Toby Foshay (eds). *Derrida and Negative Theology*. Albany: SUNY Press, 73–142.

Mémoires: for Paul de Man.
Cecile Lindsay, Jonathan Culler, Eduardo Cadava, and Peggy Kamuf (trans.). New York: Columbia University Press.

Not Everybody Loves a Parade (interview with Scott L. Malcomson).
Village Voice. 25 July 25, 29–32.

Of Spirit: Heidegger and the Question.
Geoffrey Bennington and Rachel Bowlby (trans.). Chicago: Chicago University Press.

On Colleges and Philosophy.
G. Bennington (trans.) in Lisa Appignanesi (ed.). *Postmodernism: ICA Documents*. New York: Columbia University Press, 66–71.

Post-Scriptum: Aporias, Ways and Voices.
John P. Leavey (trans.) in Harold Coward and Toby Foshay (eds). *Derrida and Negative Theology* Albany: SUNY Press, 283–323.

Psyche: Inventions of the Other.
Catherine Porter (trans.) in Waters and Godzich (eds). *Reading De Man Reading*. Minneapolis: University of Minnesota Press, 25–65.

1990

A Discussion with Jacques Derrida.
Peggy Kamuf (trans.). *Writing Instructor* (University of Southern California) 9(1), 7–18.

Jacques Derrida.
In Raoul Mortley (trans. and ed.). *French Philosophers in Conversation*. London: Routledge, 1990, 93–107.

Let Us Not Forget – Psychoanalysis.
Geoffrey Bennington (trans.). *Oxford Literary Review* 12(1), 3–7.

Sendoffs.
Thomas Pepper (trans.). *Yale French Studies* 77, 7–43.

Some Statements and Truisms about Neologisms, Newisms, Postisms, Parasitisms, and other small Seismisms.
Anne Tomiche (trans.) in David Carroll (ed.). *The States of Theory*. New York: Columbia University Press, 63–94.

Women in the Beehive: A Seminar with Jacques Derrida.
James Adner (trans.) in Jardine and Smith (eds). *Men in Feminism*. London: MIT Press, 189–203.

1991

At This Very Moment in This Work Here I Am.
Ruben Berezdivin (trans.) in Robert Bernasconi and Simon Critchley (eds). *Re-Reading Lévinas*. Bloomington: Indiana University Press, 11–48.

Summary of Impromptu Remarks, 58 minutes, 41 seconds.
Noha Khalaf (trans.) in Cynthia Davidson (ed) *Anyone*. New York: Rizzoli, 54–60.

This is Not an Oral Footnote.
Stephen Barney and Michael Hanly (trans.) in Stephen Barney (ed.). *Annotation and its Texts*. Oxford: Oxford University Press, 192–205.

1992

Acts of Literature.
Peggy Kamuf, *et al.* (trans.), Derek Attridge (ed.). New York: Routledge.

Afterwords.
Geoffrey Bennington (trans.) in Nicholas Royle (ed.). *Afterwords*. Tampere: Outside Books, 197–203.

Canons and Metonymies.
Richard Rand (trans. and ed.). *Logomachia*. Lincoln: University of Nebraska Press, 59–71.

Mochlos, or The Conflict of the Faculties.
Richard Rand and Amy Wygant (trans.) in Richard Rand (ed.). *Logomachia*. Lincoln: University of Nebraska Press, 3–34.

Onto-Theology of National-Humanism. (Prolegomena to a Hypothesis).
Geoffrey Bennington (trans.). *Oxford Literary Review* 14(1), 3–24.

Schibboleth.
Joshua Wilner (trans.) in Aris Fioretis (ed.). *Word Traces*. Baltimore: Johns Hopkins University Press, 3–72.

The Other Heading: Reflections on Today's Europe.
Pascale-Anne Brault and Michael B. Naas (trans.). Bloomington: Indiana University Press.

1993

Aporias.
Thomas Dutoit (trans.). Stanford: Stanford University Press.

Back from Moscow, in the USSR.
Mary Quaintaire (trans.) in Mark Poster (ed.). *Politics, Theory, and Contemporary Culture*. New York: Columbia University Press, 197–235.

Circonfessions.
Geoffrey Bennington (trans.) in Jacques Derrida and Geoffrey Bennington (eds). *Jacques Derrida*. Chicago: University of Chicago Press.

Given Time 1: Counterfeit Money .
Peggy Kamuf (trans.). Chicago: University of Chicago Press.

Heidegger's Ears. Geschlecht IV: Philopolemology.
John P. Leavey (trans.) in John Sallis (ed.). *Reading Heidegger – Commemorations*. Indianapolis: University of Indiana Press, 163–218.

Le toucher: Touch/to touch him.
Peggy Kamuf (trans.). *Paragraph* 16(2), 124–57.

Memoirs of the Blind: The Self-Portrait and Other Ruins.
Pascale-Anne Brault and Michael Naas (trans.). Chicago: University of Chicago Press.

On a Newly Arisen Apocalyptic Tone in Philosophy.
John P. Leavey, Jr (trans.) in Peter Fenves (ed.). *Raising the Tone of Philosophy*. Baltimore: Johns Hopkins University Press, 117–72.

1994

Foreword.
Eric Prenowitz (trans.) in Susan Sellers (ed.). *The Helene Cixous Reader*. London:
Routledge, vii–xii.

Specters of Marx: The State of the Debt, the Work of Mourning, and the New International.
Peggy Kamuf (trans.). London: Routledge.

1995

Archive Fever – A Freudian Impression.
Eric Prenowitz (trans.). Chicago: University of Chicago Press.

The Gift of Death.
David Wills (trans.). Chicago: University of Chicago Press.

On the Name.
David Wood, John P. Leavey and Ian McLeod (trans.), Thomas Dutoit (ed.). Stanford: Stanford University Press.

Points . . . : Interviews 1974–1994.
Peggy Kamuf, *et al.* (trans.), Elisabeth Weber (ed.). Stanford: Stanford University Press.

Tense.
David Farrell Krell (trans.) in Kenneth Maly (ed.). *The Path of Archaic Thinking –
Unfolding the Work of John Sallis*. Albany: SUNY Press.

1996

Monolingualism of the Other, or the Prosthesis of Origin.
Patrick Mensah (trans.). Stanford: Stanford University Press.

Remarks on Deconstruction and Pragmatism.
Chantalle Mouffe (trans. and ed.). *Deconstruction and Pragmatism*. New York,
Routledge.

1997

Adieu to Emmanuel Lévinas
Pascale-Anne Brault and Michael Naas (trans.). Stanford: Stanford University Press.

'As if I were Dead': An Interview with Jacques Derrida.
In John Brannigan (ed.). *Applying: to Derrida*. London: Macmillan, 212–26.

Politics of Friendship.
George Collins (trans.). London: Verso Books.

The Villanova Roundtable: A Conversation with Jacques Derrida.
In John Caputo (ed.). *Deconstruction in a Nutshell*. New York: Fordham University
Press, 4–28.

1998

Resistances – To Psychoanalysis
Peggy Kamuf, Pascale-Anne Brault and Michael Naas (trans.). Stanford: Stanford
University Press.

The Retrait of Metaphor.
In Julian Wolfreys (ed.). *The Derrida Reader: Writing Performances*. Nebraska: University of Nebraska Press, 102–29.

Right of Inspection with photography by Marie-Françoise Plissart.
David Wills (trans.). New York: The Monacelli Press.

The Secret Art of Antonin Artaud with Paule Thévenin.
Mary Ann Caws (trans.). Cambridge: MIT Press.

1999

Marx and Sons.
In M. Sprinker (ed.). *Ghostly Demarcations: A Symposium on Jacques Derrida's* Specters
of Marx. London: Verso, 213–69.

2000

Of Hospitality with Anne Dufourmantelle.
Rachel Bowlby (trans.). Stanford: Stanford University Press.

Word Processing.
Peggy Kamuf (trans.). *Oxford Literary Review* 21, 3–17.

2001

Acts of Religion.
Samuel Weber, *et al.* (trans.), Gil Anidjar (ed.). London: Routledge.

Arguing with Derrida.
Simon Glendinning (ed.). London: Blackwell.

Deconstruction Engaged: The Sydney Seminars.
Paul Patton and Terry Smith (eds). Sydney: Power Publications.

On Cosmopolitanism and Forgiveness.
Mark Dooley and Michael Hughes (trans.), Simon Critchley and Richard Kearney
(eds). London: Routledge.

A Taste for the Secret with Maurizio Ferraris.
Giacomo Donis (trans.), David Webb and Giacomo Donis (eds). London: Polity
Press.

What is a 'relevant' translation?
Lawrence Venuti (trans.). *Critical Inquiry* 27(2), 174–200.

The Work of Mourning.
Eds. Brault and Naas. Samuel Weber *et al.* (trans.). Chicago: University of Chicago
Press.

Veils with Hélène Cixous.
Geoffrey Bennington (trans.). Stanford: Stanford University Press.

2002

The Animal that therefore I am (more to follow).
David Wills (trans.). *Critical Inquiry* 28(2), 369–418.

Demeure: Fiction and Testimony with Maurice Blanchot.
Elizabeth Rottenberg (trans.). Stanford: Stanford University Press.

Echographies of Television: Filmed Interviews.
Jennifer Bajorek (trans.), Bernard Steigler (ed.). London: Polity Press.

Ethics, Institutions and the Right to Philosophy.
Peter Pericles Trifones (trans. and ed.). Lanham: Rowan & Littlefield.

Negotiations: Interventions and Interviews, 1971–2001.
Elizabeth Rottenberg (trans. and ed.). Stanford: Stanford University Press.

The three ages of Jacques Derrida.
LA Weekly. 8 November.

Who's Afraid of Philosophy? Right to Philosophy I.
Jan Plug (trans.). Stanford: Stanford University Press.

Without A libi.
Peggy Kamuf (trans.). Stanford: Stanford University Press.

2003

And say the animal responded?
David Wills (trans.) in Cary Wolfe (ed.). Minneapolis: University of Minnesota Press, 121–46.

Autoimmunity: Real and Symbolic Suicides.
In Giovanna Borradori (ed.). *Philosophy in a Time of Terror*. Chicago: University of Chicago Press.

ALL OTHER TEXTS CITED

St Augustine (1982) *The Literal Meaning of Genesis*. John Hammond (trans.). New York: Newman Press.
Austin, J. L. (1976) *How to do Things with Words*. Oxford: Oxford University Press.
Bataille, G. (1992) *On Nietzsche*. Bruce Boone (trans.). New York: Paragon House.
Blanchot, M. (1986) *The Writing of the Disaster*. Ann Smock (trans.). Lincoln: University of Nebraska Press.
Brunette, Peter, and David Wills (eds) (1994) *Deconstruction and the Visual Arts*. Cambridge: Cambridge University Press.
Cixous, H. (1994) *The Hélène Cixous Reader*. Susan Sellers (trans. and ed.). New York: Routledge.
Davidson, D. (1984) On The Very Idea of a Conceptual Scheme. In *Inquiries into Truth and Interpretation*. New York: Oxford University Press, 183–98.
Deleuze, G. (1983) *Nietzsche and Philosophy*. Hugh Tomlinson (trans.). London: Athlone Press.
Descartes, R. (1971) *Meditations*. F. E. Sutcliffe (trans.). Harmondsworth: Penguin Books.
Farias, V. (1989) *Heidegger and Nazism*. Paul Burrell and Gabriel Ricci (trans.). Philadelphia: Temple University Press.
Foucault, M. (1977) 'What is An Author?' In Donald F. Bouchard and Sherry Simon (trans. and ed.). *Language, Counter-Memory, Practice*. Ithaca, New York: Cornell University Press, 124–27.
Foucault, M. (1997) What is Enlightenment? Robert Hurley (trans.) in Paul Rabinow (ed.). *Essential Works of Foucault 1954–1984, Volume 1, Ethics*. New York: The New Press, 303–20.
Freud, S. (1966) *Project for a Scientific Psychology*. In James Strachey (trans. and ed.). *Standard Edition of the Complete Psychological Works of Sigmund Freud*. v. 1. London: Hogarth Press, 281–397.
Freud, S. (1975) *Beyond the Pleasure Principle*. James Strachey (trans.). New York: Norton.
Freud, S. (1976) *Interpretation of Dreams*. In James Strachey (trans. and ed.). *Standard Edition of the Complete Psychological Works of Sigmund Freud*. v. 4–5. London: Hogarth Press.
Gasché, R. (1986) *The Tain of the Mirror: Derrida and the Philosophy of Reflection*. Cambridge, MA: Harvard University Press.
Habermas, J. (1987) Beyond a Temporalized Philosophy of Origins: Jacques Derrida's Critique of Phonocentrism. Fredrick Lawrence (trans.). In *The Philosophical Discourse of Modernity: Twelve Lectures*. Cambridge, MA: MIT Press, 161–84.

Hegel, G. (1977) *Phenomenology of Spirit*. A. V. Miller (trans.). Oxford: Clarendon Press.

Heidegger, M. (1962) *Being and Time*. John Macquarie and Edward Robinson (trans.). London: SCM Press.

Heidegger, M. (1979) *Nietzsche*. David Farrell Krell (trans. and ed.). San Francisco: Harper & Row.

Heidegger, M. (1984) *Metaphysical Foundations of Logic*. Michael Heim (trans.). Bloomington: University of Indiana Press.

Husserl, E. (1964) *The Phenomenology of Internal Time-Consciousness*. James S. Churchill (trans.). Bloomington: Indiana University Press.

Husserl, E. (1970) *Logical Investigations*, 2 vols. J. N. Findlay (trans.). New York: Humanities Press.

Husserl, E. The Origin of Geometry. In Jacques Derrida (1978) *Introduction to Husserl's 'Origin of Geometry'*. Lincoln: University of Nebraska Press, 155–80.

Joyce, J. (1993) *Ulysses*. Hans Walter Gabler, Wolfhard Steppe and Claus Melchior (eds). London: The Bodley Head.

Kant, I. (1929) *Critique of Pure Reason*. Norman Kemp Smith (trans.). London: Macmillan.

Kant, I. (1952) *Critique of Judgement*. James Meredith (trans.). Oxford: Clarendon University Press.

Kant, I. (1998) *Religion within the Bounds of Mere Reason and Other Writings*. Allen Wood and George Di Giovanni (trans.). Cambridge: Cambridge University Press.

Kierkegaard, S. (1983) *Fear and Trembling*. Hong and Hong (trans.). Princeton: Princeton University Press.

Klossowski, P. (1997) *Nietzsche and the Vicious Circle*. Daniel W. Smith (trans.). Chicago: University of Chicago Press.

Lacan, J. (1977) *Ecrits*. Alan Sheridan (trans.). New York: Norton.

Le Doueff, M. (1987) Ants and Women, or Philosophy Without Borders. In Griffiths (ed.). Contemporary French Philosophy supplement to *Philosophy, Royal Institute of Philosophy Lecture Series*. Cambridge: Cambridge University Press.

Lévinas, E. (1963) *Difficile Liberté*. Paris: Presses Universitaires de France.

Lévinas, E. (1969) *Totality and Infinity*. Alphonso Lingis (trans.). Pittsburgh: Duquesne University Press.

Lévinas, E. (1991) *Otherwise than Being Or Beyond Essence*. Alphonso Lingis (trans.). Dordrecht: Kluwer Press.

Luther, Martin (1966) Ninety-five Theses (the Heidelberg *Disputatio*). In Lewis Spitz (ed.). *The Protestant Reformation*. Englewood Cliffs: Prentice Hall, 161–6.

Nietzsche, F. (1966) *Beyond Good and Evil*. Walter Kaufman (trans.). New York: Vintage.

Nietzsche, F. (1969) *Thus Spoke Zarathustra*. R. J. Hollingdale (trans.). New York: Penguin.

Nietzsche, F. (1974) *The Gay Science*. Walter Kaufman (trans.). New York: Vintage.

Nietzsche, F. (1977) *Twilight of the Idols and the Anti-Christ*. R.J. Hollingdale (trans.). New York: Vintage.

Nietzsche, F. (1982) *Ecce Homo*. R. J. Hollingdale (trans.). New York: Penguin Books.

Poe, E. A. (1975) The Purloined Letter. In A. Walton Litz (ed.). *Major American Short Stories*. New York, Oxford University Press, 14–21.

Pseudo-Dionysius (1957) *Divine Names and Mystical Theology*. C. E. Rolt (trans. and ed.). New York: Macmillan.

Rorty, R. (1982) Philosophy as a Kind of Writing: An Essay on Derrida, *Consequences of Pragmatism, Essays: 1972–1980*. Sussex: Harvester.

Wittgenstein, L. (1996). *Philosophical Investigations*. G. E. M. Anscombe (trans.). Oxford: Blackwell.

Yerushalmi, Y. (1992) *Freud's Moses – Judaism Terminable and Interminable*. New Haven: Yale University Press.

Index

MORE PHILOSOPHY FROM CONTINUUM

THE GREAT THINKERS A-Z
Edited by Julian Baggini and Jeremy Stangroom

HB • 0 82646754 7 • £45.00/$75.00
PB • 0 8264 6742 3 • £9.99/$15.95 • 256pp • 2004

WHAT PHILOSOPHERS THINK
Edited by Julian Baggini and Jeremy Stangroom

HB • 0 8264 6754 7 • £45.00/$85.00
PB • 0 8264 6180 8 • £9.99/$14.95 • 256pp • 2003

WHAT PHILOSOPHY IS
Edited by Havi Cavel and David Gamez

HB • 0 8264 7241 9 • £45.00/$85.00
PB • 0 8264 7242 7 • £9.99/$15.95 • 352pp • 2004

INFINITE THOUGHT
Truth and the Return of Philosophy
Alain Badiou

HB • 0 8264 6724 5 • £16.99/$19.95
PB • 0 8264 7320 2 • £9.99/$19.95 • 208pp • 2004

TIME FOR REVOLUTION
Antonio Negri

HB • 0 8264 5931 5 • £16.99/$29.95
PB • 0 8264 7328 8 • £9.99/$19.95 • 304pp • 2004

KILLING FREUD
Twentieth Century Culture and the Death of Psychoanalysis
Todd Dufresne

HB • 0 8264 6893 4 • £16.99/$19.95 • 224pp • 2003

LIFE.AFTER.THEORY
Interviews with Jacques Derrida, Frank Kermode, Toril Moi
and Christopher Norris
Edited by Michael Payne and John Schad

HB • 0 8264 6565 X • £16.99/$19.95
PB • 0 8264 7317 2 • £9.99/$12.95 • 208pp • 2004